SIFT

SECRETS

Study Guide
Your Key to Exam Success

SIFT Test Review for the U.S. Army's
Selection Instrument for Flight Training

Published by
Mometrix Test Preparation
SIFT Exam Secrets Test Prep Team

Written and edited by the SIFT Exam Secrets Test Prep Staff

Printed in the United States of America

This paper meets the requirements of ANSI/NISO Z39.48-1992 (Permanence of Paper).

Mometrix offers volume discount pricing to institutions. For more information or a price quote, please contact our sales department at sales@mometrix.com or 888-248-1219.

Mometrix Media LLC is not affiliated with or endorsed by any official testing organization. All organizational and test names are trademarks of their respective owners.

ISBN 13: 978-1-5167-0042-4
ISBN 10: 1-5167-0042-2

Dear Future Exam Success Story:

Congratulations on your purchase of our study guide. Our goal in writing our study guide was to cover the content on the test, as well as provide insight into typical test taking mistakes and how to overcome them.

Standardized tests are a key component of being successful, which only increases the importance of doing well in the high-pressure high-stakes environment of test day. How well you do on this test will have a significant impact on your future, and we have the research and practical advice to help you execute on test day.

The product you're reading now is designed to exploit weaknesses in the test itself, and help you avoid the most common errors test takers frequently make.

How to use this study guide

We don't want to waste your time. Our study guide is fast-paced and fluff-free. We suggest going through it a number of times, as repetition is an important part of learning new information and concepts.

First, read through the study guide completely to get a feel for the content and organization. Read the general success strategies first, and then proceed to the content sections. Each tip has been carefully selected for its effectiveness.

Second, read through the study guide again, and take notes in the margins and highlight those sections where you may have a particular weakness.

Finally, bring the manual with you on test day and study it before the exam begins.

Your success is our success

We would be delighted to hear about your success. Send us an email and tell us your story. Thanks for your business and we wish you continued success.

Sincerely,

Mometrix Test Preparation Team

TABLE OF CONTENTS

Top 15 Test Taking Tips

1. Know the test directions, duration, topics, question types, how many questions
2. Setup a flexible study schedule at least 3-4 weeks before test day
3. Study during the time of day you are most alert, relaxed, and stress free
4. Maximize your learning style; visual learner use visual study aids, auditory learner use auditory study aids
5. Focus on your weakest knowledge base
6. Find a study partner to review with and help clarify questions
7. Practice, practice, practice
8. Get a good night's sleep; don't try to cram the night before the test
9. Eat a well balanced meal
10. Wear comfortable, loose fitting, layered clothing; prepare for it to be either cold or hot during the test
11. Eliminate the obviously wrong answer choices, then guess the first remaining choice
12. Pace yourself; don't rush, but keep working and move on if you get stuck
13. Maintain a positive attitude even if the test is going poorly
14. Keep your first answer unless you are positive it is wrong
15. Check your work, don't make a careless mistake

SIFT Overview

The goal of becoming a military aviator is a noble one, and those who achieve it will have earned membership in a very elite class. Many people would like to become aviators, but few are up to the myriad demands and challenges that must be successfully met in order to reach their dream. It is a long and arduous journey, and it begins with performing well on a difficult aptitude test, above and beyond any other requirements for college degrees or percentile rank on broader military aptitude exams. These exams are known as aptitude tests, because they focus less on the knowledge a person already has and more on that person's ability to innately handle certain types of tasks.

There are two primary reasons the military requires aspiring aviators to pass these challenging exams. The first reason hinges on supply and demand. Simply put, the number of men and women interested in becoming aviators in the military is far higher than the number of pilots the various branches of the military actually need. The second primary factor is the enormous cost of training a military pilot. It has long been common knowledge that it costs well over a $1 million to train a pilot, but that now appears to be an outdated figure. It was recently reported that the Air Force spends approximately $6 million to train one fighter pilot. No matter what the exact figure is, training military pilots is extremely expensive. Before they commit to training a pilot, the military branches want to be pretty certain that he or she is up to the challenge, and won't wash out before completing training. These tests have been designed to select the candidates who are most likely to be excellent candidates for pilot training, and they have a long track record of being very accurate.

In the Army, the aptitude test is known as the SIFT, which stands for Selection Instrument for Flight Training. Although SIFT is considered to be an aptitude test, it is also a test of acquired knowledge and skills in some areas, such as aviation knowledge and math. The SIFT has only been around since 2013, when it replaced the Army's previous exam for future pilots, the Army Flight Aptitude Selection Test. There is no paper and pencil version of the SIFT; it is only given via computer. The SIFT is actually a battery of seven different exams, or subtests, and it takes about two and a half hours to complete the entire battery.

The seven sections of the SIFT are: Simple Drawings (SD), which lasts two minutes and has 100 questions, Hidden Figures (HF), which last five minutes and has 50 questions, Army Aviation Information Test (AAIT), which lasts 30 minutes and has 40 questions, Spatial Apperception Test (SAT), which lasts 10 minutes and has 25 questions, Reading Comprehension Test (RCT), which lasts 30 minutes and has 20 questions, and two sections which have a variable number of questions – Math Skills Test (MST) which lasts 40 minutes, and Mechanical Comprehension Test (MCT), which lasts 15 minutes. The reason the number of questions varies on the last two sections is that they are in a format known as computer adaptive. This means that the section will begin with a question of medium difficulty. If the test taker answers it correctly, the computer will give them a harder question. If they answer that question incorrectly, they will be given an easier question. People who answer the first question incorrectly are then given an easier one, and if they get it right, the next question will be harder. The computer will adapt to the test taker in this manner after every question, so a person who answers several of the early questions correctly may not be given as many questions in total as other test takers receive.

Keep in mind that no one will be allowed to take the SIFT more than two times. If a person takes the SIFT, and does poorly, they have one more chance to pass it, but they must first wait six months before attempting it again. If they fail the SIFT the second time, that's it – they can never take it again. So it's critical to be thoroughly prepared to do well on your first attempt at the SIFT.

The next few sections will go over the seven subtests in detail to help prepare you for what you will see on each test.

Simple Drawings Test

The Simple Drawings section of the SIFT couldn't be more simple, on the one hand, yet at the same time, it's also extremely challenging. Every problem asks you to perform one very easy task – look at the five items shown, and choose the one that doesn't match the other four. In other words, four of the five items will be exactly the same, and one will be different, and you must spot the exception and mark the corresponding answer choice.

The task itself sounds easy enough, and, in fact, it really is quite easy. As the name of the section implies, the drawings aren't at all complicated. The differences between the mismatched item and the other four items will be obvious; you won't be searching for minute differences. The problems won't involve looking at five circles and trying to determine which one of them has a circumference that is 31/32 of the circumference of the other four, or any other drawings with only tiny or subtle differences. The correct answer will be apparent. It's just a matter of how quickly you can process what's in front of you and respond correctly.

Answering any single question in this section correctly is easy enough, but answering all of them will be very challenging. That's because there's a time limit of only two minutes, and there are 100 questions. That's what turns this section, which appears disarmingly easy at first glance, into an extremely difficult task. The strictly enforced time limit means a person has a mere 1.2 seconds to spend on each problem if they're going to answer all 100 questions. That's 1.2 seconds to scan the problem, spot the item that doesn't match the others, and mark the correct answer choice, a hundred times in a row.

For the vast majority of people, this is an impossible task. So you should be aware going in that you probably won't finish all the questions in this section. You should definitely try to go as fast as you can, for as long as you can, because speed is critically important. Of course, accuracy is also critically important, and if going too fast in order to answer all 100 questions causes a drop in your accuracy, you won't have helped yourself at all. Also, if you're running out of time, do not start marking answer choices randomly, hoping to get some right by accident. Wrong answers penalize your score, so you will lower your score if you try randomly guessing.

Giving a person only two minutes to answer 100 questions may seem a bit harsh, but the Army's testing experts deliberately designed this section in such a way that hardly anyone would be able to complete all 100 questions in the allotted time. This section is mainly measuring two abilities or aptitudes – accurate observation under pressure, and reaction time under pressure. These are two of the most important skills a person must possess in order to succeed as a pilot, and the Army's test designers believe that the high pressure Simple Drawings section is an efficient way of determining which applicants have high levels of skill in these areas, and which ones don't.

It is a good idea to take advantage of the opportunity to practice this subtest before you take your official SIFT. Practicing with a two minute timer set is your best bet for increasing your chances of earning a great score in this section. You'll gain some experience in racing against the clock while trying to maintain your accuracy.

Bear in mind that the process of answering these questions on paper will not be the same as the process of answering them on a computer, as you will have to for your official SIFT. On paper, you can see the whole page's worth of questions at a time, while on the computer, you will only see one question at a time, and you will have to answer it before you are shown the next one. This may not seem like a big deal, but if each question takes even a tenth of a second longer to process, then that means your timer is effectively starting out at 110 seconds instead of 120 seconds. To try to counteract this effect, it might be a good idea to have an extra blank sheet of paper when you practice that you can use to cover up all the questions on the page except the question you're currently working on. That way, you can better simulate the actual testing experience.

Also, because of the nature of the test questions, there's no reason why you shouldn't be able to retake the same test over a few times. You couldn't do this with a test based on reading passages, of course, because you would tend to remember many of the right answers. However, because the problems in this section involve comparing groups of random symbols, and because you'll be going very fast as you work through the tests, you won't retain very much of what you see. For that reason, we recommend marking your answers on a separate sheet of paper so there will be no clues on the actual questions if you decide to practice again with the same test.

Here are a few examples of what the Simple Drawings questions might look like:

1.   (A)   (B)   (C)   (D)   (E)

2.   (A)   (B)   (C)   (D)   (E)

3.   (A)   (B)   (C)   (D)   (E)

4.   (A)   (B)   (C)   (D)   (E)

5.   (A)   (B)   (C)   (D)   (E)

Hidden Figures Test

This section of the SIFT is similar to the Simple Drawings section in that it measures your ability to quickly and accurately apprehend visual information. In Simple Drawings the information you're looking for is obvious, and the difficulty is in trying to complete all of the questions before time expires. That is not the case in the Hidden Figures section; as the name implies, your task in this part of the SIFT is to locate a figure or shape that is hidden in a larger, much more complicated drawing.

These questions are measuring where you fall on the Field Independence – Field Dependence Scale. Field independence refers to a person's ability to ignore non-important visual information, and zero in on the important information within the field. People who are high on the Field Independence end of the scale are able to do this very well, while people on the other end of the scale, the Field Dependence end, have a lot of difficulty in separating important visual information from irrelevant information. Of course, pilots need to be extremely skilled at accurately interpreting visual information instantly, ignoring everything that doesn't matter and honing in on the important data, so you'll need to do well on this section to achieve a high score on the SIFT.

Each group of questions on the test will show five complex arrangements of lines and geometric shapes, where each arrangement looks much like a puzzle that has been put together. Above these, the test will show five different figures. Each arrangement of lines and shapes is hiding one (and only one) of the figures shown above them and you must determine which figure is in each shape arrangement. Not all figures have to be used; some may be used more than once within a set of five questions, so the answer to the fifth question is not necessarily the choice that hasn't been used yet.

This section contains 50 questions, and has a time limit of five minutes. This may sound less intimidating than the Simple Drawings section, which features 100 questions with a two minute time limit, but for most people, answering all the Hidden Figures questions in the space of five minute will be even more difficult than answering all the Simple Drawings questions in two minutes. That's because in Simple Drawings, it takes a mere glance to find the right answer for each question. In this section, the figure you're looking for is well hidden, and unless you're extraordinarily gifted in field independence, you're going to have to spend some amount of time on each complex drawing to find the hidden figure.

There are a few different strategies that can be used on these questions. Some strategies will work better than others, depending on the different figures and shape arrangements you encounter, and your particular characteristics.

Strategy 1: Examine each shape arrangement in turn. For each arrangement, try to fit each of the figures into the lines in the arrangement. Once you find one that fits (size, shape, and orientation) into the arrangement, go ahead and mark it. There's no need to check the remaining figures since only one will fit into each arrangement. Remember though not to cross a figure off the list after you've used it; figures can be used multiple times in the set.

Strategy 2: Instead of starting with the shape arrangements, start with the figures. Look through the figures and check for any prominent distinguishing characteristics (e.g., a long side at a particular diagonal angle, a pair of sides that run parallel at a particular distance, a side that zigzags). For each figure with a prominent feature, scan the shape arrangements and eliminate that figure for any arrangements that cannot accommodate the prominent feature. Once you've ruled out as many figures as possible for the five arrangements, follow the steps for strategy 1, but check out only the remaining figures (the ones that you haven't eliminated for each arrangement).

You'll want to try out both strategies and see which one gives you better results within the time constraints of the section. One of the most important rules governing these questions is that the hidden figure has to be the exact same size and orientation as where it is shown above with the answer choices, so regardless of what strategy you choose to employ, keep this in mind.

On the next page is an example of a hidden figures question set.

A   B   C   D   E

1.

4.

2.

5.

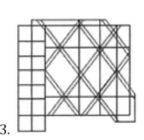

3.

Answers:

1. A
2. D
3. E
4. C
5. B

Army Aviation Information Test

The Army Aviation Information section tests your knowledge of basic aviation information. Most of the information the questions are based on can be found in the FAA Helicopter Flying Handbook. In Army Aviation Information, you'll have 30 minutes to answer 40 questions. Since these are knowledge-based questions, you can improve your success rate here by reading up on the content that will be tested on the exam. In fact, since nearly all the rest of the SIFT subtests are testing for aptitude, this is one of the few sections where good old fashioned studying can make a huge difference in your results. And unlike other sections, this section is not designed to be difficult for the average person to answer all the questions within the allotted time. With proper preparation, you should be able to finish all the questions in this section, and answer most of them correctly.

The section below consists primarily of brief excerpts from the FAA handbook on helicopter flight. The FAA helicopter handbook is a lengthy and thorough manual that covers everything you need to know to operate a helicopter. No matter what you read and retain from the excerpts we've included, you'll want to obtain a copy of the FAA helicopter manual for yourself. You can download it for free from the internet or if you like physical books, there are a variety of nominally priced options that can be purchased on Amazon. No matter which format you choose, make it a point to study this handbook thoroughly. Doing so is essential not only to your score on this section of the SIFT, but also to your attaining the necessary knowledge to become a skillful pilot. If you have time to read the whole manual, we recommend doing so, but if not, we advise that you focus your time on the following chapters:
Chapter 2: Aerodynamics of Flight
Chapter 3: Helicopter Flight Controls
Chapter 6: Weight and Balance
Chapter 9: Basic Flight Maneuvers
Chapter 10: Advanced Flight Maneuvers

Link for accessing the FAA Helicopter Handbook online or downloading it:
https://www.faa.gov/regulations_policies/handbooks_manuals/aviation/helicopter_flying_handbook/

If the link doesn't work (i.e., if the FAA decides to change the location), you can always access it by going to www.faa.gov and entering "helicopter flying handbook" in their search bar.

Aerodynamics

Forces Acting on the Aircraft

Once a helicopter leaves the ground, it is acted upon by four aerodynamic forces; thrust, drag, lift and weight. Understanding how these forces work and knowing how to control them with the use of power and flight controls are essential to flight. They are defined as follows:

- Thrust—the forward force produced by the power plant/propeller or rotor. It opposes or overcomes the force of drag. As a general rule, it acts parallel to the longitudinal axis. However, this is not always the case, as explained later.
- Drag—a rearward, retarding force caused by disruption of airflow by the wing, rotor, fuselage, and other protruding objects. Drag opposes thrust and acts rearward parallel to the relative wind.
- Weight—the combined load of the aircraft itself, the crew, the fuel, and the cargo or baggage. Weight pulls the aircraft downward because of the force of gravity. It opposes lift and acts vertically downward through the aircraft's center of gravity (CG).
- Lift—opposes the downward force of weight, is produced by the dynamic effect of the air acting on the airfoil, and acts perpendicular to the flightpath through the center of lift.

Lift

Lift is generated when an object changes the direction of flow of a fluid or when the fluid is forced to move by the object passing through it. When the object and fluid move relative to each other and the object turns the fluid flow in a direction perpendicular to that flow, the force required to do this work creates an equal and opposite force that is lift. The object may be moving through a stationary fluid, or the fluid may be flowing past a stationary object—these two are effectively identical as, in principle, it is only the frame of reference of the viewer which differs. The lift generated by an airfoil depends on such factors as:

- Speed of the airflow
- Density of the air
- Total area of the segment or airfoil
- Angle of attack (AOA) between the air and the airfoil

The AOA is the angle at which the airfoil meets the oncoming airflow (or vice versa). In the case of a helicopter, the object is the rotor blade (airfoil) and the fluid is the air. Lift is produced when a mass of air is deflected, and it always acts perpendicular to the resultant relative wind. A symmetric airfoil must have a positive AOA to generate positive lift. At a zero AOA, no lift is generated. At a negative AOA, negative lift is generated. A cambered or nonsymmetrical airfoil may produce positive lift at zero, or even small negative AOA.

The basic concept of lift is simple. However, the details of how the relative movement of air and airfoil interact to produce the turning action that generates lift are complex. In any case causing lift, an angled flat plate, revolving cylinder, airfoil, etc., the flow meeting the leading edge of the object is forced to split over and under the object. The sudden change in direction over the object causes an area of low pressure to form behind the leading edge on the upper surface of the object. In turn, due to this pressure gradient and the viscosity of the fluid, the flow over the object is accelerated down along the upper surface of the object. At the same time, the flow forced under the object is rapidly slowed or stagnated causing an area of high pressure. This also causes the flow to accelerate along the upper surface of the object. The two sections of the fluid each leave the trailing edge of the object with a downward component of momentum, producing lift.

Weight

Normally, weight is thought of as being a known, fixed value, such as the weight of the helicopter, fuel, and occupants. To lift the helicopter off the ground vertically, the rotor system must generate enough lift to overcome or offset the total weight of the helicopter and its occupants. Newton's First Law states: "Every object in a state of uniform motion tends to remain in that state of motion unless an external force is applied to it." In this case, the object is the helicopter whether at a hover or on the ground and the external force applied to it is lift, which is accomplished by increasing the pitch angle of the main rotor blades. This action forces the helicopter into a state of motion, without it the helicopter would either remain on the ground or at a hover.

The weight of the helicopter can also be influenced by aerodynamic loads. When you bank a helicopter while maintaining a constant altitude, the "G" load or load factor increases. The load factor is the actual load on the rotor blades at any time, divided by the normal load or gross weight (weight of the helicopter and its contents). Any time a helicopter flies in a constant altitude curved flightpath, the load supported by the rotor blades is greater than the total weight of the helicopter. The tighter the curved flightpath is, the steeper the bank is; the more rapid the flare or pullout from a dive is, the greater the load supported by the rotor. Therefore, the greater the load factor must be.

To overcome this additional load factor, the helicopter must be able to produce more lift. If excess engine power is not available, the helicopter either descends or has to decelerate in order to maintain the same altitude. The load factor and, hence, apparent gross weight increase is relatively small in banks up to 30°. Even so, under the right set of adverse circumstances, such as high density altitude, turbulent air, high gross weight, and poor pilot technique, sufficient or excess power may not be available to maintain altitude and airspeed. Pilots must take all of these factors into consideration throughout the entire flight from the point of ascending to a hover to landing. Above 30° of bank, the apparent increase in gross weight soars. At 30° of bank, or pitch, the apparent increase is only 16 percent, but at 60°, it is twice the load on the wings and rotor system. For example, if the weight of the helicopter is 1,600 pounds, the weight supported by the rotor disk in a 30° bank at a constant altitude would be 1,856 pounds (1,600 + 16 percent (or 256)). In a 60° bank, it would be 3,200 pounds; in an 80° bank, it would be almost six times as much, or 8,000 pounds. It is important to note that each rotor blade must support a percentage of the gross weight. In a two bladed system, each blade of the 1,600 pound helicopter as stated above would have to lift 50 percent or 800 pounds. If this same helicopter had three rotor blades, each blade would have to lift only 33 percent, or 533 pounds. One additional cause of large load factors is rough or turbulent air. The severe vertical gusts produced by turbulence can cause a sudden increase in AOA, resulting in increased rotor blade loads that are resisted by the inertia of the helicopter.

Each type of helicopter has its own limitations which are based on the aircraft structure, size, and capabilities. Regardless of how much weight one can carry or the engine power that it may have, they are all susceptible to aerodynamic overloading. Unfortunately, if the pilot attempts to push the performance envelope the consequence can be fatal. Aerodynamic forces effect every movement in a helicopter, whether it is increasing the collective or a steep bank angle. Anticipating results from a particular maneuver or adjustment of a flight control is not good piloting technique. Instead pilots need to truly understand the capabilities of the helicopter under any and all circumstances and plan to never exceed the flight envelope for any situation.

Thrust

Thrust, like lift, is generated by the rotation of the main rotor system. In a helicopter, thrust can be forward, rearward, sideward, or vertical. The resultant lift and thrust determines the direction of movement of the helicopter.

The solidity ratio is the ratio of the total rotor blade area, which is the combined area of all the main rotor blades, to the total rotor disk area. This ratio provides a means to measure the potential for a rotor system to provide thrust and lift. The mathematical calculations needed to calculate the solidity ratio for each helicopter may not be of importance to most pilots but what should be are the capabilities of the rotor system to produce and maintain lift. Many helicopter accidents are caused from the rotor system being overloaded. Simply put, pilots attempt maneuvers that require more lift than the rotor system can produce or more power than the helicopter's powerplant can provide. Trying to land with a nose high attitude along with any other unfavorable condition (i.e., high gross weight or wind gusts) is most likely to end in disaster.

The tail rotor also produces thrust. The amount of thrust is variable through the use of the antitorque pedals and is used to control the helicopter's yaw.

Drag

The force that resists the movement of a helicopter through the air and is produced when lift is developed is called drag. Drag must be overcome by the engine to turn the rotor. Drag always acts parallel to the relative wind. Total drag is composed of three types of drag: profile, induced, and parasite.

Profile Drag
Profile drag develops from the frictional resistance of the blades passing through the air. It does not change significantly with the airfoil's AOA, but increases moderately when airspeed increases. Profile drag is composed of form drag and skin friction. Form drag results from the turbulent wake caused by the separation of airflow from the surface of a structure. The amount of drag is related to both the size and shape of the structure that protrudes into the relative wind. Skin friction is caused by surface roughness. Even though the surface appears smooth, it may be quite rough when viewed under a microscope. A thin layer of air clings to the rough surface and creates small eddies that contribute to drag.

Induced Drag
Induced drag is generated by the airflow circulation around the rotor blade as it creates lift. The high pressure area beneath the blade joins the low pressure area above the blade at the trailing edge and at the rotor tips. This causes a spiral, or vortex, which trails behind each blade whenever lift is being produced. These vortices deflect the airstream downward in

the vicinity of the blade, creating an increase in downwash. Therefore, the blade operates in an average relative wind that is inclined downward and rearward near the blade. Because the lift produced by the blade is perpendicular to the relative wind, the lift is inclined aft by the same amount. The component of lift that is acting in a rearward direction is induced drag.

As the air pressure differential increases with an increase in AOA, stronger vortices form, and induced drag increases. Since the blade's AOA is usually lower at higher airspeeds, and higher at low speeds, induced drag decreases as airspeed increases and increases as airspeed decreases. Induced drag is the major cause of drag at lower airspeeds.

Parasite Drag
Parasite drag is present any time the helicopter is moving through the air. This type of drag increases with airspeed. Non-lifting components of the helicopter, such as the cabin, rotor mast, tail, and landing gear, contribute to parasite drag. Any loss of momentum by the airstream, due to such things as openings for engine cooling, creates additional parasite drag. Because of its rapid increase with increasing airspeed, parasite drag is the major cause of drag at higher airspeeds. Parasite drag varies with the square of the velocity; therefore, doubling the airspeed increases the parasite drag four times.

Total Drag
Total drag for a helicopter is the sum of all three drag forces. As airspeed increases, parasite drag increases, while induced drag decreases. Profile drag remains relatively constant throughout the speed range with some increase at higher airspeeds. Combining all drag forces results in a total drag curve. The low point on the total drag curve shows the airspeed at which drag is minimized. This is the point where the lift-to-drag ratio is greatest and is referred to as L/DMAX. At this speed, the total lift capacity of the helicopter, when compared to the total drag of the helicopter, is most favorable. This is an important factor in helicopter performance.

Flight Controls

Collective Pitch Control

The collective pitch control (or simply "collective" or "thrust lever") is located on the left side of the pilot's seat and is operated with the left hand. The collective is used to make changes to the pitch angle of the main rotor blades and does this simultaneously, or collectively, as the name implies. As the collective pitch control is raised, there is a simultaneous and equal increase in pitch angle of all main rotor blades; as it is lowered, there is a simultaneous and equal decrease in pitch angle. This is done through a series of mechanical linkages and the amount of movement in the collective lever determines the amount of blade pitch change. An adjustable friction control helps prevent inadvertent collective pitch movement.

Changing the pitch angle on the blades changes the angle of incidence on each blade. With a change in angle of incidence comes a change in drag, which affects the speed or revolutions per minute (rpm) of the main rotor. As the pitch angle increases, angle of incidence increases, drag increases, and rotor rpm decreases. Decreasing pitch angle decreases both angle of incidence and drag, while rotor rpm increases. In order to maintain a constant rotor rpm, which is essential in helicopter operations, a proportionate change in power is required to compensate for the change in drag. This is accomplished with the throttle control or governor, which automatically adjusts engine power.

Throttle Control

The function of the throttle is to regulate engine rpm. If the correlator or governor system does not maintain the desired rpm when the collective is raised or lowered, or if those systems are not installed, the throttle must be moved manually with the twist grip in order to maintain rpm. The throttle control is much like a motorcycle throttle, and works in virtually the same way. Twisting the throttle to the left increases rpm; twisting the throttle to the right decreases rpm.

Governor/Correlator

A governor is a sensing device that senses rotor and engine rpm and makes the necessary adjustments in order to keep rotor rpm constant. In normal operations, once the rotor rpm is set, the governor keeps the rpm constant, and there is no need to make any throttle adjustments. Governors are common on all turbine helicopters (as it is a function of the fuel control system of the turbine engine), and used on some piston powered helicopters.

A correlator is a mechanical connection between the collective lever and the engine throttle. When the collective lever is raised, power is automatically increased; when lowered, power is decreased. This system maintains rpm close to the desired value, but still requires adjustment of the throttle for fine tuning.

Some helicopters do not have correlators or governors and require coordination of all collective and throttle movements. When the collective is raised, the throttle must be increased; when the collective is lowered, the throttle must be decreased. As with any aircraft control, large adjustments of either collective pitch or throttle should be avoided. All corrections should be made through the use of smooth pressure.

In piston helicopters, the collective pitch is the primary control for manifold pressure, and the throttle is the primary control for rpm. However, the collective pitch control also influences rpm, and the throttle also influences manifold pressure; therefore, each is considered to be a secondary control of the other's function. Both the tachometer (rpm indicator) and the manifold pressure gauge must be analyzed to determine which control to use.

Cyclic Pitch Control

The cyclic pitch control is usually projected upward from the cockpit floor, between the pilot's legs or between the two pilot seats in some models. This primary flight control allows the pilot to fly the helicopter in any direction of travel: forward, rearward, left, and right. As discussed in Chapter 3, Aerodynamics of Flight, the total lift force is always perpendicular to the tip-path plane of the main rotor. The purpose of the cyclic pitch control is to tilt the tip-path plane in the direction of the desired horizontal direction. The cyclic controls the rotor disk tilt versus the horizon, which directs the rotor disk thrust to enable the pilot to control the direction of travel of the helicopter.

The rotor disk tilts in the same direction the cyclic pitch control is moved. If the cyclic is moved forward, the rotor disk tilts forward; if the cyclic is moved aft, the disk tilts aft, and so on. Because the rotor disk acts like a gyro, the mechanical linkages for the cyclic control rods are rigged in such a way that they decrease the pitch angle of the rotor blade approximately 90° before it reaches the direction of cyclic displacement, and increase the pitch angle of the rotor blade approximately 90° after it passes the direction of displacement. An increase in pitch angle increases AOA; a decrease in pitch angle decreases AOA. For example, if the cyclic is moved forward, the AOA decreases as the rotor blade passes the right side of the helicopter and increases on the left side. This results in maximum downward deflection of the rotor blade in front of the helicopter and maximum upward deflection behind it, causing the rotor disk to tilt forward.

Antitorque Pedals

The antitorque pedals, located on the cabin floor by the pilot's feet, control the pitch and therefore the thrust of the tail rotor blades or other antitorque system. Newton's Third Law applies to the helicopter fuselage and its rotation in the opposite direction of the main rotor blades unless counteracted and controlled. To make flight possible and to compensate for this torque, most helicopter designs incorporate an antitorque rotor or tail rotor. The antitorque pedals allow the pilot to control the pitch angle of the tail rotor blades, which in forward flight puts the helicopter in longitudinal trim and, while at a hover, enables the pilot to turn the helicopter 360°. The antitorque pedals are connected to the pitch change mechanism on the tail rotor gearbox and allow the pitch angle on the tail rotor blades to be increased or decreased.

<u>Heading Control</u>
The tail rotor is used to control the heading of the helicopter while hovering or when making hovering turns, as well as counteracting the torque of the main rotor. Hovering turns are commonly referred to as "pedal turns."

At speeds above translational lift, the pedals are used to compensate for torque to put the helicopter in longitudinal trim so that coordinated flight can be maintained. The cyclic control is used to change heading by making a turn to the desired direction.

The thrust of the tail rotor depends on the pitch angle of the tail rotor blades. This pitch angle can be positive, negative, or zero. A positive pitch angle tends to move the tail to the right. A negative pitch angle moves the tail to the left, while no thrust is produced with a zero pitch angle. The maximum positive pitch angle of the tail rotor is generally greater than the maximum negative pitch angle available. This is because the primary purpose of the tail rotor is to counteract the torque of the main rotor. The capability for tail rotors to produce thrust to the left (negative pitch angle) is necessary, because during autorotation the drag of the transmission tends to yaw the nose to the left, or in the same direction the main rotor is turning.

From the neutral position, applying right pedal causes the nose of the helicopter to yaw right and the tail to swing to the left. Pressing on the left pedal has the opposite effect: the nose of the helicopter yaws to the left and the tail swings right.

With the antitorque pedals in the neutral position, the tail rotor has a medium positive pitch angle. In medium positive pitch, the tail rotor thrust approximately equals the torque of the main rotor during cruise flight, so the helicopter maintains a constant heading in level flight.

A vertical fin or stabilizer is used in many single-rotor helicopters to help aid in heading control. The fin is designed to optimize directional stability in flight with a zero tail rotor thrust setting. The size of the fin is crucial to this design. If the surface is too large, the tail rotor thrust may be blocked. Heading control would be more difficult at slower airspeeds and at a hover and the vertical fin would then weathervane.

Helicopters that are designed with tandem rotors do not have an antitorque rotor. The helicopter is designed with both rotor systems rotating in opposite directions to counteract the torque rather than a tail rotor. Directional antitorque pedals are used for directional control of the aircraft while in flight, as well as while taxiing with the forward gear off the ground.

In intermeshing rotor systems, which are a set of two rotors turning in opposite directions with each rotor mast mounted on the helicopter with a slight angle to the other so that the blades intermesh without colliding, and a coaxial rotor systems, which are a pair of rotors mounted one above the other on the same shaft and turning in opposite directions, the heading pedals control the heading of the helicopter while at a hover by imbalancing torque between the rotors, allowing for the torque to turn the helicopter.

Weight and Balance

Weight

When determining if a helicopter is within the weight limits, consider the weight of the basic helicopter, crew, passengers, cargo, and fuel. Although the effective weight (load factor) varies during maneuvering flight, this chapter primarily considers the weight of the loaded helicopter while at rest.

It is critical to understand that the maximum allowable weight may change during the flight. When operations include OGE hovers and confined areas, planning must be done to ensure that the helicopter is capable of lifting the weight during all phases of flight. The weight may be acceptable during the early morning hours, but as the density altitude increases during the day, the maximum allowable weight may have to be reduced to keep the helicopter within its capability.

The following terms are used when computing a helicopter's weight:

Basic Empty Weight
The starting point for weight computations is the basic empty weight, which is the weight of the standard helicopter, optional equipment, unusable fuel, and all operating fluids including engine and transmission oil, and hydraulic fluid for those aircraft so equipped. Some helicopters might use the term "licensed empty weight," which is nearly the same as basic empty weight, except that it does not include full engine and transmission oil, just undrainable oil. If flying a helicopter that lists a licensed empty weight, be sure to add the weight of the oil to computations.

Maximum Gross Weight
The maximum weight of the helicopter. Most helicopters have an internal maximum gross weight, which refers to the weight within the helicopter structure and an external maximum gross weight, which refers to the weight of the helicopter with an external load. The external maximum weight may vary depending on where it is attached to the helicopter. Some large cargo helicopters may have several attachment points for sling load or winch operations. These helicopters can carry a tremendous amount of weight when the attachment point is directly under the CG of the aircraft.

Weight Limitations
Weight limitations are necessary to guarantee the structural integrity of the helicopter and enable pilots to predict helicopter performance accurately. Although aircraft manufacturers build in safety factors, a pilot should never intentionally exceed the load limits for which a helicopter is certificated. Operating below a minimum weight could adversely affect the handling characteristics of the helicopter. During single-pilot operations in some helicopters, a pilot needs to use a large amount of forward cyclic in order to maintain a hover. By adding ballast to the helicopter, the cyclic position is closer to the CG, which gives a greater range of control motion in every direction. When operating at or below the minimum weight of the helicopter, additional weight also improves autorotational characteristics since the autorotational descent can be established sooner. In addition, operating below minimum weight could prevent achieving the desirable rotor revolutions per minute (rpm) during autorotations.

Operating above a maximum weight could result in structural deformation or failure during flight, if encountering excessive load factors, strong wind gusts, or turbulence. Weight and maneuvering limitations also are factors considered for establishing fatigue life of components. Overweight, meaning overstressed, parts fail sooner than anticipated. Therefore, premature failure is a major consideration in determination of fatigue life and life cycles of parts.

Although a helicopter is certificated for a specified maximum gross weight, it is not safe to take off with this load under some conditions. Anything that adversely affects takeoff, climb, hovering, and landing performance may require off-loading of fuel, passengers, or baggage to some weight less than the published maximum. Factors that can affect performance include high altitude, high temperature, and high humidity conditions, which result in a high density altitude. In-depth performance planning is critical when operating in these conditions.

Balance

Helicopter performance is not only affected by gross weight, but also by the position of that weight. It is essential to load the aircraft within the allowable CG range specified in the RFM's weight and balance limitations.

Center of Gravity
Ideally, a pilot should try to balance a helicopter perfectly so that the fuselage remains horizontal in hovering flight, with no cyclic pitch control needed except for wind correction. Since the fuselage acts as a pendulum suspended from the rotor, changing the CG changes the angle at which the aircraft hangs from the rotor. When the CG is directly under the rotor

mast, the helicopter hangs horizontally; if the CG is too far forward of the mast, the helicopter hangs with its nose tilted down; if the CG is too far aft of the mast, the nose tilts up.

CG Forward of Forward Limit
A forward CG may occur when a heavy pilot and passenger take off without baggage or proper ballast located aft of the rotor mast. This situation becomes worse if the fuel tanks are located aft of the rotor mast because as fuel burns the CG continues to shift forward.

This condition is easily recognized when coming to a hover following a vertical takeoff. The helicopter has a nose-low attitude, and excessive rearward displacement of the cyclic control is needed to maintain a hover in a no-wind condition. Do not continue flight in this condition, since a pilot could rapidly lose rearward cyclic control as fuel is consumed. A pilot may also find it impossible to decelerate sufficiently to bring the helicopter to a stop. In the event of engine failure and the resulting autorotation, there may not be enough cyclic control to flare properly for the landing.

A forward CG is not as obvious when hovering into a strong wind, since less rearward cyclic displacement is required than when hovering with no wind. When determining whether a critical balance condition exists, it is essential to consider the wind velocity and its relation to the rearward displacement of the cyclic control.

CG Aft of Aft Limit
Without proper ballast in the cockpit, exceeding the aft CG may occur when:
- A lightweight pilot takes off solo with a full load of fuel located aft of the rotor mast.
- A lightweight pilot takes off with maximum baggage allowed in a baggage compartment located aft of the rotor mast.
- A lightweight pilot takes off with a combination of baggage and substantial fuel where both are aft of the rotor mast.

A pilot can recognize the aft CG condition when coming to a hover following a vertical takeoff. The helicopter will have a tail-low attitude, and will need excessive forward displacement of cyclic control to maintain a hover in a no-wind condition. If there is a wind, even greater forward cyclic is needed.

If flight is continued in this condition, it may be impossible to fly in the upper allowable airspeed range due to inadequate forward cyclic authority to maintain a nose-low attitude. In addition, with an extreme aft CG, gusty or rough air could accelerate the helicopter to a speed faster than that produced with full forward cyclic control. In this case, dissymmetry of lift and blade flapping could cause the rotor disk to tilt aft. With full forward cyclic control already applied, a pilot might not be able to lower the rotor disk, resulting in possible loss of control, or the rotor blades striking the tailboom.

Lateral Balance
For smaller helicopters, it is generally unnecessary to determine the lateral CG for normal flight instruction and passenger flights. This is because helicopter cabins are relatively narrow and most optional equipment is located near the centerline. However, some helicopter manuals specify the seat from which a pilot must conduct solo flight. In addition, if there is an unusual situation that could affect the lateral CG, such as a heavy pilot and a full load of fuel on one side of the helicopter, its position should be checked against the CG

envelope. If carrying external loads in a position that requires large lateral cyclic control displacement to maintain level flight, fore and aft cyclic effectiveness could be limited dramatically. Manufacturers generally account for known lateral CG displacements by locating external attachment points opposite the lateral imbalance. Examples are placement of hoist systems attached to the side, and wing stores commonly used on military aircraft for external fuel pods or armament systems.

Basic Maneuvers

The Four Fundamentals

There are four fundamentals of flight upon which all maneuvers are based: straight-and-level flight, turns, climbs, and descents. All controlled flight maneuvers consist of one or more of the four fundamentals of flight. If a student pilot is able to perform these maneuvers well, and the student's proficiency is based on accurate "feel" and control analysis rather than mechanical movements, the ability to perform any assigned maneuver is only a matter of obtaining a clear visual and mental conception of it. The flight instructor must impart a good knowledge of these basic elements to the student, and must combine them and plan their practice so that perfect performance of each is instinctive without conscious effort. The importance of this to the success of flight training cannot be overemphasized. As the student progresses to more complex maneuvers, discounting any difficulties in visualizing the maneuvers, most student difficulties are caused by a lack of training, practice, or understanding of the principles of one or more of these fundamentals.

Guidelines
Good practices to follow during maneuvering flight include:
1. Move the cyclic only as fast as trim, torque, and rotor can be maintained. When entering a maneuver and the trim, rotor, or torque reacts quicker than anticipated, pilot limitations have been exceeded. If continued, an aircraft limitation will be exceeded. Perform the maneuver with less intensity until all aspects of the machine can be controlled. The pilot must be aware of the sensitivity of the flight controls due to the high speed of the main rotor.
2. Anticipate changes in aircraft performance due to loading or environmental condition. The normal collective increase to check rotor speed at sea level standard (SLS) may not be sufficient at 4,000 feet pressure altitude (PA) and 95 °F.
3. Anticipate the following characteristics during aggressive maneuvering flight, and adjust or lead with collective as necessary to maintain trim and torque:
   - Left turns, torque increases (more antitorque). This applies to most helicopters, but not all.
   - Right turns, torque decreases (less antitorque). This applies to most helicopters, but not all.
   - Application of aft cyclic, torque decreases and rotor speed increases.
   - Application of forward cyclic (especially when immediately following aft cyclic application), torque increases and rotor speed decreases.
   - Always leave a way out.
   - Know where the winds are.
   - Engine failures occur during power changes and cruise flight.

- 19 -

- Crew coordination is critical. Everyone needs to be fully aware of what is going on, and each crewmember has a specific duty.
- In steep turns, the nose drops. In most cases, energy (airspeed) must be traded to maintain altitude as the required excess engine power may not be available (to maintain airspeed in a 2G/60° turn, rotor thrust/engine power must increase by 100 percent). Failure to anticipate this at low altitude endangers the crew and passengers. The rate of pitch change is proportional to gross weight and density altitude.
- Many overtorques during flight occur as the aircraft unloads from high G maneuvers. This is due to insufficient collective reduction following the increase to maintain consistent torque and rotor rpm as G-loading increased (dive recovery or recovery from high G-turn to the right).
- Normal helicopter landings usually require high power settings, with terminations to a hover requiring the highest power setting.
- The cyclic position relative to the horizon determines the helicopter's travel and attitude.

Vertical Takeoff to a Hover

A vertical takeoff to a hover involves flying the helicopter from the ground vertically to a skid height of two to three feet, while maintaining a constant heading. Once the desired skid height is achieved, the helicopter should remain nearly motionless over a reference point at a constant altitude and on a constant heading. The maneuver requires a high degree of concentration and coordination.

Technique
The pilot on the controls needs to clear the area left, right, and above to perform a vertical takeoff to a hover. The pilot should remain focused outside the aircraft and obtain clearance to take off from the controlling tower. If necessary, the pilot who is not on the controls assists in clearing the aircraft and provides adequate warning of any obstacles and any unannounced or unusual drift/altitude changes.

Heading control, direction of turn, and rate of turn at hover are all controlled by using the pedals. Hover height, rate of ascent, and the rate of descent are controlled by using the collective. Helicopter position and the direction of travel are controlled by the cyclic.

After receiving the proper clearance and ensuring that the area is clear of obstacles and traffic, begin the maneuver with the collective in the down position and the cyclic in a neutral position, or slightly into the wind. Very slowly increase the collective until the helicopter becomes light on the skids or wheels. At the same time apply pressure and counter pressure on the pedals to ensure the heading remains constant. Continue to apply pedals as necessary to maintain heading and coordinate the cyclic for a vertical ascent. As the helicopter slowly leaves the ground, check for proper attitude control response and helicopter center of gravity. A slow ascent will allow stopping if responses are outside the normal parameters indicating hung or entangled landing gear, center of gravity problems, or control issues. If a roll or tilt begin, decrease the collective and determine the cause of the roll or tilt. Upon reaching the desired hover altitude, adjust the flight controls as necessary to maintain position over the intended hover area. Student pilots should be reminded that while at a hover, the helicopter is rarely ever level. Helicopters usually hover left side low due to the tail rotor thrust being counteracted by the main rotor tilt. A nose low or high condition is generally caused by loading. Once stabilized, check the engine instruments and note the power required to hover.

Excessive movement of any flight control requires a change in the other flight controls. For example, if the helicopter drifts to one side while hovering, the pilot naturally moves the cyclic in the opposite direction. When this is done, part of the vertical thrust is diverted, resulting in a loss of altitude. To maintain altitude, increase the collective. This increases drag on the blades and tends to slow them down. To counteract the drag and maintain rpm, increase the throttle. Increased throttle means increased torque, so the pilot must add more pedal pressure to maintain the heading. This can easily lead to overcontrolling the helicopter. However, as level of proficiency increases, problems associated with overcontrolling decrease. Helicopter controls are usually more driven by pressure than by gross control movements.

Common Errors
1. Failing to ascend vertically as the helicopter becomes airborne.
2. Pulling excessive collective to become airborne, causing the helicopter to gain too much altitude.
3. Overcontrolling the antitorque pedals, which not only changes the heading of the helicopter, but also changes the rpm.
4. Reducing throttle rapidly in situations in which proper rpm has been exceeded, usually resulting in exaggerated heading changes and loss of lift, resulting in loss of altitude.
5. Failing to ascend slowly.

Hovering

Hovering is a maneuver in which the helicopter is maintained in nearly motionless flight over a reference point at a constant altitude and on a constant heading.

Technique
To maintain a hover over a point, use sideview and peripheral vision to look for small changes in the helicopter's attitude and altitude. When these changes are noted, make the necessary control inputs before the helicopter starts to move from the point. To detect small variations in altitude or position, the main area of visual attention needs to be some distance from the aircraft, using various points on the helicopter or the tip-path plane as a reference. Looking too closely or looking down leads to overcontrolling. Obviously, in order to remain over a certain point, know where the point is, but do not focus all attention there.

As with a takeoff, the pilot controls altitude with the collective and maintains a constant rpm with the throttle. The cyclic is used to maintain the helicopter's position; the pedals, to control heading. To maintain the helicopter in a stabilized hover, make small, smooth, coordinated corrections. As the desired effect occurs, remove the correction in order to stop the helicopter's movement. For example, if the helicopter begins to move rearward, apply a small amount of forward cyclic pressure. However, neutralize this pressure just before the helicopter comes to a stop, or it will begin to move forward.

After experience is gained, a pilot develops a certain "feel" for the helicopter. Small deviations can be felt and seen, so you can make the corrections before the helicopter actually moves. A certain relaxed looseness develops, and controlling the helicopter becomes second nature, rather than a mechanical response.

Common Errors
1. Tenseness and slow reactions to movements of the helicopter.
2. Failure to allow for lag in cyclic and collective pitch, which leads to overcontrolling. It is very common for a student to get ahead of the helicopter. Due to inertia, it requires some small time period for the helicopter to respond.
3. Confusing attitude changes for altitude changes, which results in improper use of the controls.
4. Hovering too high, creating a hazardous flight condition. The height velocity chart should be referenced to determine the maximum skid height to hover and safely recover the helicopter should a malfunction occur.
5. Hovering too low, resulting in occasional touchdown.
6. Becoming overly confident over prepared surfaces when taking off to a hover. Be aware that dynamic rollover accidents usually occur over a level surface.

Hovering Turn

A hovering turn is a maneuver performed at hovering altitude in which the nose of the helicopter is rotated either left or right while maintaining position over a reference point on the surface. Hovering turns can also be made around the mast or tail of the aircraft. The maneuver requires the coordination of all flight controls and demands precise control near the surface. A pilot should maintain a constant altitude, rate of turn, and rpm.

Technique
Initiate the turn in either direction by applying anti-torque pedal pressure toward the desired direction. It should be noted that during a turn to the left, more power is required because left pedal pressure increases the pitch angle of the tail rotor, which, in turn, requires additional power from the engine. A turn to the right requires less power. (On helicopters with a clockwise rotating main rotor, right pedal increases the pitch angle and, therefore, requires more power.)

As the turn begins, use the cyclic as necessary (usually into the wind) to keep the helicopter over the desired spot. To continue the turn, add more pedal pressure as the helicopter turns to the crosswind position. This is because the wind is striking the tail surface and tail rotor area, making it more difficult for the tail to turn into the wind. As pedal pressures increase due to crosswind forces, increase the cyclic pressure into the wind to maintain position. Use the collective with the throttle to maintain a constant altitude and rpm.

After the 90° portion of the turn, decrease pedal pressure slightly to maintain the same rate of turn. Approaching the 180°, or downwind portion, anticipate opposite pedal pressure due to the tail moving from an upwind position to a downwind position. At this point, the rate of turn has a tendency to increase at a rapid rate due to the tendency of the tail surfaces to weathervane. Because of the tailwind condition, hold rearward cyclic pressure to keep the helicopter over the same spot.

The horizontal stabilizer has a tendency to lift the tail during a tailwind condition. This is the most difficult portion of the hovering turn. Horizontal and vertical stabilizers have several different designs and locations, including the canted stabilizers used on some Hughes and Schweizer helicopters. The primary purpose of the vertical stabilizer is to unload the work of the antitorque system and to aid in trimming the helicopter in flight should the antitorque system fail. The horizontal stabilizer provides for a more usable CG range and aids in trimming the helicopter longitudinally.

Because of the helicopter's tendency to weathervane, maintaining the same rate of turn from the 180° position actually requires some pedal pressure opposite the direction of turn. If a pilot does not apply opposite pedal pressure, the helicopter tends to turn at a faster rate. The amount of pedal pressure and cyclic deflection throughout the turn depends on the wind velocity. As the turn is finished on the upwind heading, apply opposite pedal pressure to stop the turn. Gradually apply forward cyclic pressure to keep the helicopter from drifting.

Control pressures and direction of application change continuously throughout the turn. The most dramatic change is the pedal pressure (and corresponding power requirement) necessary to control the rate of turn as the helicopter moves through the downwind portion of the maneuver.

Turns can be made in either direction; however, in a high wind condition, the tail rotor may not be able to produce enough thrust, which means the pilot cannot control a turn to the right in a counterclockwise rotor system. Therefore, if control is ever questionable, first attempt to make a 90° turn to the left. If sufficient tail rotor thrust exists to turn the helicopter crosswind in a left turn, a right turn can be successfully controlled. The opposite applies to helicopters with clockwise rotor systems. In this case, start the turn to the right. Hovering turns should be avoided in winds strong enough to preclude sufficient aft cyclic control to maintain the helicopter on the selected surface reference point when headed downwind. Check the flight manual for the manufacturer's recommendations for this limitation.

Common Errors
1. Failing to maintain a slow, constant rate of turn.
2. Failing to maintain position over the reference point.
3. Failing to maintain rpm within normal range.
4. Failing to maintain constant altitude.
5. Failing to use the antitorque pedals properly

Hovering—Forward Flight

Forward hovering flight is normally used to move a helicopter to a specific location, and it may begin from a stationary hover. During the maneuver, constant groundspeed, altitude, and heading should be maintained.

Technique
Before starting, pick out two references directly in front and in line with the helicopter. These reference points should be kept in line throughout the maneuver.

Begin the maneuver from a normal hovering altitude by applying forward pressure on the cyclic. As movement begins, return the cyclic toward the neutral position to maintain low groundspeed—no faster than a brisk walk. Throughout the maneuver, maintain a constant groundspeed and path over the ground with the cyclic, a constant heading with the antitorque pedals, altitude with the collective, and the proper rpm with the throttle.

To stop the forward movement, apply rearward cyclic pressure until the helicopter stops. As forward motion stops, return the cyclic to the neutral position to prevent rearward movement. Forward movement can also be stopped by simply applying rearward pressure to level the helicopter and allowing it to drift to a stop.

Common Errors
1. Exaggerated movement of the cyclic, resulting in erratic movement over the surface.
2. Failure to use proper antitorque pedal control, resulting in excessive heading change.
3. Failure to maintain desired hovering altitude.
4. Failure to maintain proper rpm.
5. Failure to maintain alignment with direction of travel

Hovering—Sideward Flight

Sideward hovering flight may be necessary to move the helicopter to a specific area when conditions make it impossible to use forward flight. During the maneuver, a constant groundspeed, altitude, and heading should be maintained.

Technique
Before starting sideward hovering flight, ensure the area for the hover is clear, especially at the tail rotor. Constantly monitor hover height and tail rotor clearance during all hovering maneuvers to prevent dynamic rollover or tail rotor strikes to the ground. Then, pick two points of in-line reference in the direction of sideward hovering flight to help maintain the proper ground track. These reference points should be kept in line throughout the maneuver.

Begin the maneuver from a normal hovering altitude by applying cyclic toward the side in which the movement is desired. As the movement begins, return the cyclic toward the neutral position to maintain low groundspeed—no faster than a brisk walk. Throughout the maneuver, maintain a constant groundspeed and ground track with cyclic. Maintain heading, which in this maneuver is perpendicular to the ground track, with the antitorque pedals, and a constant altitude with the collective. Use the throttle to maintain the proper operating rpm. Be aware that the nose tends to weathervane into the wind. Changes in the pedal position will change the rpm and must be corrected by collective and/or throttle changes to maintain altitude.

To stop the sideward movement, apply cyclic pressure in the direction opposite to that of movement and hold it until the helicopter stops. As motion stops, return the cyclic to the neutral position to prevent movement in the opposite direction. Applying sufficient opposite cyclic pressure to level the helicopter may also stop sideward movement. The helicopter then drifts to a stop.

Common Errors
1. Exaggerated movement of the cyclic, resulting in overcontrolling and erratic movement over the surface.
2. Failure to use proper antitorque pedal control, resulting in excessive heading change.
3. Failure to maintain desired hovering altitude.
4. Failure to maintain proper rpm.
5. Failure to make sure the area is clear prior to starting the maneuver.

Hovering—Rearward Flight

Rearward hovering flight may be necessary to move the helicopter to a specific area when the situation is such that forward or sideward hovering flight cannot be used. During the maneuver, maintain a constant groundspeed, altitude, and heading. Due to the limited visibility behind a helicopter, it is important that the area behind the helicopter be cleared before beginning the maneuver. Use of ground personnel is recommended.

Technique
Before starting rearward hovering flight, pick out two reference points in front of, and in line with the helicopter just like hovering forward. The movement of the helicopter should be such that these points remain in line. Begin the maneuver from a normal hovering altitude by applying rearward pressure on the cyclic. After the movement has begun, position the cyclic to maintain a slow groundspeed—no faster than a brisk walk. Throughout the maneuver, maintain constant groundspeed and ground track with the cyclic, a constant heading with the antitorque pedals, constant altitude with the collective, and the proper rpm with the throttle. To stop the rearward movement, apply forward cyclic and hold it until the helicopter stops. As the motion stops, return the cyclic to the neutral position. Also, as in the case of forward and sideward hovering flight, opposite cyclic can be used to level the helicopter and let it drift to a stop. Tail rotor clearance must be maintained. Generally, a higher-than-normal hover altitude is preferred.

Common Errors
1. Exaggerated movement of the cyclic resulting in overcontrolling and an uneven movement over the surface.
2. Failure to use proper antitorque pedal control, resulting in excessive heading change.
3. Failure to maintain desired hovering altitude.
4. Failure to maintain proper rpm.
5. Failure to make sure the area is clear prior to starting the maneuver.

Taxiing

Taxiing refers to operations on or near the surface of taxiways or other prescribed routes. Helicopters utilize three different types of taxiing.

Hover Taxi
A hover taxi is used when operating below 25 feet above ground level (AGL). Since hover taxi is just like forward, sideward, or rearward hovering flight, the technique to perform it is not presented here.

Air Taxi
An air taxi is preferred when movements require greater distances within an airport or heliport boundary. In this case, fly to the new location; however, it is expected that the helicopter will remain below 100 feet AGL with an appropriate airspeed and will avoid over flight of other aircraft, vehicles, and personnel.

Technique
Before starting, determine the appropriate airspeed and altitude combination to remain out of the cross-hatched or shaded areas of the height-velocity diagram. Additionally, be aware of crosswind conditions that could lead to loss of tail rotor effectiveness. Pick out two

references directly in front of the helicopter for the ground path desired. These reference points should be kept in line throughout the maneuver.

Begin the maneuver from a normal hovering altitude by applying forward pressure on the cyclic. As movement begins, attain the desired airspeed with the cyclic. Control the desired altitude with the collective and rpm with the throttle. Throughout the maneuver, maintain a desired groundspeed and ground track with the cyclic, a constant heading with antitorque pedals, the desired altitude with the collective, and proper operating rpm with the throttle.

To stop the forward movement, apply aft cyclic pressure to reduce forward speed. Simultaneously lower the collective to initiate a descent to hover altitude. As forward motion stops, return the cyclic to the neutral position to prevent rearward movement. As approaching the proper hover altitude, increase the collective as necessary to stop descent at hover altitude (much like a quick stop maneuver).

Common Errors
1. Erratic movement of the cyclic, resulting in improper airspeed control and erratic movement over the surface.
2. Failure to use proper antitorque pedal control, resulting in excessive heading change.
3. Failure to maintain desired altitude.
4. Failure to maintain proper rpm.
5. Overflying parked aircraft causing possible damage from rotor downwash.
6. Flying in the cross-hatched or shaded area of the height-velocity diagram.
7. Flying in a crosswind that could lead to loss of tail rotor effectiveness.
8. Excessive tail-low attitudes.
9. Excessive power used or required to stop.
10. Failure to maintain alignment with direction of travel

Surface Taxi
A surface taxi is used to minimize the effects of rotor downwash. Avoid excessive cyclic displacement while surface taxiing or on the ground which can lead to main rotor blades contacting the helicopter or rotor mast. This technique may be used with wheeled aircraft, or with those that have floats, skids or skis.

Technique
The helicopter should be in a stationary position on the surface with the collective full down and the rpm the same as that used for a hover. This rpm should be maintained throughout the maneuver. Then, move the cyclic slightly forward and apply gradual upward pressure on the collective to move the helicopter forward along the surface. Use the antitorque pedals to maintain heading and the cyclic to maintain ground track. The collective controls starting, stopping, and speed while taxiing. The higher the collective pitch, the faster the taxi speed; however, do not taxi faster than a brisk walk. If the helicopter is equipped with brakes, use them to help slow down. Do not use the cyclic to control groundspeed.

During a crosswind taxi, hold the cyclic into the wind a sufficient amount to eliminate any drifting movement.

Common Errors
1. Improper use of cyclic.
2. Failure to use antitorque pedals for heading control.
3. Improper use of the controls during crosswind operations.
4. Failure to maintain proper rpm

Normal Takeoff from a Hover

A normal takeoff from a hover is an orderly transition to forward flight and is executed to increase altitude safely and expeditiously. During the takeoff, fly a profile that avoids the cross-hatched or shaded areas of the height-velocity diagram.

Technique
Bring the helicopter to a hover (position 1) and make a performance check, which includes power, balance, and flight controls. The power check should include an evaluation of the amount of excess power available; that is, the difference between the power being used to hover and the power available at the existing altitude and temperature conditions. The balance condition of the helicopter is indicated by the position of the cyclic when maintaining a stationary hover. Wind necessitates some cyclic deflection, but there should not be an extreme deviation from neutral. Flight controls must move freely, and the helicopter should respond normally. Then, visually clear the surrounding area.

Start the helicopter moving by smoothly and slowly easing the cyclic forward (position 2). As the helicopter starts to move forward, increase the collective, as necessary, to prevent the helicopter from sinking and adjust the throttle to maintain rpm. The increase in power requires an increase in the proper antitorque pedal to maintain heading. Maintain a straight takeoff path throughout the takeoff.

While accelerating through effective translational lift (position 3), the helicopter begins to climb and the nose tends to rise due to increased lift. At this point, adjust the collective to obtain normal climb power and apply enough forward cyclic to overcome the tendency of the nose to rise. At position 4, hold an attitude that allows a smooth acceleration toward climbing airspeed and a commensurate gain in altitude so that the takeoff profile does not take the helicopter through any of the cross-hatched or shaded areas of the height-velocity diagram. As airspeed increases (position 5), place the aircraft in trim and allow a crab to take place to maintain ground track and a more favorable climb configuration. As the helicopter continues to climb and accelerate to best rate-of-climb, apply aft cyclic pressure to raise the nose smoothly to the normal climb attitude.

Common Errors
1. Failing to use sufficient collective pitch to prevent loss of altitude prior to attaining translational lift.
2. Adding power too rapidly at the beginning of the transition from hovering to forward flight without forward cyclic compensation, causing the helicopter to gain excessive altitude before acquiring airspeed.
3. Assuming an extreme nose-down attitude near the surface in the transition from hovering to forward flight.
4. Failing to maintain a straight flightpath over the surface (ground track).

5. Failing to maintain proper airspeed during the climb.
6. Failing to adjust the throttle to maintain proper rpm.
7. Failing to transition to a level crab to maintain ground track.

Normal Takeoff from the Surface

Normal takeoff from the surface is used to move the helicopter from a position on the surface into effective translational lift and a normal climb using a minimum amount of power. If the surface is dusty or covered with loose snow, this technique provides the most favorable visibility conditions and reduces the possibility of debris being ingested by the engine.

Technique
Place the helicopter in a stationary position on the surface. Lower the collective to the full down position, and reduce the rpm below operating rpm. Visually clear the area and select terrain features or other objects to aid in maintaining the desired track during takeoff and climb out. Increase the throttle to the proper rpm, and raise the collective slowly until the helicopter is light on the skids. Hesitate momentarily and adjust the cyclic and antitorque pedals, as necessary, to prevent any surface movement. Continue to apply upward collective. As the helicopter leaves the ground, use the cyclic, as necessary, to begin forward movement as altitude is gained. Continue to accelerate, and as effective translational lift is attained, the helicopter begins to climb. Adjust attitude and power, if necessary, to climb in the same manner as a takeoff from a hover. A second less efficient but acceptable technique is to attempt a vertical takeoff to evaluate if power or lift is sufficient to clear obstructions. This allows the helicopter to be returned to the takeoff position if required.

Common Errors
1. Departing the surface in an attitude that is too nose-low. This situation requires the use of excessive power to initiate a climb.
2. Using excessive power combined with a level attitude, which causes a vertical climb, unless needed for obstructions and landing considerations.
3. Application of the collective that is too abrupt when departing the surface, causing rpm and heading control errors.

Crosswind Considerations during Takeoffs

If the takeoff is made during crosswind conditions, the helicopter is flown in a slip during the early stages of the maneuver. The cyclic is held into the wind a sufficient amount to maintain the desired ground track for the takeoff. The heading is maintained with the use of the antitorque pedals. In other words, the rotor is tilted into the wind so that the sideward movement of the helicopter is just enough to counteract the crosswind effect. To prevent the nose from turning in the direction of the rotor tilt, it is necessary to increase the antitorque pedal pressure on the side opposite the cyclic.

Straight-and-Level Flight

Straight-and-level flight is flight in which constant altitude and heading are maintained. The attitude of the rotor disk relative to the horizon determines the airspeed. The horizontal stabilizer design determines the helicopter's attitude when stabilized at an airspeed and altitude. Altitude is primarily controlled by use of the collective.

<u>Technique</u>
To maintain forward flight, the rotor tip-path plane must be tilted forward to obtain the necessary horizontal thrust component from the main rotor. By doing this, it causes the nose of the helicopter to lower which in turn will cause the airspeed to increase. In order to counteract this, the pilot must find the correct power setting to maintain level flight by adjusting the collective. The horizontal stabilizer aids in trimming the helicopter longitudinally and reduces the amount of nose tuck that would occur. On several helicopters, it is designed as a negative lift airfoil, which produces a lifting force in a downward direction.

When in straight-and-level flight, any increase in the collective, while holding airspeed constant, causes the helicopter to climb. A decrease in the collective, while holding airspeed constant, causes the helicopter to descend. A change in the collective requires a coordinated change of the throttle to maintain a constant rpm. Additionally, the antitorque pedals need to keep the helicopter in trim around the vertical axis.

To increase airspeed in straight-and-level flight, apply forward pressure on the cyclic and raise the collective as necessary to maintain altitude. To decrease airspeed, apply rearward pressure on the cyclic and lower the collective, as necessary, to maintain altitude.

Although the cyclic is sensitive, there is a slight delay in control reaction, and it is necessary to anticipate actual movement of the helicopter. When making cyclic inputs to control the altitude or airspeed of a helicopter, take care not to overcontrol. If the nose of the helicopter rises above the level-flight attitude, apply forward pressure to the cyclic to bring the nose down. If this correction is held too long, the nose drops too low. Since the helicopter continues to change attitude momentarily after the controls reach neutral, return the cyclic to neutral slightly before the desired attitude is reached. This principle holds true for any cyclic input.

Since helicopters are not very stable, but are inherently very controllable, if a gust or turbulence causes the nose to drop, the nose tends to continue to drop instead of returning to a straight-and-level attitude as it would on a fixed-wing aircraft. Therefore, a pilot must remain alert and fly the helicopter at all times.

<u>Common Errors</u>
1. Failure to trim the helicopter properly, tending to hold antitorque pedal pressure and opposite cyclic. This is commonly called cross-controlling.
2. Failure to maintain desired airspeed.
3. Failure to hold proper control position to maintain desired ground track.
4. Failure to allow helicopter to stabilize at new airspeed

Turns

A turn is a maneuver used to change the heading of the helicopter.

<u>Technique</u>
Before beginning any turn, the area in the direction of the turn must be cleared not only at the helicopter's altitude, but also above and below. To enter a turn from straight-and-level flight, apply sideward pressure on the cyclic in the direction the turn is to be made. This is

the only control movement needed to start the turn. Do not use the pedals to assist the turn. Use the pedals only to compensate for torque to keep the helicopter in trim around the vertical axis. Keeping the fuselage in the correct streamlined position around the vertical axis facilitates the helicopter flying forward with the least drag. Trim is indicated by a yaw string in the center, or a centered ball on a turn and slip indicator.

How fast the helicopter banks depends on how much lateral cyclic pressure is applied. How far the helicopter banks (the steepness of the bank) depends on how long the cyclic is displaced. After establishing the proper bank angle, return the cyclic toward the neutral position. When the bank is established, returning the cyclic to neutral or holding it inclined relative to the horizon will maintain the helicopter at that bank angle. Increase the collective and throttle to maintain altitude and rpm. As the torque increases, increase the proper antitorque pedal pressure to maintain longitudinal trim. Depending on the degree of bank, additional forward cyclic pressure may be required to maintain airspeed.

Rolling out of the turn to straight-and-level flight is the same as the entry into the turn except that pressure on the cyclic is applied in the opposite direction. Since the helicopter continues to turn as long as there is any bank, start the rollout before reaching the desired heading.

The discussion on level turns is equally applicable to making turns while climbing or descending. The only difference is that the helicopter is in a climbing or descending attitude rather than that of level flight. If a simultaneous entry is desired, merely combine the techniques of both maneuvers—climb or descent entry and turn entry. When recovering from a climbing or descending turn, the desired heading and altitude are rarely reached at the same time. If the heading is reached first, stop the turn and maintain the climb or descent until reaching the desired altitude. On the other hand, if the altitude is reached first, establish the level flight attitude and continue the turn to the desired heading.

Slips
A slip occurs when the helicopter slides sideways toward the center of the turn. It is caused by an insufficient amount of antitorque pedal in the direction of the turn, or too much in the direction opposite the turn, in relation to the amount of power used. In other words, if you hold improper antitorque pedal pressure, which keeps the nose from following the turn, the helicopter slips sideways toward the center of the turn.

Skids
A skid occurs when the helicopter slides sideways away from the center of the turn. It is caused by too much antitorque pedal pressure in the direction of the turn, or by too little in the direction opposite the turn in relation to the amount of power used. If the helicopter is forced to turn faster with increased pedal pressure instead of by increasing the degree of the bank, it skids sideways away from the center of the turn instead of flying in its normal curved path.

In summary, a skid occurs when the rate of turn is too great for the amount of bank being used, and a slip occurs when the rate of turn is too low for the amount of bank being used.

Normal Climb

The entry into a climb from a hover has already been described in the Normal Takeoff from a Hover subsection; therefore, this discussion is limited to a climb entry from cruising flight.

<u>Technique</u>
To enter a climb in a helicopter while maintaining airspeed, the first actions are increasing the collective and throttle, and adjusting the pedals as necessary to maintain a centered ball in the slip/skid indicator. Moving the collective up requires a slight aft movement of the cyclic to direct all of the increased power into lift and maintain the airspeed. Remember, a helicopter can climb with the nose down and descend with the nose up. Helicopter attitude changes mainly reflect acceleration or deceleration, not climb or descent. Therefore, the climb attitude is approximately the same as level flight in a stable climb, depending on the aircraft's horizontal stabilizer design.

If the pilot wishes to climb faster, with a decreased airspeed, then the climb can be initiated with aft cyclic. Depending on initial or entry airspeed for the climb, the climb can be accomplished without increasing the collective, if a much slower airspeed is acceptable. However, as the airspeed decreases, the airflow over the vertical fin decreases necessitating more antitorque (left) pedal application.

To level off from a climb, start adjusting the attitude to the level flight attitude a few feet prior to reaching the desired altitude. The amount of lead depends on the rate of climb at the time of level-off (the higher the rate of climb, the more the lead). Generally, the lead is 10 percent of the climb rate. For example, if the climb rate is 500 feet per minute (fpm), you should lead the level-off by 50 feet.

To begin the level-off, apply forward cyclic to adjust and maintain a level flight attitude, which can be slightly nose low. Maintain climb power until the airspeed approaches the desired cruising airspeed, then lower the collective to obtain cruising power and adjust the throttle to obtain and maintain cruising rpm. Throughout the level-off, maintain longitudinal trim with the antitorque pedals.

<u>Common Errors</u>
1. Failure to maintain proper power and airspeed.
2. Holding too much or too little antitorque pedal.
3. In the level-off, decreasing power before adjusting the nose to cruising attitude.

Normal Descent

A normal descent is a maneuver in which the helicopter loses altitude at a controlled rate in a controlled attitude.

<u>Technique</u>
To establish a normal descent from straight-and-level flight at cruising airspeed, lower the collective to obtain proper power, adjust the throttle to maintain rpm, and increase right antitorque pedal pressure to maintain heading in a counterclockwise rotor system, or left pedal pressure in a clockwise system. If cruising airspeed is the same as or slightly above descending airspeed, simultaneously apply the necessary cyclic pressure to obtain the approximate descending attitude. If the pilot wants to decelerate, the cyclic must be moved

aft. If the pilot desires to descend with increased airspeed, then forward cyclic is all that is required if airspeed remains under the limit. As the helicopter stabilizes at any forward airspeed, the fuselage attitude will streamline due to the airflow over the horizontal stabilizer. As the airspeed changes, the airflow over the vertical stabilizer or fin changes, so the pedals must be adjusted for trim.

The pilot should always remember that the total lift and thrust vectoring is controlled by the cyclic. If a certain airspeed is desired, it will require a certain amount of cyclic and collective movement for level flight. If the cyclic is moved, the thrust-versus-lift ration is changed. Aft cyclic directs more power to lift, and altitude increases. Forward cyclic directs more power to thrust, and airspeed increases. If the collective is not changed and there is a change only in cyclic, the total thrust to lift ration does not change; aft cyclic results in a climb, and forward cyclic results in a descent with the corresponding airspeed changes.

To level off from the descent, lead the desired altitude by approximately 10 percent of the rate of descent. For example, a 500 fpm rate of descent would require a 50 foot lead. At this point, increase the collective to obtain cruising power, adjust the throttle to maintain rpm, and increase left antitorque pedal pressure to maintain heading (right pedal pressure in a clockwise rotor system). Adjust the cyclic to obtain cruising airspeed and a level flight attitude as the desired altitude is reached.

Common Errors
1. Failure to maintain constant angle of descent during training.
2. Failure to level-off the aircraft sufficiently, which results in recovery below the desired altitude.
3. Failure to adjust antitorque pedal pressures for changes in power.

Conclusion

Once again, please note that these are merely excerpts from the FAA helicopter handbook. The full text of the handbook is freely available and you would do well to study it, both for improving your performance on the test and for augmenting your background knowledge should you be accepted into the Army's flight training program.

Spatial Apperception Test

The Spatial Apperception section of the SIFT lasts 10 minutes and features 25 questions. This is another test based on visual information rather than written text, or mathematical problems. The word *apperception* refers to the process by which you interpret some new information using the knowledge you already possess.

This section of the SIFT is measuring your ability to translate visual information from one perspective into an accurate mental representation of the same information from a completely different perspective. Military test developers have determined that this ability is critical to success in flight school and as a pilot, and they have also determined that the Spatial Apperception test is very accurate at measuring a person's aptitude and abilities in this area.

For each question, you'll first be shown a drawing of a terrain with a horizon, from the point of view of a pilot in the cockpit of an aircraft above the terrain. Then you'll be shown five more drawings of the aircraft from the perspective of someone on the ground observing the craft, each showing the aircraft in a different attitude. You will be required to determine which of the five drawings shows the aircraft in the attitude that would provide the view of the terrain shown in the first illustration to someone looking straight out of the cockpit of the aircraft.

The most important thing to keep in mind is that you're really only looking for three pieces of information. The three questions you'll need to answer for each drawing are:
- What is the vertical orientation of the aircraft? Is it climbing, diving, or flying straight ahead?
- Are the wings level, is the aircraft banking left, or is it banking right?
- In which direction is the aircraft heading?

Answering these three questions correctly will enable you to choose the right answer for any question in this section. Let's look at how to answer each of these questions a bit more in depth.

You should probably start in the same order, so first you want to determine the orientation of the plane. The key to answering this question is the placement of the horizon in the illustration. The horizon is where the sky meets one of the shaded areas, either land or sea. Is the horizon right in the middle of the drawing? Or in other words, is there about the same amount of space above the horizon as below it? If so, then the aircraft is flying straight ahead, or level. If most of the drawing is above the horizon, then the aircraft is climbing, and if most of the drawing is below the horizon, the aircraft is diving.

Next, is the plane flying level or is it banking to one side? If the horizon is level, then the plane's wings are level. If the horizon goes from the upper left to the lower right, the plane is banking left. If it goes from the lower left to the upper right, it's banking right. On whichever side of the picture the horizon is elevated, that's the direction that the plane is banking.

The final piece of the puzzle is determining which way the aircraft is headed. Is it headed toward the sea, toward the land, or flying along the coastline? Keep in mind that the plane doesn't have to be flying at a 90 degree angle to the coastline; if it's headed toward sea or land, it could be approaching at another angle.

One common mistake people make in the Spatial Apperception section of the SIFT is confusing the coastline with the horizon in some of the drawings. Always keep in mind the difference between these two, especially when looking at angled drawings. Another thing to keep in mind is that for every view out of the cockpit, there are two possible ways to view the aircraft: from coastline left and from coastline right. All of the answer choices on a given question will be from the same side, so before you start visualizing how you think the plane will appear, it would be useful to check the answer choices and see which side you need to picture it from.

Do not underestimate the difficulty of this section of the SIFT. The questions seem relatively simple in concept, and the steps for solving them are straightforward, but they require very close attention to detail. If you're not prepared or not focused, it is very easy to do poorly on this section without realizing it. The key is practice. Be sure to work through all the practice questions for this section.

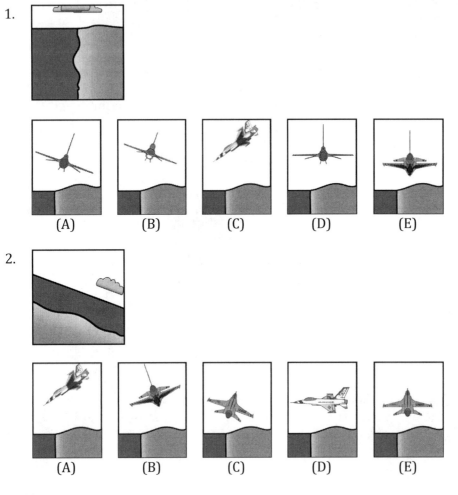

Answers: 1. E; 2. D

- 34 -

Reading Comprehension Test

Possessing excellent reading skills is a necessity for anyone hoping to become a military aviator. The Reading Comprehension section of the SIFT is designed to measure your abilities in this area.

This section tests your ability to read and understand written passages of the level of difficulty you can expect to encounter in your aviation training and career. Many of the passages used in our practice test were taken directly from helicopter operation instructional material.

You've probably taken numerous tests of reading comprehension in your educational career, and may have already identified the strategy that works best for you. If that's the case, you can go ahead and skip this next section. We're going to outline some of the strategies that we've found to be effective, but the key is finding the one or ones that work best for you.

Strategies

Read the question(s) before reading the passage
By identifying what you need to look for ahead of time, you can more quickly read the passage to find the information you need. In addition, reading the question will give you an idea of its complexity. If the question is simply asking you to find a detail in a passage, it probably won't take nearly as long as a question that requires you to make a conclusion about a hypothetical scenario. If it looks like the question will be very time-consuming, you can skip it and come back.

Systematically eliminate answers that are obviously wrong
This will make it easier to focus on the remaining choices, and more importantly, you will improve your chances of correctly answering the question if you have to randomly guess.

Use context clues to understand difficult words
You may encounter words and phrases that are new to you, and whose meanings you must decipher in order to answer a question correctly. If you don't know what they mean, you will have to use clues in the sentence to understand their meaning.

General Reading Comprehension Skills

Topics and main ideas

One of the most important skills in reading comprehension is the identification of **topics** and **main ideas.** There is a subtle difference between these two features. The topic is the subject of a text (i.e., what the text is all about). The main idea, on the other hand, is the most important point being made by the author. The topic is usually expressed in a few words at the most while the main idea often needs a full sentence to be completely defined. As an example, a short passage might have the topic of penguins and the main idea could be written as *Penguins are different from other birds in many ways*. In most nonfiction writing, the topic and the main idea will be stated directly and often appear in a sentence at the very beginning or end of the text. When being tested on an understanding of the author's topic, you may be able to skim the passage for the general idea, by reading only the first sentence of each paragraph. A body paragraph's first sentence is often--but not always--the main topic sentence which gives you a summary of the content in the paragraph.

However, there are cases in which the reader must figure out an unstated topic or main idea. In these instances, you must read every sentence of the text and try to come up with an overarching idea that is supported by each of those sentences.

> ➤ **Review Video:** <u>Topics and Main Ideas</u>
> Visit ***mometrix.com/academy*** and enter ***Code: 407801***

Supporting details

Supporting details provide evidence and backing for the main point. In order to show that a main idea is correct, or valid, authors add details that help prove their point. All texts contain details, but they are only classified as supporting details when they serve to reinforce some larger point. Supporting details are most commonly found in informative and persuasive texts. In some cases, they will be clearly indicated with terms like *for example* or *for instance*, or they will be enumerated with terms like *first*, *second*, and *last*. However, you need to be prepared for texts that do not contain those indicators. As a reader, you should consider whether the author's supporting details really back up his or her main point. Supporting details can be factual and correct, yet they may not be relevant to the author's point. Conversely, supporting details can seem pertinent, but they can be ineffective because they are based on opinion or assertions that cannot be proven.

Topic and summary sentences

Topic and summary sentences are a convenient way to encapsulate the main idea of a text. In some textbooks and academic articles, the author will place a topic or summary sentence at the beginning of each section as a means of preparing the reader for what is to come. Research suggests that the brain is more receptive to new information when it has been prepared by the presentation of the main idea or some key words. The phenomenon is somewhat akin to the primer coat of paint that allows subsequent coats of paint to absorb more easily. A good topic sentence will be clear and not contain any jargon. When topic or summary sentences are not provided, good readers can jot down their own so that they can find their place in a text and refresh their memory.

Predictions based on prior knowledge

A prediction is a guess about what will happen next. Readers constantly make predictions based on what they have read and what they already know. Consider the following sentence: *Staring at the computer screen in shock, Kim blindly reached over for the brimming glass of water on the shelf to her side.* The sentence suggests that Kim is agitated, and that she is not looking at the glass that she is going to pick up. So, a reader might predict that Kim is going to knock over the glass. Of course, not every prediction will be accurate: perhaps Kim will pick the glass up cleanly. Nevertheless, the author has certainly created the expectation that the water might be spilled. Predictions are always subject to revision as the reader acquires more information.

Making inferences

Readers are often required to understand a text that claims and suggests ideas without stating them directly. An **inference** is a piece of information that is implied but not written outright by the author. For instance, consider the following sentence: *After the final out of the inning, the fans were filled with joy and rushed the field.* From this sentence, a reader can infer that the fans were watching a baseball game and their team won the game. Readers should take great care to avoid using information beyond the provided passage before making inferences. As you practice with drawing inferences, you will find that they require concentration and attention.

Drawing conclusions

In addition to inference and prediction, readers must often **draw conclusions** about the information they have read. When asked for a *conclusion* that may be drawn, look for critical "hedge" phrases, such as *likely, may, can, will often,* among many others. When you are being tested on this knowledge, remember the question that writers insert into these hedge phrases to cover every possibility. Often an answer will be wrong simply because there is no room for exception. Extreme positive or negative answers (such as always or never) are usually not correct. You **should not** rely on any outside knowledge that is not gathered from the passage to answer the related questions. Correct answers can be derived straight from the passage.

Sequence

Readers must be able to identify a text's **sequence**, or the order in which things happen. Often, when the sequence is very important to the author, the text is indicated with signal words like *first, then, next,* and *last.* However, a sequence can be merely implied and must be noted by the reader. Consider the sentence *He walked through the garden and gave water and fertilizer to the plants.* Clearly, the man did not walk through the garden before he collected water and fertilizer for the plants. So, the implied sequence is that he first collected water and fertilizer, next he walked through the garden, and last he gave water or fertilizer as necessary to the plants.

Texts do not always proceed in an orderly sequence from first to last. Sometimes they begin at the end and start over at the beginning. As a reader, you can enhance your understanding of the passage by taking brief notes to clarify the sequence.

> ➤ **Review Video:** <u>Sequence</u>
> Visit *mometrix.com/academy* and enter *Code:* **489027**

Comparison and contrast

Authors will use different stylistic and writing devices to make their meaning clear for readers. One of those devices is comparison and contrast. As mentioned previously, when an author describes the ways in which two things are alike, he or she is comparing them. When the author describes the ways in which two things are different, he or she is contrasting them. The "compare and contrast" essay is one of the most common forms in nonfiction. These passages are often signaled with certain words: a comparison may have indicating terms such as *both*, *same*, *like*, *too*, and *as well*; while a contrast may have terms like *but*, *however*, *on the other hand*, *instead*, and *yet*. Of course, comparisons and contrasts may be implicit without using any such signaling language. A single sentence may both compare and contrast. Consider the sentence *Brian and Sheila love ice cream, but Brian prefers vanilla and Sheila prefers strawberry*. In one sentence, the author has described both a similarity (love of ice cream) and a difference (favorite flavor).

> ➤ **Review Video:** <u>Compare and Contrast</u>
> Visit *mometrix.com/academy* and enter *Code:* **798319**

Cause and effect

One of the most common text structures is cause and effect. A cause is an act or event that makes something happen, and an effect is the thing that happens as a result of the cause. A cause-and-effect relationship is not always explicit, but there are some terms in English that signal causes, such as *since*, *because*, and *due to*. Furthermore, terms that signal effects include *consequently*, *therefore*, *this lead(s) to*. As an example, consider the sentence *Because the sky was clear, Ron did not bring an umbrella*. The cause is the clear sky, and the effect is that Ron did not bring an umbrella. However, readers may find that sometimes the cause-and-effect relationship will not be clearly noted. For instance, the sentence *He was late and missed the meeting* does not contain any signaling words, but the sentence still contains a cause (he was late) and an effect (he missed the meeting).

> ➤ **Review Video:** <u>Cause and Effect</u>
> Visit *mometrix.com/academy* and enter *Code:* **725944**

Identifying an author's position

In order to be an effective reader, one must pay attention to the author's **position** and purpose. Even those texts that seem objective and impartial, like textbooks, have a position and bias. Readers need to take these positions into account when considering the author's message. When an author uses emotional language or clearly favors one side of an argument, his or her position is clear. However, the author's position may be evident not only in what he or she writes, but also in what he or she doesn't write. In a normal setting, a reader would want to review some other texts on the same topic in order to develop a view of the author's position. If this was not possible, then you would want to acquire some background about the author. However, since you are in the middle of an exam and the only source of information is the text, you should look for language and argumentation that seems to indicate a particular stance on the subject.

Purpose

Usually, identifying the **purpose** of an author is easier than identifying his or her position. In most cases, the author has no interest in hiding his or her purpose. A text that is meant to entertain, for instance, should be written to please the reader. Most narratives, or stories, are written to entertain, though they may also inform or persuade. Informative texts are easy to identify, while the most difficult purpose of a text to identify is persuasion because the author has an interest in making this purpose hard to detect. When a reader discovers that the author is trying to persuade, he or she should be skeptical of the argument. For this reason persuasive texts often try to establish an entertaining tone and hope to amuse the reader into agreement. On the other hand, an informative tone may be implemented to create an appearance of authority and objectivity.

An author's purpose is evident often in the organization of the text (e.g., section headings in bold font points to an informative text). However, you may not have such organization available to you in your exam. Instead, if the author makes his or her main idea clear from the beginning, then the likely purpose of the text is to inform. If the author begins by making a claim and provides various arguments to support that claim, then the purpose is probably to persuade. If the author tells a story or seems to want the attention of the reader more than to push a particular point or deliver information, then his or her purpose is most likely to entertain. As a reader, you must judge authors on how well they accomplish their purpose. In other words, you need to consider the type of passage (e.g., technical, persuasive, etc.) that the author has written and if the author has followed the requirements of the passage type.

Word meaning from context

One of the benefits of reading is the expansion of one's vocabulary. In order to obtain this benefit, however, one needs to know how to identify the definition of a word from its context. This means defining a word based on the words around it and the way it is used in a sentence. Consider the following sentence: *The elderly scholar spent his evenings hunched over arcane texts that few other people even knew existed.* The adjective *arcane* is uncommon, but you can obtain significant information about it based on its use in the sentence. The fact that few other people know of their existence allows you to assume that "arcane texts" must be rare and be of interest to a few people. Also, the texts are being read by an elderly scholar. So, you can assume that they focus on difficult academic subjects. Sometimes, words can be defined by what they are not. Consider the following sentence: *Ron's fealty to his parents was not shared by Karen, who disobeyed their every command.* Someone who disobeys is not demonstrating *fealty*. So, you can infer that the word means something like *obedience* or *respect*.

Identifying the logical conclusion

Identifying a logical conclusion can help you determine whether you agree with the writer or not. Coming to this conclusion is much like making an inference: the approach requires you to combine the information given by the text with what you already know in order to make a logical conclusion. If the author intended the reader to draw a certain conclusion, then you can expect the author's argumentation and detail to be leading in that direction. One way to approach the task of drawing conclusions is to make brief notes of all the points made by the author. When the notes are arranged on paper, they may clarify the logical conclusion. Another way to approach conclusions is to consider whether the reasoning of the author raises any pertinent questions. Sometimes you will be able to draw several conclusions from a passage. On occasion these will be conclusions that were never imagined by the author. Therefore, be aware that these conclusions must be supported directly by the text.

Math Skills Test

On this section of the SIFT, you'll be tested for your knowledge, skill, and aptitude in math. Being highly skilled at math is very important for anyone seeking to become a pilot, for many reasons. In order to make it successfully through aviator training, and then to succeed as a pilot, a person will need to be able to solve basic math problems rapidly, and in their head, without having time to work them out on a calculator or with a pencil and paper. Beyond this, however, the highly developed analytical skills that enable a person to quickly solve math problems will be useful in all sorts of different ways and in all kinds of different situations. So, while this section of the SIFT does test knowledge and abilities, it's also testing for general learning aptitude.

To do well on this section, you'll need to have a solid mastery of some of the math subjects taught through all four years of high school, and some lower level college courses. This subtest lasts 40 minutes, and you are not allowed to use a calculator. It's very important to keep in mind that the MST section is adaptive, and factor this into your approach.

The math section will begin with a question of medium difficulty. If you answer it correctly, you will then be given a harder question. If you answer that question correctly, the next question will be even more difficult. This process will continue until you get an answer wrong, at which point you will be given an easier question. Answer it right, and the questions will start getting harder again, but if you answer it wrong, the computer will keep giving you easier questions until you get one right.

If you answer the first question incorrectly, the process works in reverse, giving you an easier question right off the bat. The computer will adapt to a test taker's answers in this manner after every question, so the next question that will be displayed is not determined until after an answer has been submitted for the previous question.

Because of this, it's important to take the time to do your best on every question. Don't skip a question just because it seems hard. If you're answering questions right, the questions are supposed to get harder. At the same time though, you want to make sure you answer enough questions so that the computer can accurately identify your skill level. Not answering enough questions can hurt you even more than answering some questions incorrectly. As with everything, there is a balance to be struck, but with computer adaptive testing, that balance leans more heavily toward answering correctly than answering as many questions as possible.

The following sections outline the basic math concepts needed to excel on the Math Skills subtest. As someone who is interested in flight training, you've probably taken a lot of math tests in your educational career, but just in case, here is one of the most important things to remember as you study math concepts:
More so than in almost any other subject, **practice matters**. Math concepts are explained in ways that make you think you understand them well, but until you can quickly work practice problems several days after you read about the underlying concepts without referring back to them, you haven't actually internalized them.

Numbers and Their Classifications

Numbers are the basic building blocks of mathematics. Specific features of numbers are identified by the following terms:

- Integers – The set of whole positive and negative numbers, including zero. Integers do not include fractions $\left(\frac{1}{3}\right)$, decimals (0.56), or mixed numbers $\left(7\frac{3}{4}\right)$.
- Prime number – A whole number greater than 1 that has only two factors, itself and 1; that is, a number that can be divided evenly only by 1 and itself.
- Composite number – A whole number greater than 1 that has more than two different factors; in other words, any whole number that is not a prime number. For example: The composite number 8 has the factors of 1, 2, 4, and 8.
- Even number – Any integer that can be divided by 2 without leaving a remainder. For example: 2, 4, 6, 8, and so on.
- Odd number – Any integer that cannot be divided evenly by 2. For example: 3, 5, 7, 9, and so on.
- Decimal number – a number that uses a decimal point to show the part of the number that is less than one. Example: 1.234.
- Decimal point – a symbol used to separate the ones place from the tenths place in decimals or dollars from cents in currency.
- Decimal place – the position of a number to the right of the decimal point. In the decimal 0.123, the 1 is in the first place to the right of the decimal point, indicating tenths; the 2 is in the second place, indicating hundredths; and the 3 is in the third place, indicating thousandths.

> ➤ **Review Video: Numbers and Their Classifications**
> *Visit* **mometrix.com/academy** *and enter* **Code: 461071**

The decimal, or base 10, system is a number system that uses ten different digits (0, 1, 2, 3, 4, 5, 6, 7, 8, 9). An example of a number system that uses something other than ten digits is the binary, or base 2, number system, used by computers, which uses only the numbers 0 and 1. It is thought that the decimal system originated because people had only their 10 fingers for counting.

Rational, irrational, and real numbers can be described as follows:

- Rational numbers include all integers, decimals, and fractions. Any terminating or repeating decimal number is a rational number.
- Irrational numbers cannot be written as fractions or decimals because the number of decimal places is infinite and there is no recurring pattern of digits within the number. For example, pi (π) begins with 3.141592 and continues without terminating or repeating, so pi is an irrational number.
- Real numbers are the set of all rational and irrational numbers.

Operations

There are four basic mathematical operations:

1. Addition increases the value of one quantity by the value of another quantity. *Example*: $2 + 4 = 6$; $8 + 9 = 17$. The result is called the sum. With addition, the order does not matter. $4 + 2 = 2 + 4$.

2. Subtraction is the opposite operation to addition; it decreases the value of one quantity by the value of another quantity. *Example*: $6 - 4 = 2$; $17 - 8 = 9$. The result is called the difference. Note that with subtraction, the order does matter. $6 - 4 \neq 4 - 6$.

3. Multiplication can be thought of as repeated addition. One number tells how many times to add the other number to itself. *Example*: 3×2 (three times two) $= 2 + 2 + 2 = 6$. With multiplication, the order does not matter. $2 \times 3 = 3 \times 2$ or $3 + 3 = 2 + 2 + 2$.

4. Division is the opposite operation to multiplication; one number tells us how many parts to divide the other number into. *Example*: $20 \div 4 = 5$; if 20 is split into 4 equal parts, each part is 5. With division, the order of the numbers does matter. $20 \div 4 \neq 4 \div 20$.

An exponent is a superscript number placed next to another number at the top right. It indicates how many times the base number is to be multiplied by itself. Exponents provide a shorthand way to write what would be a longer mathematical expression. *Example*: $a^2 = a \times a$; $2^4 = 2 \times 2 \times 2 \times 2$. A number with an exponent of 2 is said to be "squared," while a number with an exponent of 3 is said to be "cubed."

The value of a number raised to an exponent is called its power. So, 8^4 is read as "8 to the 4th power," or "8 raised to the power of 4." A negative exponent is the same as the reciprocal of a positive exponent. *Example*: $a^{-2} = \frac{1}{a^2}$.

> ➤ **Review Video: Exponents**
> *Visit **mometrix.com/academy** and enter **Code**: **600998***

Parentheses are used to designate which operations should be done first when there are multiple operations. *Example*: $4 - (2 + 1) = 1$; the parentheses tell us that we must add 2 and 1, and then subtract the sum from 4, rather than subtracting 2 from 4 and then adding 1 (this would give us an answer of 3).

Order of Operations is a set of rules that dictates the order in which we must perform each operation in an expression so that we will evaluate it accurately. If we have an expression that includes multiple different operations, Order of Operations tells us which operations to do first. The most common mnemonic for Order of Operations is PEMDAS, or "Please Excuse My Dear Aunt Sally." PEMDAS stands for Parentheses, Exponents, Multiplication, Division, Addition, Subtraction. It is important to understand that multiplication and division have equal precedence, as do addition and subtraction, so those pairs of operations are simply worked from left to right in order.

> ➤ **Review Video: Order of Operations**
> *Visit **mometrix.com/academy** and enter **Code**: **259675***

Example: Evaluate the expression $5 + 20 \div 4 \times (2 + 3)^2 - 6$ using the correct order of operations.

P: Perform the operations inside the parentheses, $(2 + 3) = 5$.
E: Simplify the exponents, $(5)^2 = 25$.
The equation now looks like this: $5 + 20 \div 4 \times 25 - 6$.
MD: Perform multiplication and division from left to right, $20 \div 4 = 5$; then $5 \times 25 = 125$. The equation now looks like this: $5 + 125 - 6$.
AS: Perform addition and subtraction from left to right, $5 + 125 = 130$; then $130 - 6 = 124$.

The laws of exponents are as follows:
1) Any number to the power of 1 is equal to itself: $a^1 = a$.
2) The number 1 raised to any power is equal to 1: $1^n = 1$.
3) Any number raised to the power of 0 is equal to 1: $a^0 = 1$.
4) Add exponents to multiply powers of the same base number: $a^n \times a^m = a^{n+m}$.
5) Subtract exponents to divide powers of the same number; that is $a^n \div a^m = a^{n-m}$.
6) Multiply exponents to raise a power to a power: $(a^n)^m = a^{n \times m}$.
7) If multiplied or divided numbers inside parentheses are collectively raised to a power, this is the same as each individual term being raised to that power: $(a \times b)^n = a^n \times b^n$; $(a \div b)^n = a^n \div b^n$.
Note: Exponents do not have to be integers. Fractional or decimal exponents follow all the rules above as well.

Example: $5^{\frac{1}{4}} \times 5^{\frac{3}{4}} = 5^{\frac{1}{4} + \frac{3}{4}} = 5^1 = 5$.

A root, such as a square root, is another way of writing a fractional exponent. Instead of using a superscript, roots use the radical symbol ($\sqrt{}$) to indicate the operation. A radical will have a number underneath the bar, and may sometimes have a number in the upper left: $\sqrt[n]{a}$, read as "the nth root of a." The relationship between radical notation and exponent notation can be described by this equation: $\sqrt[n]{a} = a^{\frac{1}{n}}$. The two special cases of $n = 2$ and $n = 3$ are called square roots and cube roots. If there is no number to the upper left, it is understood to be a square root ($n = 2$). Nearly all of the roots you encounter will be square roots. A square root is the same as a number raised to the one-half power. When we say that a is the square root of b ($a = \sqrt{b}$), we mean that a multiplied by itself equals b: ($a \times a = b$).

> ➤ **Review Video:** <u>Square Root and Perfect Square</u>
> *Visit* **mometrix.com/academy** *and enter* **Code: 648063**

A perfect square is a number that has an integer for its square root. There are 10 perfect squares from 1 to 100: 1, 4, 9, 16, 25, 36, 49, 64, 81, 100 (the squares of integers 1 through 10).

Scientific notation is a way of writing large numbers in a shorter form. The form $a \times 10^n$ is used in scientific notation, where a is greater than or equal to 1, but less than 10, and n is the number of places the decimal must move to get from the original number to a. *Example*: The number 230,400,000 is cumbersome to write. To write the value in scientific notation, place a decimal point between the first and second numbers, and include all digits through the last non-zero digit ($a = 2.304$). To find the appropriate power of 10, count the number of places the decimal point had to move ($n = 8$). The number is positive if the decimal moved to the left, and negative if it moved to the right. We can then write 230,400,000 as 2.304×10^8. If we look instead at the number 0.00002304, we have the same value for a, but this time the decimal moved 5 places to the right ($n = -5$). Thus, 0.00002304 can be written as 2.304×10^{-5}. Using this notation makes it simple to compare very large or very small numbers. By comparing exponents, it is easy to see that 3.28×10^4 is smaller than 1.51×10^5, because 4 is less than 5.

> ➤ **Review Video: Scientific Notation**
> *Visit* ***mometrix.com/academy*** *and enter* ***Code*: 976454**

Positive and Negative Numbers

A precursor to working with negative numbers is understanding what absolute values are. A number's absolute value is simply the distance away from zero a number is on the number line. The absolute value of a number is always positive and is written $|x|$.

When adding signed numbers, if the signs are the same simply add the absolute values of the addends and apply the original sign to the sum. For example, $(+4) + (+8) = +12$ and $(-4) + (-8) = -12$. When the original signs are different, take the absolute values of the addends and subtract the smaller value from the larger value, then apply the original sign of the larger value to the difference. For instance, $(+4) + (-8) = -4$ and $(-4) + (+8) = +4$.

For subtracting signed numbers, change the sign of the number after the minus symbol and then follow the same rules used for addition. For example, $(+4) - (+8) = (+4) + (-8) = -4$.

If the signs are the same the product is positive when multiplying signed numbers. For example, $(+4) \times (+8) = +32$ and $(-4) \times (-8) = +32$. If the signs are opposite, the product is negative. For example, $(+4) \times (-8) = -32$ and $(-4) \times (+8) = -32$. When more than two factors are multiplied together, the sign of the product is determined by how many negative factors are present. If there are an odd number of negative factors then the product is negative, whereas an even number of negative factors indicates a positive product. For instance, $(+4) \times (-8) \times (-2) = +64$ and $(-4) \times (-8) \times (-2) = -64$.

The rules for dividing signed numbers are similar to multiplying signed numbers. If the dividend and divisor have the same sign, the quotient is positive. If the dividend and divisor have opposite signs, the quotient is negative. For example, $(-4) \div (+8) = -0.5$.

Factors and Multiples

Factors are numbers that are multiplied together to obtain a product. For example, in the equation $2 \times 3 = 6$, the numbers 2 and 3 are factors. A prime number has only two factors (1 and itself), but other numbers can have many factors.

A common factor is a number that divides exactly into two or more other numbers. For example, the factors of 12 are 1, 2, 3, 4, 6, and 12, while the factors of 15 are 1, 3, 5, and 15.

The common factors of 12 and 15 are 1 and 3. A prime factor is also a prime number. Therefore, the prime factors of 12 are 2 and 3. For 15, the prime factors are 3 and 5.

The greatest common factor (GCF) is the largest number that is a factor of two or more numbers. For example, the factors of 15 are 1, 3, 5, and 15; the factors of 35 are 1, 5, 7, and 35. Therefore, the greatest common factor of 15 and 35 is 5.

> **Review Video: Greatest Common Factor (GCF)**
> *Visit mometrix.com/academy and enter Code: 838699*

The least common multiple (LCM) is the smallest number that is a multiple of two or more numbers. For example, the multiples of 3 include 3, 6, 9, 12, 15, etc.; the multiples of 5 include 5, 10, 15, 20, etc. Therefore, the least common multiple of 3 and 5 is 15.

Fractions, Percentages, and Related Concepts

A fraction is a number that is expressed as one integer written above another integer, with a dividing line between them $\left(\frac{x}{y}\right)$. It represents the quotient of the two numbers "x divided by y." It can also be thought of as x out of y equal parts.

The top number of a fraction is called the numerator, and it represents the number of parts under consideration. The 1 in $\frac{1}{4}$ means that 1 part out of the whole is being considered in the calculation. The bottom number of a fraction is called the denominator, and it represents the total number of equal parts. The 4 in $\frac{1}{4}$ means that the whole consists of 4 equal parts. A fraction cannot have a denominator of zero; this is referred to as "undefined."

> **Review Video: Fractions**
> *Visit mometrix.com/academy and enter Code: 262335*

Fractions can be manipulated, without changing the value of the fraction, by multiplying or dividing (but not adding or subtracting) both the numerator and denominator by the same number. If you divide both numbers by a common factor, you are reducing or simplifying the fraction. Two fractions that have the same value, but are expressed differently are known as equivalent fractions. For example, $\frac{2}{10}, \frac{3}{15}, \frac{4}{20}$, and $\frac{5}{25}$ are all equivalent fractions. They can also all be reduced or simplified to $\frac{1}{5}$.

When two fractions are manipulated so that they have the same denominator, this is known as finding a common denominator. The number chosen to be that common denominator should be the least common multiple of the two original denominators. *Example*: $\frac{3}{4}$ and $\frac{5}{6}$; the least common multiple of 4 and 6 is 12. Manipulating to achieve the common denominator: $\frac{3}{4} = \frac{9}{12}; \frac{5}{6} = \frac{10}{12}$.

If two fractions have a common denominator, they can be added or subtracted simply by adding or subtracting the two numerators and retaining the same denominator. *Example*: $\frac{1}{2} + \frac{1}{4} = \frac{2}{4} + \frac{1}{4} = \frac{3}{4}$. If the two fractions do not already have the same denominator, one or

- 46 -

both of them must be manipulated to achieve a common denominator before they can be added or subtracted.

Two fractions can be multiplied by multiplying the two numerators to find the new numerator and the two denominators to find the new denominator. *Example*: $\frac{1}{3} \times \frac{2}{3} = \frac{1 \times 2}{3 \times 3} = \frac{2}{9}$.

> ➤ **Review Video: <u>Multiplying Fractions</u>**
> *Visit mometrix.com/academy and enter Code: **638849***

Two fractions can be divided by flipping the numerator and denominator of the second fraction and then proceeding as though it were a multiplication. *Example*: $\frac{2}{3} \div \frac{3}{4} = \frac{2}{3} \times \frac{4}{3} = \frac{8}{9}$.

> ➤ **Review Video: <u>Dividing Fractions</u>**
> *Visit mometrix.com/academy and enter Code: **300874***

A fraction whose denominator is greater than its numerator is known as a proper fraction, while a fraction whose numerator is greater than its denominator is known as an improper fraction. Proper fractions have values less than one and improper fractions have values greater than one.

A mixed number is a number that contains both an integer and a fraction. Any improper fraction can be rewritten as a mixed number. *Example*: $\frac{8}{3} = \frac{6}{3} + \frac{2}{3} = 2 + \frac{2}{3} = 2\frac{2}{3}$. Similarly, any mixed number can be rewritten as an improper fraction. *Example*: $1\frac{3}{5} = 1 + \frac{3}{5} = \frac{5}{5} + \frac{3}{5} = \frac{8}{5}$.

> ➤ **Review Video: <u>Improper Fractions and Mixed Numbers</u>**
> *Visit mometrix.com/academy and enter Code: **731507***

Percentages can be thought of as fractions that are based on a whole of 100; that is, one whole is equal to 100%. The word percent means "per hundred." Fractions can be expressed as percents by finding equivalent fractions with a denomination of 100. *Example*: $\frac{7}{10} = \frac{70}{100} = 70\%$; $\frac{1}{4} = \frac{25}{100} = 25\%$.

To express a percentage as a fraction, divide the percentage number by 100 and reduce the fraction to its simplest possible terms. *Example*: $60\% = \frac{60}{100} = \frac{3}{5}$; $96\% = \frac{96}{100} = \frac{24}{25}$. Converting decimals to percentages and percentages to decimals is as simple as moving the decimal point. To convert from a decimal to a percent, move the decimal point two places to the right. To convert from a percent to a decimal, move it two places to the left. *Example*: 0.23 = 23%; 5.34 = 534%; 0.007 = 0.7%; 700% = 7.00; 86% = 0.86; 0.15% = 0.0015.

It may be helpful to remember that the percentage number will always be larger than the equivalent decimal number.

A percentage problem can be presented three main ways: (1) Find what percentage of some number another number is. *Example*: What percentage of 40 is 8? (2) Find what number is some percentage of a given number. *Example*: What number is 20% of 40? (3) Find what number another number is a given percentage of. *Example*: What number is 8 20% of? The three components in all of these cases are the same: a whole (W), a part (P), and a percentage (%). These are related by the equation: $P = W \times \%$. This is the form of the equation you would use to solve problems of type (2). To solve types (1) and (3), you would use these two forms: $\% = \frac{P}{W}$ and $W = \frac{P}{\%}$.

➢ **Review Video:** <u>Percentages</u>
Visit mometrix.com/academy and enter Code: **141911**

The thing that frequently makes percentage problems difficult is that they are most often also word problems, so a large part of solving them is figuring out which quantities are what. Here's an example: *In a school cafeteria, 7 students choose pizza, 9 choose hamburgers, and 4 choose tacos. Find the percentage that chooses tacos.* To find the whole, you must first add all of the parts: 7 + 9 + 4 = 20. The percentage can then be found by dividing the part by the whole($\% = \frac{P}{W}$): $\frac{4}{20} = \frac{20}{100} = 20\%$.

A ratio is a comparison of two quantities in a particular order. *Example*: If there are 14 computers in a lab, and the class has 20 students, there is a student to computer ratio of 20 to 14, commonly written as 20:14. Ratios are normally reduced to their smallest whole number representation, so 20:14 would be reduced to 10:7 by dividing both sides by 2.

A proportion is a relationship between two quantities that dictates how one changes when the other changes. A direct proportion describes a relationship in which a quantity increases by a set amount for every increase in the other quantity, or decreases by that same amount for every decrease in the other quantity. *Example*: Assuming a constant driving speed, the time required for a car trip increases as the distance of the trip increases. The distance to be traveled and the time required to travel are directly proportional.

Inverse proportion is a relationship in which an increase in one quantity is accompanied by a decrease in the other, or vice versa. *Example*: the time required for a car trip decreases as the speed increases, and increases as the speed decreases, so the time required is inversely proportional to the speed of the car.

Systems of Equations

Systems of Equations are a set of simultaneous equations that all use the same variables. A solution to a system of equations must be true for each equation in the system. *Consistent Systems* are those with at least one solution. *Inconsistent Systems* are systems of equations that have no solution.

➢ **Review Video:** <u>Systems of Equations</u>
Visit mometrix.com/academy and enter Code: **658153**

To solve a system of linear equations by *substitution*, start with the easier equation and solve for one of the variables. Express this variable in terms of the other variable. Substitute this expression in the other equation, and solve for the other variable. The solution should be expressed in the form (x, y). Substitute the values into both of the original equations to check your answer. Consider the following problem.

Solve the system using substitution:
$$x + 6y = 15$$
$$3x - 12y = 18$$

Solve the first equation for x:
$$x = 15 - 6y$$

Substitute this value in place of x in the second equation, and solve for y:
$$3(15 - 6y) - 12y = 18$$
$$45 - 18y - 12y = 18$$
$$30y = 27$$
$$y = \frac{27}{30} = \frac{9}{10} = 0.9$$

Plug this value for y back into the first equation to solve for x:
$$x = 15 - 6(0.9) = 15 - 5.4 = 9.6$$

Check both equations if you have time:
$$9.6 + 6(0.9) = 9.6 + 5.4 = 15$$
$$3(9.6) - 12(0.9) = 28.8 - 10.8 = 18$$
Therefore, the solution is $(9.6, 0.9)$.

To solve a system of equations using *elimination*, begin by rewriting both equations in standard form $Ax + By = C$. Check to see if the coefficients of one pair of like variables add to zero. If not, multiply one or both of the equations by a non-zero number to make one set of like variables add to zero. Add the two equations to solve for one of the variables. Substitute this value into one of the original equations to solve for the other variable. Check your work by substituting into the other equation. Next we will solve the same problem as above, but using the addition method.

Solve the system using elimination:
$$x + 6y = 15$$
$$3x - 12y = 18$$

If we multiply the first equation by 2, we can eliminate the y terms:
$$2x + 12y = 30$$
$$3x - 12y = 18$$

Add the equations together and solve for x:
$$5x = 48$$
$$x = \frac{48}{5} = 9.6$$

- 49 -

Plug the value for *x* back into either of the original equations and solve for *y*:

$$9.6 + 6y = 15$$

$$y = \frac{15 - 9.6}{6} = 0.9$$

Check both equations if you have time:

$$9.6 + 6(0.9) = 9.6 + 5.4 = 15$$
$$3(9.6) - 12(0.9) = 28.8 - 10.8 = 18$$

Therefore, the solution is (9.6, 0.9).

Polynomial Algebra

To multiply two binomials, follow the *FOIL* method. FOIL stands for:

- First: Multiply the first term of each binomial

- Outer: Multiply the outer terms of each binomial

- Inner: Multiply the inner terms of each binomial

- Last: Multiply the last term of each binomial

Using FOIL, $(Ax + By)(Cx + Dy) = ACx^2 + ADxy + BCxy + BDy^2$.

> **Review Video:** <u>Multiplying Terms Using the FOIL Method</u>
> Visit *mometrix.com/academy* and enter *Code:* **854792**

To divide polynomials, begin by arranging the terms of each polynomial in order of one variable. You may arrange in ascending or descending order, but be consistent with both polynomials. To get the first term of the quotient, divide the first term of the dividend by the first term of the divisor. Multiply the first term of the quotient by the entire divisor and subtract that product from the dividend. Repeat for the second and successive terms until you either get a remainder of zero or a remainder whose degree is less than the degree of the divisor. If the quotient has a remainder, write the answer as a mixed expression in the form: quotient $+ \frac{\text{remainder}}{\text{divisor}}$.

Rational Expressions are fractions with polynomials in both the numerator and the denominator; the value of the polynomial in the denominator cannot be equal to zero. To add or subtract rational expressions, first find the common denominator, then rewrite each fraction as an equivalent fraction with the common denominator. Finally, add or subtract the numerators to get the numerator of the answer, and keep the common denominator as the denominator of the answer. When multiplying rational expressions, factor each polynomial and cancel like factors (a factor which appears in both the numerator and the denominator). Then, multiply all remaining factors in the numerator to get the numerator of the product, and multiply the remaining factors in the denominator to get the denominator of the product. Remember – cancel entire factors, not individual terms. To divide rational expressions, take the reciprocal of the divisor (the rational expression you are dividing by) and multiply by the dividend.

Below are patterns of some special products to remember: *perfect trinomial squares*, the *difference between two squares*, the *sum and difference of two cubes*, and *perfect cubes*.

- Perfect Trinomial Squares: $x^2 + 2xy + y^2 = (x + y)^2$ or $x^2 - 2xy + y^2 = (x - y)^2$

- Difference between Two Squares: $x^2 - y^2 = (x + y)(x - y)$

- Sum of Two Cubes: $x^3 + y^3 = (x + y)(x^2 - xy + y^2)$

  Note: the second factor is NOT the same as a perfect trinomial square, so do not try to factor it further.

- Difference between Two Cubes: $x^3 - y^3 = (x - y)(x^2 + xy + y^2)$

  Again, the second factor is NOT the same as a perfect trinomial square.

- Perfect Cubes: $x^3 + 3x^2y + 3xy^2 + y^3 = (x + y)^3$ and $x^3 - 3x^2y + 3xy^2 - y^3 = (x - y)^3$

In order to *factor* a polynomial, first check for a common monomial factor. When the greatest common monomial factor has been factored out, look for patterns of special products: differences of two squares, the sum or difference of two cubes for binomial factors, or perfect trinomial squares for trinomial factors. If the factor is a trinomial but not a perfect trinomial square, look for a factorable form, such as $x^2 + (a + b)x + ab = (x + a)(x + b)$ or $(ac)x^2 + (ad + bc)x + bd = (ax + b)(cx + d)$. For factors with four terms, look for groups to factor. Once you have found the factors, write the original polynomial as the product of all the factors. Make sure all of the polynomial factors are prime. Monomial factors may be prime or composite. Check your work by multiplying the factors to make sure you get the original polynomial.

Solving Quadratic Equations

The *Quadratic Formula* is used to solve quadratic equations when other methods are more difficult. To use the quadratic formula to solve a quadratic equation, begin by rewriting the equation in standard form $ax^2 + bx + c = 0$, where a, b, and c are coefficients. Once you have identified the values of the coefficients, substitute those values into the quadratic formula $= \frac{-b \pm \sqrt{b^2 - 4ac}}{2a}$. Evaluate the equation and simplify the expression. Again, check each root by substituting into the original equation. In the quadratic formula, the portion of the formula under the radical ($b^2 - 4ac$) is called the *Discriminant*. If the discriminant is zero, there is only one root: zero. If the discriminant is positive, there are two different real roots. If the discriminant is negative, there are no real roots.

To solve a quadratic equation by *Factoring*, begin by rewriting the equation in standard form, if necessary. Factor the side with the variable then set each of the factors equal to zero and solve the resulting linear equations. Check your answers by substituting the roots you found into the original equation. If, when writing the equation in standard form, you have an equation in the form $x^2 + c = 0$ or $x^2 - c = 0$, set $x^2 = -c$ or $x^2 = c$ and take the square root of c. If $c = 0$, the only real root is zero. If c is positive, there are two real roots—the positive and negative square root values. If c is negative, there are no real roots because you cannot take the square root of a negative number.

> **Review Video:** <u>Factoring Quadratic Equations</u>
> Visit *mometrix.com/academy* and enter *Code:* **336566**

To solve a quadratic equation by *Completing the Square*, rewrite the equation so that all terms containing the variable are on the left side of the equal sign, and all the constants are on the right side of the equal sign. Make sure the coefficient of the squared term is 1. If there is a coefficient with the squared term, divide each term on both sides of the equal side by that number. Next, work with the coefficient of the single-variable term. Square half of this coefficient, and add that value to both sides. Now you can factor the left side (the side containing the variable) as the square of a binomial. $x^2 + 2ax + a^2 = C \Rightarrow (x + a)^2 = C$, where x is the variable, and a and C are constants. Take the square root of both sides and solve for the variable. Substitute the value of the variable in the original problem to check your work.

Basic Geometry

<u>Angles</u>
An angle is formed when two lines or line segments meet at a common point. It may be a common starting point for a pair of segments or rays, or it may be the intersection of lines. Angles are represented by the symbol $\angle$.

The vertex is the point at which two segments or rays meet to form an angle. If the angle is formed by intersecting rays, lines, and/or line segments, the vertex is the point at which four angles are formed. The pairs of angles opposite one another are called vertical angles, and their measures are equal. In the figure below, angles ABC and DBE are congruent, as are angles ABD and CBE.

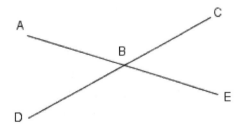

An acute angle is an angle with a degree measure less than 90°.
A right angle is an angle with a degree measure of exactly 90°.
An obtuse angle is an angle with a degree measure greater than 90° but less than 180°.
A straight angle is an angle with a degree measure of exactly 180°. This is also a semicircle.
A reflex angle is an angle with a degree measure greater than 180° but less than 360°.
A full angle is an angle with a degree measure of exactly 360°.

Two angles whose sum is exactly 90° are said to be complementary. The two angles may or may not be adjacent. In a right triangle, the two acute angles are complementary.

Two angles whose sum is exactly 180° are said to be supplementary. The two angles may or may not be adjacent. Two intersecting lines always form two pairs of supplementary angles. Adjacent supplementary angles will always form a straight line.

Circles
The center is the single point inside the circle that is equidistant from every point on the circle. (Point *O* in the diagram below.)

The radius is a line segment that joins the center of the circle and any one point on the circle. All radii of a circle are equal. (Segments *OX*, *OY*, and *OZ* in the diagram below.)

The diameter is a line segment that passes through the center of the circle and has both endpoints on the circle. The length of the diameter is exactly twice the length of the radius. (Segment *XZ* in the diagram below.)

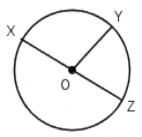

Triangles
A triangle is a polygon with three sides and three angles. Triangles can be classified according to the length of their sides or magnitude of their angles.

An acute triangle is a triangle whose three angles are all less than 90°. If two of the angles are equal, the acute triangle is also an isosceles triangle. If the three angles are all equal, the acute triangle is also an equilateral triangle.

A right triangle is a triangle with exactly one angle equal to 90°. All right triangles follow the Pythagorean Theorem. A right triangle can never be acute or obtuse.

An obtuse triangle is a triangle with exactly one angle greater than 90°. The other two angles may or may not be equal. If the two remaining angles are equal, the obtuse triangle is also an isosceles triangle.

An equilateral triangle is a triangle with three congruent sides. An equilateral triangle will also have three congruent angles, each 60°. All equilateral triangles are also acute triangles.

An isosceles triangle is a triangle with two congruent sides. An isosceles triangle will also have two congruent angles opposite the two congruent sides.

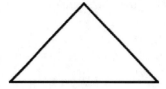

A scalene triangle is a triangle with no congruent sides. A scalene triangle will also have three angles of different measures. The angle with the largest measure is opposite the longest side, and the angle with the smallest measure is opposite the shortest side.

The Triangle Inequality Theorem states that the sum of the measures of any two sides of a triangle is always greater than the measure of the third side. If the sum of the measures of two sides were equal to the third side, a triangle would be impossible because the two sides would lie flat across the third side and there would be no vertex. If the sum of the measures of two of the sides was less than the third side, a closed figure would be impossible because the two shortest sides would never meet.

Similar triangles are triangles whose corresponding angles are congruent to one another. Their corresponding sides may or may not be equal, but they are proportional to one another. Since the angles in a triangle always sum to 180°, it is only necessary to determine that two pairs of corresponding angles are congruent, since the third will be also in that case.

Congruent triangles are similar triangles whose corresponding sides are all equal. Congruent triangles can be made to fit on top of one another by rotation, reflection, and/or translation. When trying to determine whether two triangles are congruent, there are several criteria that can be used.

Area formulas
Rectangle: $A = wl$, where w is the width and l is the length

Square: $A = s^2$, where s is the length of a side.

Triangle: $A = \frac{1}{2}bh$, where b is the length of one side (base) and h is the distance from that side to the opposite vertex measured perpendicularly (height).

Circle: $A = \pi r^2$, where π is the mathematical constant approximately equal to 3.14 and r is the distance from the center of the circle to any point on the circle (radius).

<u>Volume formulas</u>
Rectangular Prism – all 6 sides are rectangles. The volume can be calculated as $V = s_1 \times s_2 \times s_3$, or the lengths of the three different sides multiplied together.

Cube – a special type of prism in which all faces are squares. The volume can be calculated as $V = s^3$, where s is the length of any side.

Sphere – a round solid consisting of one continuous, uniformly-curved surface. The volume can be calculated as $V = \frac{4}{3}\pi r^3$, where r is the distance from the center of the sphere to any point on the surface (radius).

Mechanical Comprehension Test

The Mechanical Comprehension Test (MCT) isn't as long as the Math Skills or Reading Comprehension sections. It has a time limit of only 15 minutes. Keep in mind that this section is computer adaptive like the Math Skills subtest. Once again, this means that there is no fixed number of questions on the test. The questions get progressively harder each time you answer a question correctly, and progressively easier each time you answer a question incorrectly. This is an ongoing process throughout the test, and this format allows the computer software to tailor the questions to your current perceived skill level. Do not guess on this section unless you've exhausted all other options because incorrect answers will have a negative impact on your final score.

If you've ever taken the ASVAB, the Mechanical Comprehension subtest on the SIFT should not be all that foreign to you. The two tests cover a very similar breadth of concepts and in very similar ways. You'll see questions about gears, pulleys, levers, simple machines, mechanical advantage, and so on. Most questions in this section will be accompanied by a drawing to help illustrate the physical situation that is being asked about. None of the questions should baffle you, nor should any of them require knowledge of physics or mechanics beyond the high school level. The emphasis in Mechanical Comprehension is much more on aptitude and intuition than on acquired knowledge.

That is not to say that you shouldn't take an inventory of your knowledge and skills in physics and mechanics as part of your SIFT test preparation. On the contrary, developing a strong background in those areas is one of the best ways to make these concepts intuitive to you. If it has been a while since you've interacted with these topics on a regular basis, a refresher is probably in order. Since few applicants for military aviation training are engaged in the kind of jobs or academic studies which require them to rely on their knowledge of physics on a daily basis, we've included an extensive primer on all the basics that might show up on the SIFT.

Kinematics

To begin, we will look at the basics of physics. At its heart, physics is just a set of explanations for the ways in which matter and energy behave. There are three key concepts used to describe how matter moves:

1. Displacement
2. Velocity
3. Acceleration

Displacement

Concept: where and how far an object has gone
Calculation: final position – initial position

When something changes its location from one place to another, it is said to have undergone displacement. If a golf ball is hit across a sloped green into the hole, the displacement only takes into account the final and initial locations, not the path of the ball.

Displacement along a straight line is a very simple example of a vector quantity: that is, it has both a magnitude and a direction. Direction is as important as magnitude in many measurements. If we can determine the original and final position of the object, then we can determine the total displacement with this simple equation:

$$\text{Displacement} = \text{final position} - \text{original position}$$

The hole (final position) is at the Cartesian coordinate location (2, 0) and the ball is hit from the location (1, 0). The displacement is:

$$\text{Displacement} = (2,0) - (1,0)$$
$$\text{Displacement} = (1,0)$$

The displacement has a magnitude of 1 and a direction of the positive x direction.

Velocity

Concept: the rate of moving from one position to another
Calculation: change in position / change in time

Velocity answers the question, "How quickly is an object moving?" For example, if a car and a plane travel between two cities which are a hundred miles apart, but the car takes two hours and the plane takes one hour, the car has the same displacement as the plane, but a smaller velocity.

In order to solve some of the problems on the exam, you may need to assess the velocity of an object. If we want to calculate the average velocity of an object, we must know two things. First, we must know its displacement. Second, we must know the time it took to cover this distance. The formula for average velocity is quite simple:

$$\textbf{average velocity} = \frac{\textbf{displacement}}{\textbf{change in time}}$$

Or

$$\textbf{average velocity} = \frac{\textbf{final position} - \textbf{original position}}{\textbf{final time} - \textbf{original time}}$$

To complete the example, the velocity of the plane is calculated to be:

$$\textbf{plane average velocity} = \frac{100 \text{ miles}}{1 \text{ hour}} = 100 \text{ miles per hour}$$

The velocity of the car is less:

$$\textbf{car average velocity} = \frac{100 \text{ miles}}{2 \text{ hours}} = 50 \text{ miles per hour}$$

Often, people confuse the words *speed* and *velocity*. There is a significant difference. The average velocity is based on the amount of displacement, a vector. Alternately, the average speed is based on the distance covered or the path length. The equation for speed is:

$$\textbf{average speed} = \frac{\textbf{total distance traveled}}{\textbf{change in time}}$$

Notice that we used total distance and *not* change in position, because speed is path-dependent.

If the plane traveling between cities had needed to fly around a storm on its way, making the distance traveled 50 miles greater than the distance the car traveled, the plane would still have the same total displacement as the car.

The calculation for the speed: For this reason, average speed can be calculated:

$$\text{plane average speed} = \frac{150 \text{ miles}}{1 \text{ hour}} = 150 \text{ miles per hour}$$

$$\text{car average speed} = \frac{100 \text{ miles}}{2 \text{ hours}} = 50 \text{ miles per hour}$$

Acceleration

Concept: how quickly something changes from one velocity to another
Calculation: change in velocity / change in time

Acceleration is the rate of change of the velocity of an object. If a car accelerates from zero velocity to 60 miles per hour (88 feet per second) in two seconds, the car has an impressive acceleration. But if a car performs the same change in velocity in eight seconds, the acceleration is much lower and not as impressive.

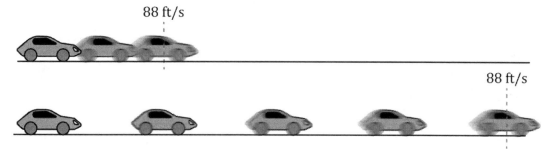

To calculate average acceleration, we may use the equation:

$$\textbf{average acceleration} = \frac{\textbf{change in velocity}}{\textbf{change in time}}$$

The acceleration of the cars is found to be:

$$\text{Car \#1 average acceleration} = \frac{88 \text{ feet per second}}{2 \text{ seconds}} = 44 \ \frac{\text{feet}}{\text{second}^2}$$

$$\text{Car \#2 average acceleration} = \frac{88 \text{ feet per second}}{8 \text{ seconds}} = 11 \ \frac{\text{feet}}{\text{second}^2}$$

Acceleration will be expressed in units of distance divided by time squared; for instance, meters per second squared or feet per second squared.

Projectile Motion

A specific application of the study of motion is projectile motion. Simple projectile motion occurs when an object is in the air and experiencing only the force of gravity. We will disregard drag for this topic. Some common examples of projectile motion are thrown balls, flying bullets, and falling rocks. The characteristics of projectile motion are:
1. The horizontal component of velocity doesn't change
2. The vertical acceleration due to gravity affects the vertical component of velocity

Because gravity only acts downwards, objects in projectile motion only experience acceleration in the y direction (vertical). The horizontal component of the object's velocity does not change in flight. This means that if a rock is thrown out off a cliff, the horizontal velocity, (think the shadow if the sun is directly overhead) will not change until the ball hits the ground.

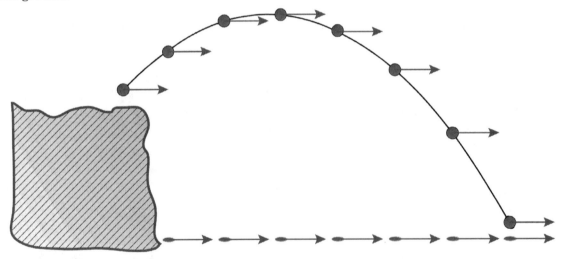

The velocity in the vertical direction is affected by gravity. Gravity imposes an acceleration of $g = 9.8 \frac{m}{s^2}$ or $32 \frac{ft}{s^2}$ downward on projectiles. The vertical component of velocity at any point is equal to:

vertical velocity = original vertical velocity − g × time

When these characteristics are combined, there are three points of particular interest in a projectile's flight. At the beginning of a flight, the object has a horizontal component and a vertical component giving it a large speed. At the top of a projectile's flight, the vertical velocity equals zero, making the top the slowest part of travel. When the object passes the same height as the launch, the vertical velocity is opposite of the initial vertical velocity making the speed equal to the initial speed.

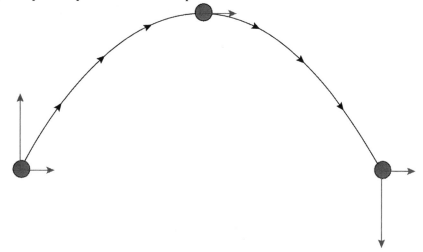

If the object continues falling below the initial height from which it was launched (e.g., it was launched from the edge of a cliff), it will have an even greater velocity than it did initially from that point until it hits the ground.

Rotational Kinematics

Concept: increasing the radius increases the linear speed
Calculation: linear speed = radius × rotational speed

Another interesting application of the study of motion is rotation. In practice, simple rotation is when an object rotates around a point at a constant speed. Most questions covering rotational kinematics will provide the distance from a rotating object to the center of rotation (radius) and ask about the linear speed of the object. A point will have a greater linear speed when it is farther from the center of rotation.

If a potter is spinning his wheel at a constant speed of one revolution per second, the clay six inches away from the center will be going faster than the clay three inches from the center. The clay directly in the center of the wheel will not have any linear velocity.

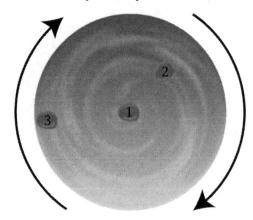

To find the linear speed of rotating objects using radians, we use the equation:

$$\textit{linear speed} = (\textit{rotational speed [in radians]}) \times (\textit{radius})$$

Using degrees, the equation is:

$$\textit{linear speed} = (\textit{rotational speed [in degrees]}) \times \frac{\pi \, radians}{180 \, degrees} \times (\textit{radius})$$

To find the speed of the pieces of clay we use the known values (rotational speed of 1 revolution per second, radii of 0 inches, 3 inches, and 6 inches) and the knowledge that one revolution = 2 pi.

$$clay \ \#1 \ speed = \left(2\pi\frac{rad}{s}\right) \times (0 \ inches) = 0 \frac{inches}{second}$$

$$clay \ \#2 \ speed = \left(2\pi\frac{rad}{s}\right) \times (3 \ inches) = 18.8 \frac{inches}{second}$$

$$clay \ \#3 \ speed = \left(2\pi\frac{rad}{s}\right) \times (6 \ inches) = 37.7 \frac{inches}{second}$$

Cams

In the study of motion, a final application often tested is the cam. A cam and follower system allows mechanical systems to have timed, specified, and repeating motion. Although cams come in varied forms, tests focus on rotary cams. In engines, a cam shaft coordinates the valves for intake and exhaust. Cams are often used to convert rotational motion into repeating linear motion.

Cams rotate around one point. The follower sits on the edge of the cam and moves along with the edge. To understand simple cams, count the number of bumps on the cam. Each bump will cause the follower to move outwards.

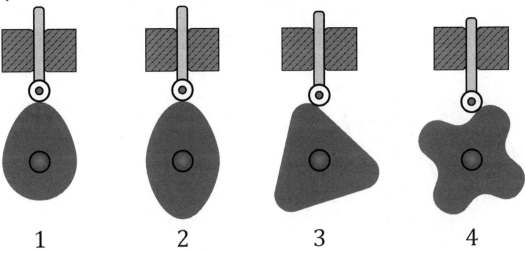

1   2   3   4

Another way to consider cams is to unravel the cam profile into a straight object. The follower will then follow the top of the profile.

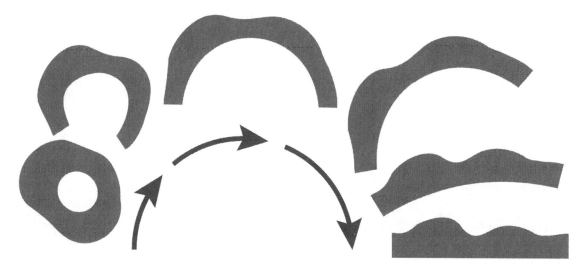

Kinetics

Newton's three laws of mechanics

The questions on the exam may require you to demonstrate familiarity with the concepts expressed in Newton's three laws of motion which relate to the concept of force.

Newton's first law – A body at rest will tend to remain at rest, while a body in motion will tend to remain in motion, unless acted upon by an external force.

Newton's second law – The acceleration of an object is directly proportional to the force being exerted on it and inversely proportional to its mass.

Newton's third law – For every force, there is an equal and opposite force.

First Law

Concept: Unless something interferes, an object won't start or stop moving

Although intuition supports the idea that objects do not start moving until a force acts on them, the idea of an object continuing forever without any forces can seem odd. Before Newton formulated his laws of mechanics, general thought held that some force had to act on an object continuously in order for it to move at a constant velocity. This seems to make sense: when an object is briefly pushed, it will eventually come to a stop. Newton, however, determined that unless some other force acted on the object (most notably friction or air resistance), it would continue in the direction it was pushed at the same velocity forever.

As time moves forward, the air resistance stops one ball, but the ball without air resistance has no stopping force.

Second Law

Concept: Acceleration increases linearly with force.

Although Newton's second law can be conceptually understood as a series of relationships describing how an increase in one factor will decrease another factor, the law can be understood best in equation format:

$$Force = mass \times acceleration$$

Or

$$Acceleration = \frac{force}{mass}$$

Or

$$Mass = \frac{force}{acceleration}$$

Each of the forms of the equation allows for a different look at the same relationships. To examine the relationships, change one factor and observe the result. If a steel ball, with a diameter of 6.3 cm, has a mass of 1 kg and an acceleration of 1 m/s², then the net force on the ball will be 1 Newton.

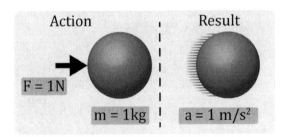

Third Law

Concept: Nothing can push or pull without being pushed or pulled in return.

When any object exerts a force on another object, the other object exerts the opposite force back on the original object. To observe this, consider two spring-based fruit scales, both tipped on their sides as shown with the weighing surfaces facing each other. If fruit scale #1 is pressing fruit scale #2 into the wall, it exerts a force on fruit scale #2, measurable by the reading on scale #2. However, because fruit scale #1 is exerting a force on scale #2, scale #2 is exerting a force on scale #1 with an opposite direction, but the same magnitude.

Force

Concept: a push or pull on an object
Calculation: $Force = mass \times acceleration$

A force is a vector which causes acceleration of a body. Force has both magnitude and direction. Furthermore, multiple forces acting on one object combine in vector addition. This can be demonstrated by considering an object placed at the origin of the coordinate plane. If it is pushed along the positive direction of the x-axis, it will move in this direction; if the force acting on it is in the positive direction of the y-axis, it will move in that direction. However, if both forces are applied at the same time, then the object will move at an angle to both the x and y axes, an angle determined by the relative amount of force exerted in each direction. In this way, we may see that the resulting force is a vector sum; that is, a net force that has both magnitude and direction.

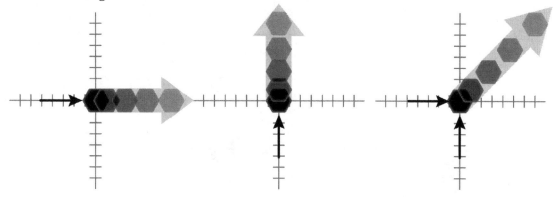

Mass

Concept: the amount of matter

Mass can be defined as the quantity of matter in an object. If we apply the same force to two objects of different mass, we will find that the resulting acceleration is different. Newton's

- 65 -

Second Law of Motion describes the relationship between mass, force, and acceleration in the equation: ***Force = mass x acceleration***. In other words, the acceleration of an object is directly proportional to the force being exerted on it and inversely proportional to its mass.

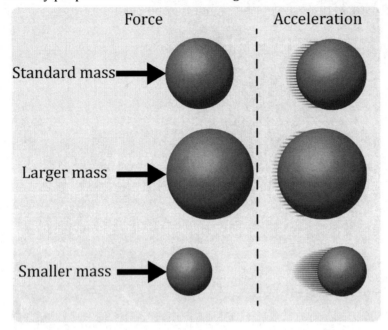

Gravity

Gravity is a force which exists between all objects with matter. Gravity is a pulling force between objects meaning that the forces on the objects point toward the opposite object. When Newton's third law is applied to gravity, the force pairs from gravity are shown to be equal in magnitude and opposite in direction.

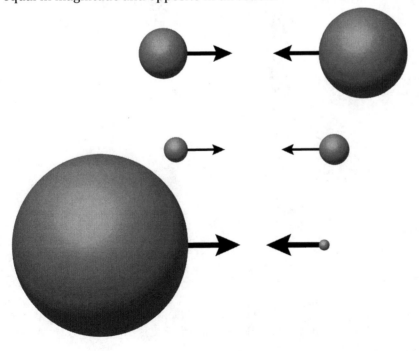

- 66 -

Weight

Weight is sometimes confused with mass. While mass is the amount of matter, weight is the force exerted by the earth on an object with matter by gravity. The earth pulls every object of mass toward its center while every object of mass pulls the earth toward its center. The object's pull on the earth is equal in magnitude to the pull which the earth exerts, but, because the mass of the earth is very large in comparison (5.97 × 10²⁴ kg), only the object appears to be affected by the force.

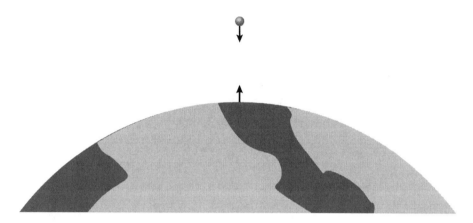

The gravity of earth causes a constant acceleration due to gravity (g) at a specific altitude. For most earthbound applications the acceleration due to gravity is 32.2 ft/s² or 9.8 m/s² in a downward direction. The equation for the force of gravity (weight) on an object is the equation from Newton's Second Law with the constant acceleration due to gravity (g).

$$Force = mass \times acceleration$$
$$Weight = mass \times acceleration\ due\ to\ gravity$$
$$W = m \times g$$

The SI (International Standard of Units) unit for weight is the Newton $\left(\frac{kg \times m}{s^2}\right)$. The English Engineering unit system uses the pound, or lb, as the unit for weight and force $\left(\frac{slug \times ft}{s^2}\right)$. Thus, a 2 kg object under the influence of gravity would have a weight of:
$$W = m \times g$$
$$W = 2 \text{ kg} \times 9.8 \frac{m}{s^2} = 18.6 \text{ N downwards}$$

Normal force

Concept: the force perpendicular to a contact surface

The word "normal" is used in mathematics to mean perpendicular, and so the force known as normal force should be remembered as the perpendicular force exerted on an object that is resting on some other surface. For instance, if a box is resting on a horizontal surface, we may say that the normal force is directed upwards through the box (the opposite, downward force is the weight of the box). If the box is resting on a wedge, the normal force from the wedge is not vertical but is perpendicular to the wedge edge.

Tension

Concept: the pulling force from a cord

Another force that may come into play on the exam is called tension. Anytime a cord is attached to a body and pulled so that it is taut, we may say that the cord is under tension. The cord in tension applies a pulling tension force on the connected objects. This force is pointed away from the body and along the cord at the point of attachment. In simple considerations of tension, the cord is assumed to be both without mass and incapable of stretching. In other words, its only role is as the connector between two bodies. The cord is also assumed to pull on both ends with the same magnitude of tension force.

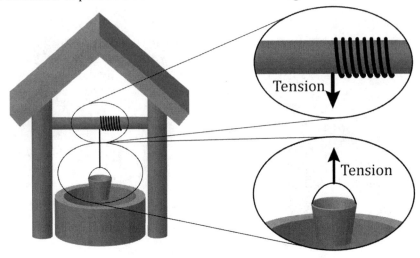

Friction

Concept: Friction is a resistance to motion between contacting surfaces

In order to illustrate the concept of friction, let us imagine a book resting on a table. As it sits, the force of its weight is equal to and opposite of the normal force. If, however, we were to exert a force on the book, attempting to push it to one side, a frictional force would arise, equal and opposite to our force. This kind of frictional force is known as static frictional force.

Static Friction Force

As we increase our force on the book, however, we will eventually cause it to accelerate in the direction of our force. At this point, the frictional force opposing us will be known as kinetic friction. For many combinations of surfaces, the magnitude of the kinetic frictional force is lower than that of the static frictional force, and consequently, the amount of force needed to maintain the movement of the book will be less than that needed to initiate the movement.

Kinetic Friction Force

Rolling Friction

Occasionally, a question will ask you to consider the amount of friction generated by an object that is rolling. If a wheel is rolling at a constant speed, then the point at which it touches the ground will not slide, and there will be no friction between the ground and the wheel inhibiting movement. In fact, the friction at the point of contact between the wheel and the ground is static friction necessary to propulsion with wheels. When a vehicle accelerates, the static friction between the wheels and ground allows the vehicle to achieve acceleration. Without this friction, the vehicle would spin its wheels and go nowhere.

Although the static friction does not impede movement for the wheels, a combination of frictional forces can resist rolling motion. One such frictional force is bearing friction. Bearing friction is the kinetic friction between the wheel and an object it rotates around, such as a stationary axle.

Most questions will consider bearing friction the only force stopping a rotating wheel. There are many other factors that affect the efficiency of a rolling wheel such as deformation of the wheel, deformation of the surface, and force imbalances, but the net resulting friction can be modeled as a simple kinetic rolling friction. Rolling friction or rolling resistance is the catch-all friction for the combination of all the losses which impede wheels in real life.

Static Friction · Bearing Friction

Drag force

Friction can also be generated when an object is moving through air or liquid. A drag force occurs when a body moves through some fluid (either liquid or gas) and experiences a force that opposes the motion of the body. The drag force is greater if the air or fluid is thicker or is moving in the direction opposite to the object. Obviously, the higher the drag force, the greater amount of positive force required to keep the object moving forward.

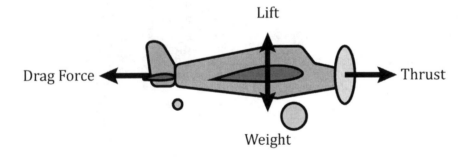

Lift · Drag Force · Thrust · Weight

Balanced Forces

An object is in equilibrium when the sum of all forces acting on the object is zero. When the forces on an object sum to zero, the object does not accelerate. Equilibrium can be obtained when forces in the y-direction sum to zero, forces in the x-direction sum to zero, or forces in both directions sum to zero.

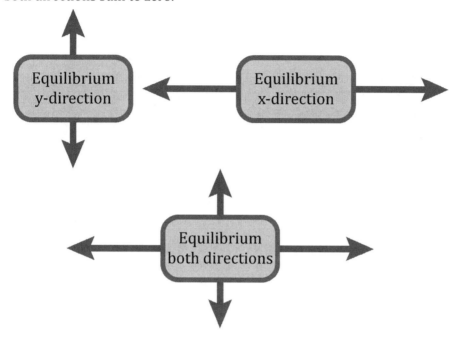

In most cases, a problem will provide one or more forces acting on object and ask for a force to balance the system. The force will be the opposite of the current force or sum of current forces.

Balance the forces

Given: Answer:

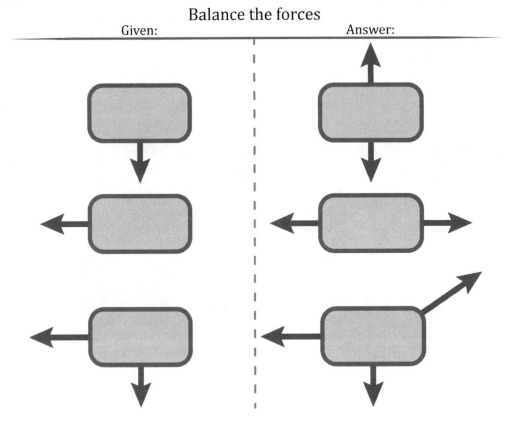

Rotational Kinetics

Many equations and concepts in linear kinematics and kinetics transfer to rotation. For example, angular position is an angle. Angular velocity, like linear velocity, is the change in the position (angle) divided by the time. Angular acceleration is the change in angular velocity divided by time. Although most tests will not require you to perform angular calculations, they will expect you to understand the angular version of force: torque.

Concept: Torque is a twisting force on an object
Calculation: $Torque = radius \times force$

Torque, like force, is a vector and has magnitude and direction. As with force, the sum of torques on an object will affect the angular acceleration of that object. The key to solving problems with torque is understanding the lever arm. A better description of the torque equation is:

Torque = force × the distance perpedicular to the force to the center of rotation

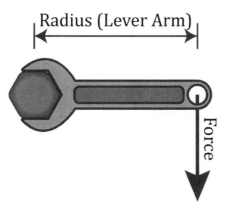

Because torque is directly proportional to the radius, or lever arm, a greater lever arm will result in a greater torque with the same amount of force. The wrench on the right has twice the radius and, as a result, twice the torque.

Alternatively, a greater force also increases torque. The wrench on the right has twice the force and twice the torque.

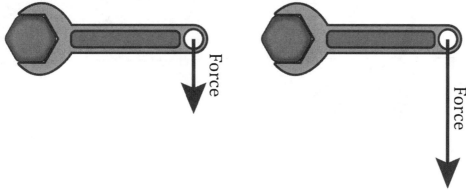

Work/Energy

Work

Concept: Work is the transfer of energy from one object to another
Calculation: Work = force × displacement

The equation for work in one dimension is fairly simple:
$$Work = Force \times displacement$$
$$W = F \times d$$

In the equation, the force and the displacement are the magnitude of the force exerted and the total change in position of the object on which the force is exerted, respectively. If force and displacement have the same direction, then the work is positive. If they are in opposite directions, however, the work is negative.

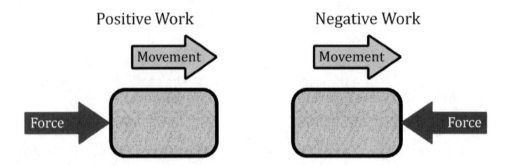

For two-dimensional work, the equation is a bit more complex:
$$Work = Force \times displacement \times cos(\theta \text{ between displacement and force})$$
$$W = F \times d \times cos(\theta)$$

The angle in the equation is the angle between the direction of the force and the direction of the displacement. Thus, the work done when a box is pulled at a 20 degree angle with a force of 100 lb for 20 ft will be less than the work done when a differently weighted box is pulled horizontally with a force of 100 lb for 20 ft.

$$W_1 = 100\text{lb} \times 20\text{ft} \times \cos(20°) = 1880 \text{ ft} \cdot \text{lb}$$
$$W_2 = 100\text{lb} \times 20\text{ft} \times \cos(0°) = 2000 \text{ ft} \cdot \text{lb}$$

The unit ft · lb is the unit for both work and energy.

Energy

Concept: the ability of a body to do work on another object

Energy is a word that has found a million different uses in the English language, but in physics it refers to the measure of a body's ability to do work. In physics, energy may not have a million meanings, but it does have many forms. Each of these forms, such as chemical, electric, and nuclear, is the capability of an object to perform work. However, for the purpose of most tests, mechanical energy and mechanical work are the only forms of energy worth understanding in depth. Mechanical energy is the sum of an object's kinetic and potential energies. Although they will be introduced in greater detail, these are the forms of mechanical energy:

Kinetic Energy – energy an object has by virtue of its motion
Gravitational Potential Energy – energy by virtue of an object's height
Elastic Potential Energy – energy stored in compression or tension

Neglecting frictional forces, mechanical energy is conserved.

- 75 -

As an example, imagine a ball moving perpendicular to the surface of the earth, with its weight the only force acting on it. As the ball rises, the weight will be doing work on the ball, decreasing its speed and its kinetic energy, and slowing it down until it momentarily stops. During this ascent, the potential energy of the ball will be rising. Once the ball begins to fall back down, it will lose potential energy as it gains kinetic energy. Mechanical energy is conserved throughout; the potential energy of the ball at its highest point is equal to the kinetic energy of the ball at its lowest point prior to impact.

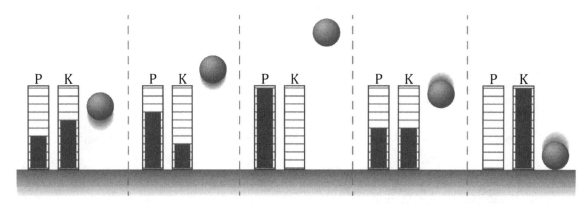

In systems where friction and air resistance are not negligible, we observe a different sort of result. For example, imagine a block sliding across the floor until it comes to a stop due to friction. Unlike a compressed spring or a ball flung into the air, there is no way for this block to regain its energy with a return trip. Therefore, we cannot say that the lost kinetic energy is being stored as potential energy. Instead, it has been dissipated and cannot be recovered. The total mechanical energy of the block-floor system has been not conserved in this case but rather reduced. The total energy of the system has not decreased, since the kinetic energy has been converted into thermal energy, but that energy is no longer useful for work.

Energy, though it may change form, will be neither created nor destroyed during physical processes. However, if we construct a system and some external force performs work on it, the result may be slightly different. If the work is positive, then the overall store of energy is increased; if it is negative, however, we can say that the overall energy of the system has decreased.

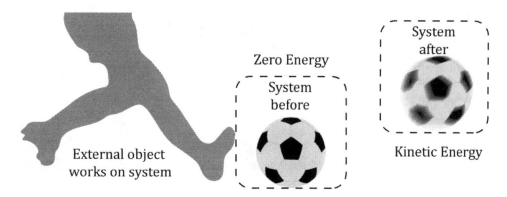

Kinetic energy

The kinetic energy of an object is the amount of energy it possesses by reason of being in motion. Kinetic energy cannot be negative. Changes in kinetic energy will occur when a force does work on an object, such that the motion of the object is altered. This change in kinetic energy is equal to the amount of work that is done. This relationship is commonly referred to as the work-energy theorem.

One interesting application of the work-energy theorem is that of objects in a free fall. To begin with, let us assert that the force acting on such an object is its weight, equal to its mass times g (the force of gravity). The work done by this force will be positive, as the force is exerted in the direction in which the object is traveling. Kinetic energy will, therefore, increase, according to the work-kinetic energy theorem.

If the object is dropped from a great enough height, it eventually reaches its terminal velocity, where the drag force is equal to the weight, so the object is no longer accelerating and its kinetic energy remains constant.

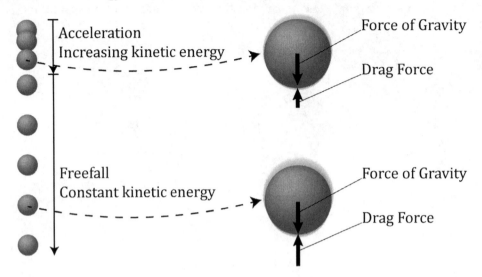

Gravitational Potential Energy

Gravitational potential energy is simply the potential for a certain amount of work to be done by one object on another using gravity. For objects on earth, the gravitational potential energy is equal to the amount of work which the earth can act on the object. The work which gravity performs on objects moving entirely or partially in the vertical direction is equal to the force exerted by the earth (weight) times the distance traveled in the direction of the force (height above the ground or reference point):

Work from gravity = weight × height above the ground

Thus, the gravitational potential energy is the same as the potential work.

Gravitational Potential Energy = weight × height

Elastic Potential Energy

Elastic potential energy is the potential for a certain amount of work to be done by one object on another using elastic compression or tension. The most common example is the spring. A spring will resist any compression or tension away from its equilibrium position (natural position). A small buggy is pressed into a large spring. The spring contains a large amount of elastic potential energy. If the buggy and spring are released, the spring will push exert a force on the buggy for a distance. This work will put kinetic energy into the buggy. The energy can be imagined as a liquid poured from one container into another. The spring pours its elastic energy into the buggy, which receives the energy as kinetic energy.

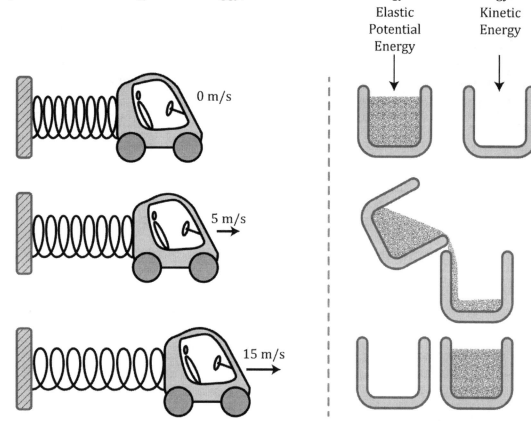

Power

Concept: the rate of work
Calculation: work/time

On occasion, you may need to demonstrate an understanding of power, as it is defined in applied physics. Power is the rate at which work is done. Power, like work and energy, is a scalar quantity. Power can be calculated by dividing the amount of work performed by the amount of time in which the work was performed.

$$\textbf{Power} = \frac{\textbf{work}}{\textbf{time}}$$

If more work is performed in a shorter amount of time, more power has been exerted. Power can be expressed in a variety of units. The preferred metric expression is one of watts or joules per seconds. For engine power, it is often expressed in horsepower.

Machines

Simple machines

Concept: Tools which transform forces to make tasks easier.

As their job is to transform forces, simple machines have an input force and an output force or forces. Simple machines transform forces in two ways: direction and magnitude. A machine can change the direction of a force, with respect to the input force, like a single stationary pulley which only changes the direction of the output force. A machine can also change the magnitude of the force like a lever.

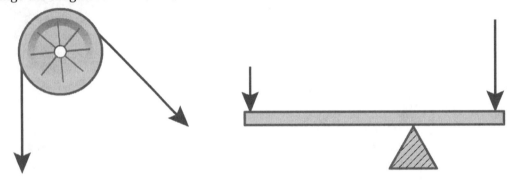

Simple machines include the inclined plane, the wedge, the screw, the pulley, the lever, and the wheel.

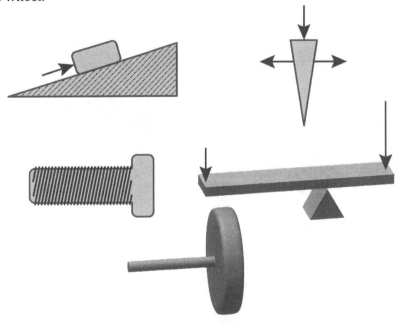

- 80 -

Mechanical Advantage

Concept: the amount of change a simple machine provides to the magnitude of a force
Calculation: output force/input force

Mechanical advantage is the measure of the output force divided by the input force. Thus, mechanical advantage measures the change performed by a machine. Machines cannot create energy, only transform it. Thus, in frictionless, ideal machines, the input work equals the output work.

$$Work_{input} = Work_{output}$$
$$force_{input} \times distance_{input} = force_{output} \times distance_{output}$$

This means that a simple machine can increase the force of the output by decreasing the distance which the output travels or it can increase the distance of the output by decreasing the force at the output.

By moving parts of the equation for work, we can arrive at the equation for mechanical advantage.

$$\textbf{Mechanical Advantage} = \frac{\textbf{force}_{\textbf{output}}}{\textbf{force}_{\textbf{input}}} = \frac{\textbf{distance}_{\textbf{input}}}{\textbf{distance}_{\textbf{output}}}$$

If the mechanical advantage is greater than one, the output force is greater than the input force and the input distance is greater than the output distance. Conversely, if the mechanical advantage is less than one, the input force is greater than the output force and the output distance is greater than the input distance. In equation form this is:

If Mechanical Advantage > 1:
$$force_{input} < force_{output} \text{ and } distance_{output} < distance_{input}$$

If Mechanical Advantage < 1:
$$force_{input} > force_{output} \text{ and } distance_{output} > distance_{input}$$

Inclined plane

The inclined plane is perhaps the most common of the simple machines. It is simply a flat surface that elevates as you move from one end to the other; a ramp is an easy example of an inclined plane. Consider how much easier it is for an elderly person to walk up a long ramp than to climb a shorter but steeper flight of stairs; this is because the force required is diminished as the distance increases. Indeed, the longer the ramp, the easier it is to ascend.

On the exam, this simple fact will most often be applied to moving heavy objects. For instance, if you have to move a heavy box onto the back of a truck, it is much easier to push it up a ramp than to lift it directly onto the truck bed. The longer the ramp, the greater the mechanical advantage, and the easier it will be to move the box. The mechanical advantage of an inclined plane is equal to the slant length divided by the rise of the plane.

$$\text{Mechanical Advantage} = \frac{\text{slant length}}{\text{rise}}$$

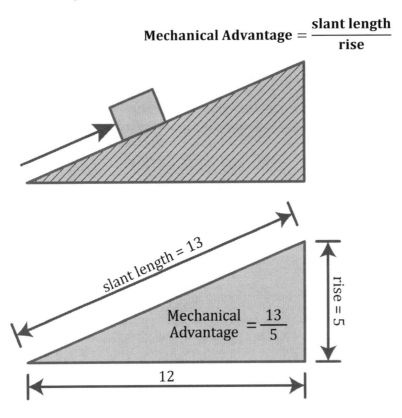

As you solve this kind of problem, however, remember that the same amount of work is being performed whether the box is lifted directly or pushed up a twenty-foot ramp; a simple machine only changes the force and the distance.

Wedge

A wedge is a variation on the inclined plane, in which the wedge moves between objects or parts and forces them apart. The unique characteristic of a wedge is that, unlike an inclined plane, it is designed to move. Perhaps the most familiar use of the wedge is in splitting wood. A wedge is driven into the wood by hitting the flat back end. The thin end of a wedge is easier to drive into the wood since it has less surface area and, therefore, transmits more force per area. As the wedge is driven in, the increased width helps to split the wood.

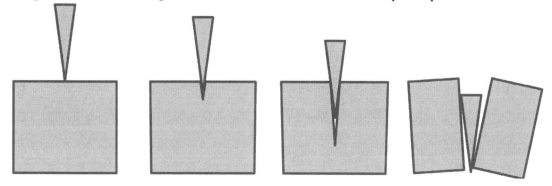

The exam may require you to select the wedge that has the highest mechanical advantage. This should be easy: the longer and thinner the wedge, the greater the mechanical advantage. The equation for mechanical advantage is:

$$\textbf{Mechanical Advantage} = \frac{\textbf{Length}}{\textbf{Width}}$$

Screw

A screw is simply an inclined plane that has been wound around a cylinder so that it forms a sort of spiral.

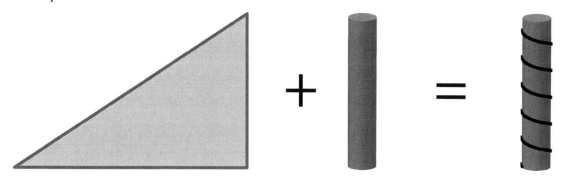

When it is placed into some medium, as for instance wood, the screw will move either forward or backward when it is rotated. The principle of the screw is used in a number of different objects, from jar lids to flashlights. On the exam, you are unlikely to see many questions regarding screws, though you may be presented with a given screw rotation and asked in which direction the screw will move. However, for consistency's sake, the equation for the mechanical advantage is a modification of the inclined plane's equation. Again, the formula for an inclined plane is:

$$Mechanical\ Advantage = \frac{slant\ length}{rise}$$

Because the rise of the inclined plane is the length along a screw, length between rotations = rise. Also, the slant length will equal the circumference of one rotation = $2\pi r$.

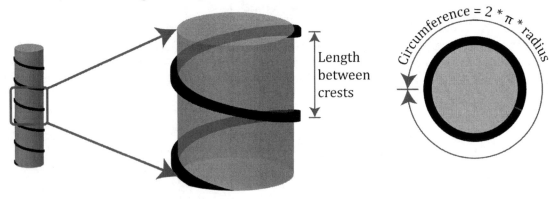

$$\textbf{Mechanical Advantage} = \frac{\textbf{2} \times \boldsymbol{\pi} \times \textbf{radius}}{\textbf{length between crests}}$$

Lever

The lever is the most common kind of simple machine. See-saws, shovels, and baseball bats are all examples of levers. There are three classes of levers which are differentiated by the relative orientations of the fulcrum, resistance, and effort. The fulcrum is the point at which the lever rotates; the effort is the point on the lever where force is applied; the resistance is the part of the lever that acts in response to the effort.

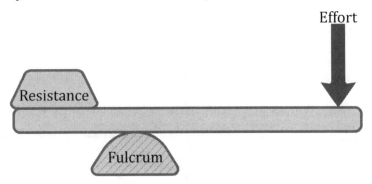

The mechanical advantage of a lever depends on the distances of the effort and resistance from the fulcrum. Mechanical advantage equals:

$$\textbf{Mechanical Advantage} = \frac{\textbf{effort distance}}{\textbf{resistance distance}}$$

For each class of lever, the location of the important distances changes:

First Class Lever

Second Class Lever

Third Class Lever

In a first class lever, the fulcrum is between the effort and the resistance. A seesaw is a good example of a first class lever: when effort is applied to force one end up, the other end goes down, and vice versa. The shorter the distance between the fulcrum and the resistance, the easier it will be to move the resistance. As an example, consider whether it is easier to lift another person on a see-saw when they are sitting close to the middle or all the way at the end. A little practice will show you that it is much more difficult to lift a person the farther away he or she is on the see-saw.

In a second class lever, the resistance is in-between the fulcrum and the effort. While a first class lever is able to increase force and distance through mechanical advantage, a second class lever is only able to increase force. A common example of a second class lever is the wheelbarrow: the force exerted by your hand at one end of the wheelbarrow is magnified at the load. Basically, with a second class lever you are trading distance for force; by moving your end of the wheelbarrow a bit farther, you produce greater force at the load.

Third class levers are used to produce greater distance. In a third class lever, the force is applied in between the fulcrum and the resistance. A baseball bat is a classic example of a third class lever; the bottom of the bat, below where you grip it, is considered the fulcrum. The end of the bat, where the ball is struck, is the resistance. By exerting effort at the base of the bat, close to the fulcrum, you are able to make the end of the bat fly quickly through the air. The closer your hands are to the base of the bat, the faster you will be able to make the other end of the bat travel.

Pulley

The pulley is a simple machine in which a rope is carried by the rotation of a wheel. Another name for a pulley is a block. Pulleys are typically used to allow the force to be directed from a convenient location. For instance, imagine you are given the task of lifting a heavy and tall bookcase. Rather than tying a rope to the bookcase and trying to lift it up, it would make sense to tie a pulley system to a rafter above the bookcase and run the rope through it, so that you could pull down on the rope and lift the bookcase. Pulling down allows you to incorporate your weight (normal force) into the act of lifting, thereby making it easier.

If there is just one pulley above the bookcase, you have created a first-class lever which will not diminish the amount of force that needs to be applied to lift the bookcase. There is another way to use a pulley, however, that can make the job of lifting a heavy object considerably easier. First, tie the rope directly to the rafter. Then, attach a pulley to the top of the bookcase and run the rope through it. If you can then stand so that you are above the bookcase, you will have a much easier time lifting this heavy object. Why? Because the weight of the bookcase is now being distributed: half of it is acting on the rafter, and half of it is acting on you. In other words, this arrangement allows you to lift an object with half the force. This simple pulley system, therefore, has a mechanical advantage of 2. Note that in this arrangement, the unfixed pulley is acting like a second-class lever. The price you pay for your mechanical advantage is that whatever distance you raise your end of the rope, the bookcase will only be lifted half as much.

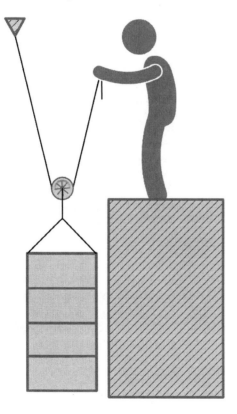

Of course, it might be difficult for you to find a place high enough to enact this system. If this is the case, you can always tie another pulley to the rafter and run the rope through it and back down to the floor. Since this second pulley is fixed, the mechanical advantage will remain the same.

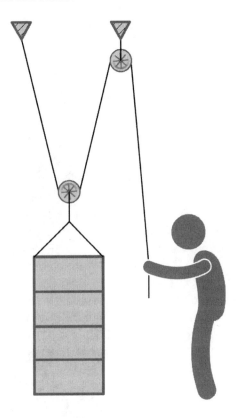

There are other, slightly more complex ways to obtain an even greater mechanical advantage with a system of pulleys. On the exam, you may be required to determine the pulley and tackle (rope) arrangement that creates the greatest mechanical advantage. The easiest way to determine the answer is to count the number of ropes that are going to and from the unfixed pulley; the more ropes coming and going, the greater the mechanical advantage.

Wheel and axle

Another basic arrangement that makes use of simple machines is called the wheel and axle. When most people think of a wheel and axle, they immediately envision an automobile tire. The steering wheel of the car, however, operates on the same mechanical principle, namely that the force required to move the center of a circle is much greater than the force require to move the outer rim of a circle. When you turn the steering wheel, you are essentially using a second-class lever by increasing the output force by increasing the input distance. The force required to turn the wheel from the outer rim is much less than would be required to turn the wheel from its center. Just imagine how difficult it would be to drive a car if the steering wheel was the size of a saucer!

Conceptually, the mechanical advantage of a wheel is easy to understand. For instance, all other things being equal, the mechanical advantage created by a system will increase along with the radius. In other words, a steering wheel with a radius of 12 inches has a greater mechanical advantage than a steering wheel with a radius of ten inches; the same amount of force exerted on the rim of each wheel will produce greater force at the axis of the larger wheel.

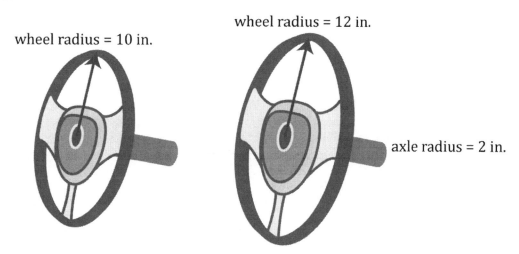

wheel radius = 10 in.

wheel radius = 12 in.

axle radius = 2 in.

The equation for the mechanical advantage of a wheel and axle is:

$$\textbf{Mechanical Advantage} = \frac{\textbf{radius}_\textbf{wheel}}{\textbf{radius}_\textbf{axle}}$$

Thus, the mechanical advantage of the steering wheel with a larger radius will be:

$$Mechanical\ Advantage = \frac{12\ inches}{2\ inches} = 6$$

Gears

The exam may ask you questions involving some slightly more complex mechanisms. It is very common, for instance, for there to be a couple of questions concerning gears. Gears are a system of interlocking wheels that can create immense mechanical advantages. The amount of mechanical advantage, however, will depend on the gear ratio; that is, on the relation in size between the gears.

When a small gear is driving a big gear, the speed of the big gear is relatively slow; when a big gear is driving a small gear, the speed of the small gear is relatively fast.

The equation for the mechanical advantage is:

$$\textbf{Mechanical Advantage} = \frac{\textbf{Torque}_{\textbf{output}}}{\textbf{Torque}_{\textbf{input}}} = \frac{\textbf{r}_{\textbf{output}}}{\textbf{r}_{\textbf{input}}} = \frac{\textbf{\# of teeth}_{\textbf{output}}}{\textbf{\# of teeth}_{\textbf{input}}}$$

Note that mechanical advantage is greater than 1 when the output gear is larger. In these cases, the output velocity (ω) will be lower. The equation for the relative speed of a gear system is:

$$\frac{\omega_{\text{input}}}{\omega_{\text{output}}} = \frac{r_{\text{output}}}{r_{\text{input}}}$$

$$Mechanical\ Advantage = \frac{teeth_{output}}{teeth_{input}} = \frac{20}{10} = 2$$

$$Mechanical\ Advantage = \frac{teeth_{output}}{teeth_{input}} = \frac{16}{8} = 2$$

Uses of Gears

Gears are used to change direction of output torque, change location of output torque, change amount of output torque, and change angular velocity of output.

Change output direction

Change torque location

Change torque amount

Change output velocity

Gear Ratios

A gear ratio is a measure of how much the speed and torque are changing in a gear system. It is the ratio of output speed to input speed. Because the number of teeth is directly proportional to the speed in meshing gears, a gear ratio can also be calculated using the number of teeth on the gears. When the driving gear has 30 teeth and the driven gear has 10 teeth, the gear ratio is 3:1.

$$Gear\ Ratio = \frac{\#\ of\ teeth_{driving}}{\#\ of\ teeth_{driven}} = \frac{30}{10} = \frac{3}{1} = 3:1$$

This means that the smaller, driven gear rotates 3 times for every 1 rotation of the driving gear.

The Hydraulic Jack

The hydraulic jack is a simple machine using two tanks and two pistons to change the amount of an output force.

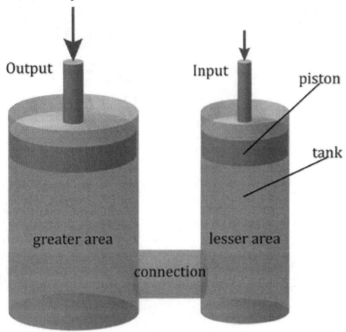

Since fluids are effectively incompressible, when you apply pressure to one part of a contained fluid, that pressure will have to be relieved in equal measure elsewhere in the container. Supposed the input piston has half the surface area of the output piston (10 in² compared to 20 in²), and it is being pushed downward with 50 pounds of force. The pressure being applied to the fluid is $50\ lb \div 10\ in^2 = 5\frac{lb}{in^2}$ or 5 psi. When that 5 psi of pressure is applied to the output piston, it pushes that piston upward with a force of $5\frac{lb}{in^2} \times 20\ in^2 = 100\ lb$.

The hydraulic jack functions similarly to a first class lever, but with the important factor being the area of the pistons rather than the length of the lever arms. Note that the mechanical advantage is based on the relative areas, not the relative radii, of the pistons. The radii must be squared to compute the relative areas.

$$\textbf{Mechanical Advantage} = \frac{\textbf{Force}_{output}}{\textbf{Force}_{input}} = \frac{\textbf{area}_{output}}{\textbf{area}_{input}} = \frac{\textbf{radius}_{output}^{2}}{\textbf{radius}_{input}^{2}}$$

Pulleys and Belts

Another system involves two pulleys connected by a drive belt (a looped band that goes around both pulleys). The operation of this system is similar to that of gears, with the exception that the pulleys will rotate in the same direction, while interlocking gears will rotate in opposite directions. A smaller pulley will always spin faster than a larger pulley, though the larger pulley will generate more torque.

The speed ratio between the pulleys can be determined by comparing their radii; for instance, a 4-inch pulley and a 12-inch pulley will have a speed ratio of 3:1.

Momentum/Impulse

Linear momentum

Concept: how much a body will resist stopping
Calculation: $momentum = mass \times velocity$

In physics, linear momentum can be found by multiplying the mass and velocity of an object:

$$\textbf{Momentum} = \textbf{mass} \times \textbf{velocity}$$

Momentum and velocity will always be in the same direction. Newton's second law describes momentum, stating that the rate of change of momentum is proportional to the force exerted and is in the direction of the force. If we assume a closed and isolated system (one in which no objects leave or enter, and upon which the sum of external forces is zero), then we can assume that the momentum of the system will neither increase nor decrease. That is, we will find that the momentum is a constant. The law of conservation of linear momentum applies universally in physics, even in situations of extremely high velocity or with subatomic particles.

Collisions

This concept of momentum takes on new importance when we consider collisions. A collision is an isolated event in which a strong force acts between each of two or more colliding bodies for a brief period of time. However, a collision is more intuitively defined as one or more objects hitting each other.

When two bodies collide, each object exerts a force on the opposite member. These equal and opposite forces change the linear momentum of the objects. However, when both bodies are considered, the net momentum in collisions is conserved.

There are two types of collisions: elastic and inelastic. The difference between the two lies in whether kinetic energy is conserved. If the total kinetic energy of the system is conserved, the collision is elastic. Visually, elastic collisions are collisions in which objects bounce perfectly. If some of the kinetic energy is transformed into heat or another form of energy, the collision is inelastic. Visually, inelastic collisions are collisions in which the objects do not bounce perfectly or even stick to each other.

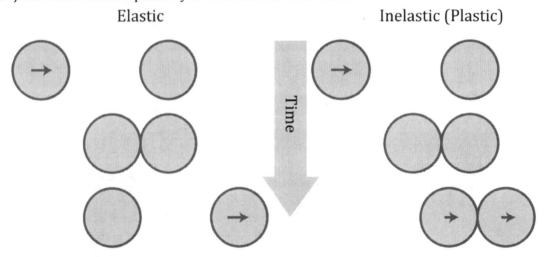

If the two bodies involved in an elastic collision have the same mass, then the body that was moving will stop completely, and the body that was at rest will begin moving at the same velocity as the projectile was moving before the collision.

Fluids

Fluids

Concept: liquids and gasses

A few of the questions on the exam will probably require you to consider the behavior of fluids. It sounds obvious, perhaps, but fluids can best be defined as substances that flow. A fluid will conform, slowly or quickly, to any container in which it is placed. Both liquids and gasses are considered to be fluids. Fluids are essentially those substances in which the atoms are not arranged in any permanent, rigid way. In ice, for instance, atoms are all lined up in what is known as a crystalline lattice, while in water and steam the only intermolecular arrangements are haphazard connections between neighboring molecules.

Flow Rates

When liquids flow in and out of containers with certain rates, the change in volume is the volumetric flow in minus the volumetric flow out. Volumetric flow is essentially the amount of volume moved past some point divided by the time it took for the volume to pass.

$$\textbf{Volumetric flow rate} = \frac{\textbf{volume moved}}{\textbf{time for the movement}}$$

If the flow into a container is greater than the flow out, the container will fill with the fluid. However, if the flow out of a container is greater than the flow into a container, the container will drain of the fluid.

- 95 -

Density

Concept: how much mass is in a specific volume of a substance

Calculation: $density = \rho = \dfrac{mass}{volume}$

Density is essentially how much stuff there is in a volume or space. The density of a fluid is generally expressed with the symbol ρ (the Greek letter rho.) The density may be found with the simple equation:

$$density = \rho = \frac{mass}{volume}$$

Density is a scalar property, meaning that it has no direction component.

Pressure

Concept: The amount of force applied per area

Calculation: $Pressure = \dfrac{force}{area}$

Pressure, like fluid density, is a scalar and does not have a direction. The equation for pressure is concerned only with the magnitude of that force, not with the direction in which it is pointing. The SI unit of pressure is the Newton per square meter, or Pascal.

$$Pressure = \frac{force}{area}$$

As every deep-sea diver knows, the pressure of water becomes greater the deeper you go below the surface; conversely, experienced mountain climbers know that air pressure decreases as they gain a higher altitude. These pressures are typically referred to as hydrostatic pressures because they involve fluids at rest.

Pascal's principle

The exam may also require you to demonstrate some knowledge of how fluids move. Anytime you squeeze a tube of toothpaste, you are demonstrating the idea known as Pascal's principle. This principle states that a change in the pressure applied to an enclosed fluid is transmitted undiminished to every portion of the fluid as well as to the walls of the containing vessel.

Buoyant force

If an object is submerged in water, it will have a buoyant force exerted on it in the upward direction. Often, of course, this buoyant force is much too small to keep an object from sinking to the bottom. Buoyancy is summarized in Archimedes' principle; a body wholly or partially submerged in a fluid will be buoyed up by a force equal to the weight of the fluid that the body displaces.

If the buoyant force is greater than the weight of an object, the object will go upward. If the weight of the object is greater than the buoyant force, the object will sink. When an object is floating on the surface, the buoyant force has the same magnitude as the weight.

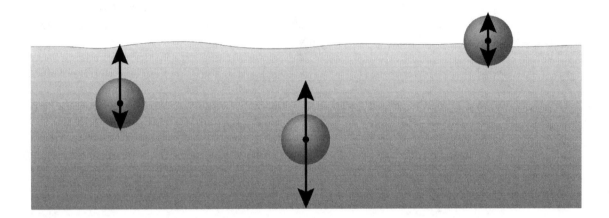

Even though the weight of a floating object is precisely balanced by a buoyant force, these forces will not necessarily act at the same point. The weight will act from the center of mass of the object, while the buoyancy will act from the center of mass of the hole in the water made by the object (known as the center of buoyancy). If the floating object is tilted, then the center of buoyancy will shift and the object may be unstable. In order to remain in equilibrium, the center of buoyancy must always shift in such a way that the buoyant force and weight provide a restoring torque, one that will restore the body to its upright position. This concept is, of course, crucial to the construction of boats which must always be made to encourage restoring torque.

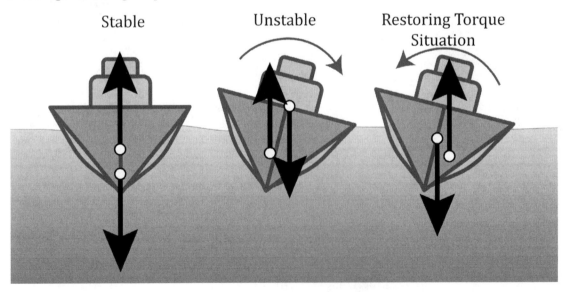

Ideal fluids

Because the motion of actual fluids is extremely complex, the exam usually assumes ideal fluids when they set up their problems. Using ideal fluids in fluid dynamics problems is like discounting friction in other problems. Therefore, when we deal with ideal fluids, we are making four assumptions. It is important to keep these in mind when considering the behavior of fluids on the exam. First, we are assuming that the flow is steady; in other words, the velocity of every part of the fluid is the same. Second, we assume that fluids are incompressible, and, therefore, have a consistent density. Third, we assume that fluids are nonviscous, meaning that they flow easily and without resistance. Fourth, we assume that the flow of ideal fluids is irrotational: that is, particles in the fluid will not rotate around a center of mass.

Bernoulli's principle

When fluids move, they do not create or destroy energy; this modification of Newton's second law for fluid behavior is called Bernoulli's principle. It is essentially just a reformulation of the law of conservation of mechanical energy for fluid mechanics.

The most common application of Bernoulli's principle is that pressure and speed are inversely related, assuming constant altitude. Thus if the elevation of the fluid remains constant and the speed of a fluid particle increases as it travels along a streamline, the pressure will decrease. If the fluid slows down, the pressure will increase.

Heat Transfer

Heat is a type of energy. Heat transfers from the hot object to the cold object through the three forms of heat transfer: conduction, convection, and radiation.

Conduction · · · · · · Convection · · · · · · Radiation

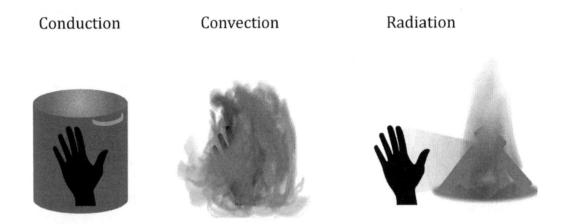

Conduction is the transfer of heat by physical contact. When you touch a hot pot, the pot transfers heat to your hand by conduction.

Convection is the transfer of heat by the movement of fluids. When you put your hand in steam, the steam transfers heat to your hand by convection.

Radiation is the transfer of heat by electromagnetic waves. When you put your hand near a campfire, the fire heats your hand by radiation.

Phase Changes

Materials exist in four phases or states: solid, liquid, gas, and plasma. However, as most tests will not cover plasma, we will focus on solids, liquids, and gases. The solid state is the densest in almost all cases (water is the most notable exception), followed by liquid, and then gas.

Solid · · · · · · · · · · Liquid · · · · · · · · · · Gas

The impetus for phase change (changing from one phase to another) is heat. When a solid is heated, it will change into a liquid. The same process of heating will change a liquid into a gas.

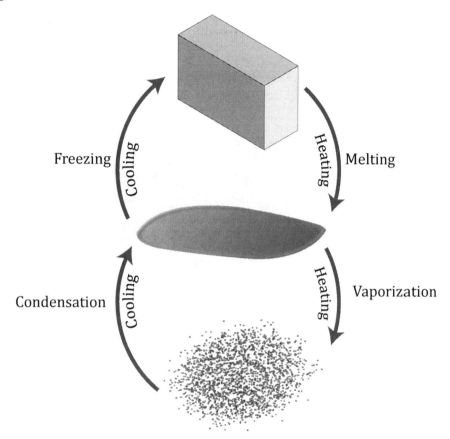

Optics

Lenses change the way light travels. Lenses are able to achieve this by the way in which light travels at different speeds in different mediums. The essentials to optics with lenses deal with concave and convex lenses. Concave lenses make objects appear smaller, while convex lenses make objects appear larger.

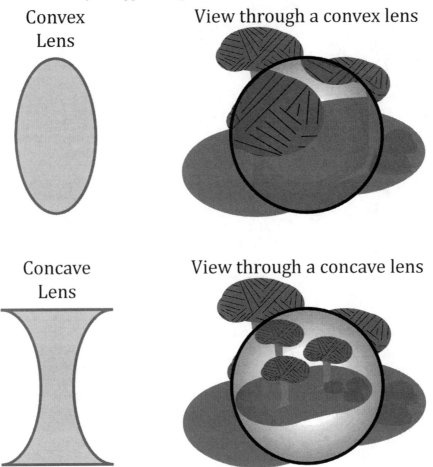

Electricity

Electric Charge

Much like gravity, electricity is an everyday observable phenomenon which is very complex, but may be understood as a set of behaviors. As the gravitational force exists between objects with mass, the electric force exists between objects with electrical charge. In all atoms, the protons have a positive charge, while the electrons have a negative charge. An imbalance of electrons and protons in an object results in a net charge. Unlike gravity, which only pulls, electrical forces can push objects apart as well as pulling them together.

Similar electric charges repel each other. Opposite charges attract each other.

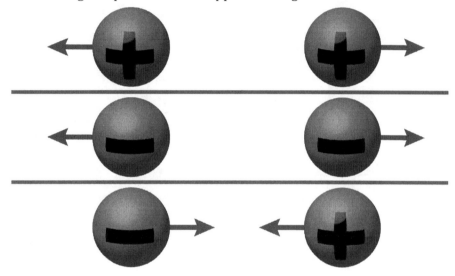

Current

Electrons (and electrical charge with it) move through conductive materials by switching quickly from one atom to another. This electrical flow can manipulate energy like mechanical systems.

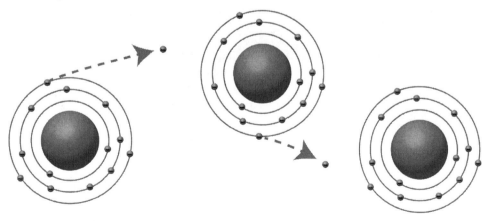

The term for the rate at which the charge flows through a conductive material is current. Because each electron carries a specific charge, current can be thought of as the number of electrons passing a point in a length of time. Current is measured in Amperes (A), each unit of which is approximately 6.24×10^{18} electrons per second.

Electric current carries energy much like moving balls carry energy.

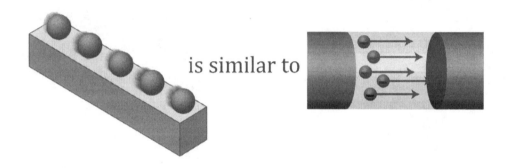

is similar to

Voltage

Voltage is the potential for electric work. Voltage is the push behind electrical work. Voltage is similar to gravitational potential energy.

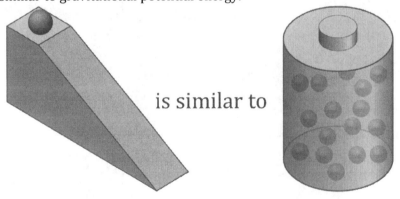

is similar to

Anything used to generate a voltage, such as a battery or a generator, is called a voltage source. Voltage is conveniently measured in Volts (V).

Resistance

Resistance is the amount of pressure to slow electrical current. Electrical resistance is much like friction, resisting flow and dissipating energy.

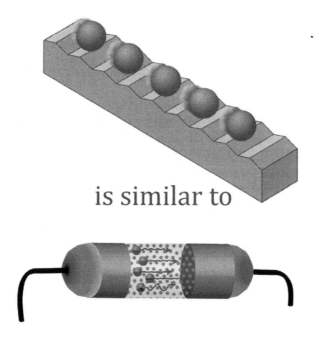

is similar to

Different objects have different resistances. A resistor is an electrical component designed to have a specific resistance, measured in Ohms (Ω).

Basic Circuits

A circuit is a closed loop through which current can flow. A simple circuit contains a voltage source and a resistor. The current flows from the positive side of the voltage source through the resistor to the negative side of the voltage source.

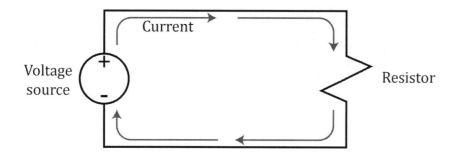

If we plot the voltage of a simple circuit, the similarities to gravitational potential energy appear.

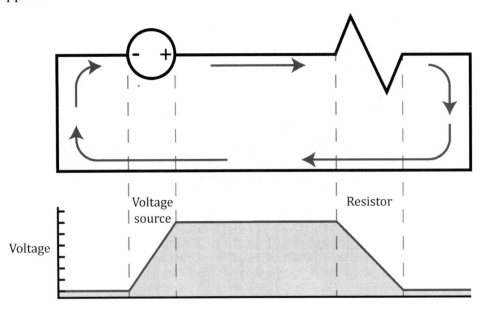

If we consider the circuit to be a track, the electrons would be balls, the voltage source would be a powered lift, and the resistor would be a sticky section of the track. The lift raises the balls, increasing their potential energy. This potential energy is expended as the balls roll down the sticky section of the track.

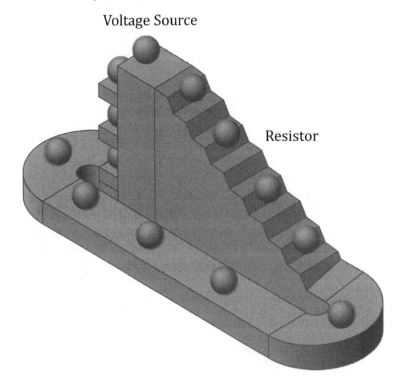

Ohm's Law

A principle called Ohm's Law explains the relationship between the voltage, current, and resistance. The voltage drop over a resistance is equal to the amount of current times the resistance:

Voltage (V) = current (I) × resistance (R)

We can gain a better understanding of this equation by looking at a reference simple circuit and then changing one variable at a time to examine the results.

Voltage = Current * Resistance
1V = 1A * 1Ω

Increased Resistance	Increased Current	Increased Voltage

Voltage = Current * Resistance   Voltage = Current * Resistance   Voltage = Current * Resistance
1V = 0.25A * 4Ω   1V = 4A * 0.25Ω   4V = 2A * 2Ω

Series Circuits

A series circuit is a circuit with two or more resistors on the same path. The same current runs through both resistors. However, the total voltage drop splits between the resistors. The resistors in series can be added together to make an equivalent basic circuit.

$$R_{equiv} = R_1 + R_2$$

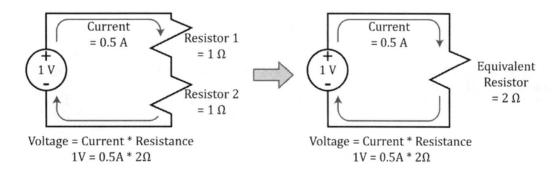

Voltage = Current * Resistance   Voltage = Current * Resistance
1V = 0.5A * 2Ω   1V = 0.5A * 2Ω

Parallel Circuits

A parallel circuit is a circuit with two or more resistors on different, parallel paths. Unlike the series circuit, the current splits between the different paths in a parallel circuit. Resistors in parallel can be reduced to an equivalent circuit, but not by simply adding the resistances. The inverse of the equivalent resistance of parallel resistors is equal to the sum of the inverses of the resistance of each leg of the parallel circuit. In equation form that means:

$$\frac{1}{R_{equiv}} = \frac{1}{R_1} + \frac{1}{R_2}$$

Or when solved for equivalent resistance:

$$\mathbf{R_{equiv}} = \frac{1}{\frac{1}{\mathbf{R_1}} + \frac{1}{\mathbf{R_2}}}$$

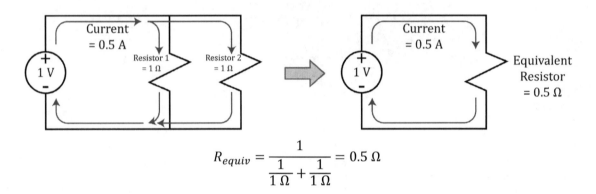

$$R_{equiv} = \frac{1}{\frac{1}{1\,\Omega} + \frac{1}{1\,\Omega}} = 0.5\,\Omega$$

Electrical Power

Electrical power, or the energy output over time, is equal to the current resulting from a voltage source times the voltage of that source:

Power(P) = current (I) × voltage (V)

Thanks to Ohm's Law, we can write this relation in two other ways:

$$P = I^2 R$$

$$P = \frac{V^2}{R}$$

For instance, if a circuit is composed of a 9 Volt battery and a 3 Ohm resistor, the power output of the battery will be:

$$Power = \frac{V^2}{R} = \frac{9^2}{3} = 27\ Watts$$

AC vs. DC

Up until this point, current has been assumed to flow in one direction. One directional flow is called Direct Current (DC). However, there is another type of electric current: Alternating Current (AC). Many circuits use AC power sources, in which the current flips back and forth rapidly between directions.

Capacitors

Capacitors are electrical components which store voltage. Capacitors are made from two conductive surfaces separated from each other by a space and/or insulation. Capacitors resist changes to voltage. Capacitors don't stop AC circuits (although they do affect the current flow), but they do stop DC circuits, acting as open circuits.

Inductors

Inductors are electrical components which effectively store current. Inductors use the relationship between electricity and magnetism to resist changes in current by running the current through coils of wire. Inductors don't stop DC circuits, but they do resist AC circuits as AC circuits utilize changing currents.

Diodes

Diodes are electrical components which limit the flow of electricity to one direction. If current flows through a diode in the intended direction, the diode will allow the flow. However, a diode will stop current if it runs the wrong way.

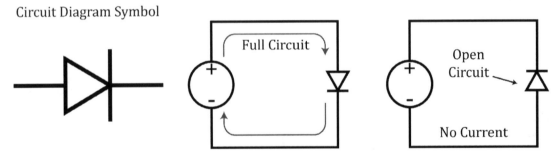

Magnetism

Magnetism is an attraction between opposite poles of magnetic materials and a repulsion between similar poles of magnetic materials. Magnetism can be natural or induced with the use of electric currents. Magnets almost always exist with two polar sides: north and south. A magnetic force exists between two poles on objects. Different poles attract each other. Like poles repel each other.

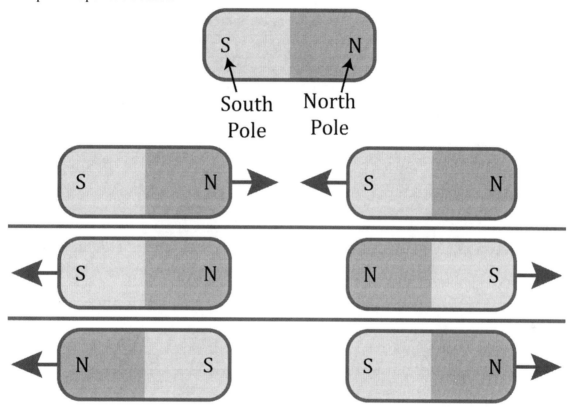

Final Notes

This concludes our review of the content of the SIFT subtests. Hopefully, a lot of this material was familiar to you, but if not, be sure to reread any sections you had difficulty with until you have a solid grasp of the important concepts. As you read, try to imagine the types of questions that will be asked on the test, and take frequent breaks to let the ideas sink in.

The SIFT tests a wide variety of knowledge and skills, so getting prepared for it is necessarily a difficult task, but so is training to be a pilot. If you can work hard enough to ace the SIFT, that's enough to convince the Army you can make it through flight training.

Good luck and good studying!

SIFT Practice Tests

Simple Drawings Test

Instructions: Select the answer letter of the image that is different from the other four images shown. There are 100 questions in this section and the allotted time is 2 minutes.

1.   (A)   (B)   (C)   (D)   (E)

2.   (A)   (B)   (C)   (D)   (E)

3.   (A)   (B)   (C)   (D)   (E)

4.   (A)   (B)   (C)   (D)   (E)

5.   (A)   (B)   (C)   (D)   (E)

6.   (A)   (B)   (C)   (D)   (E)

7.   (A)   (B)   (C)   (D)   (E)

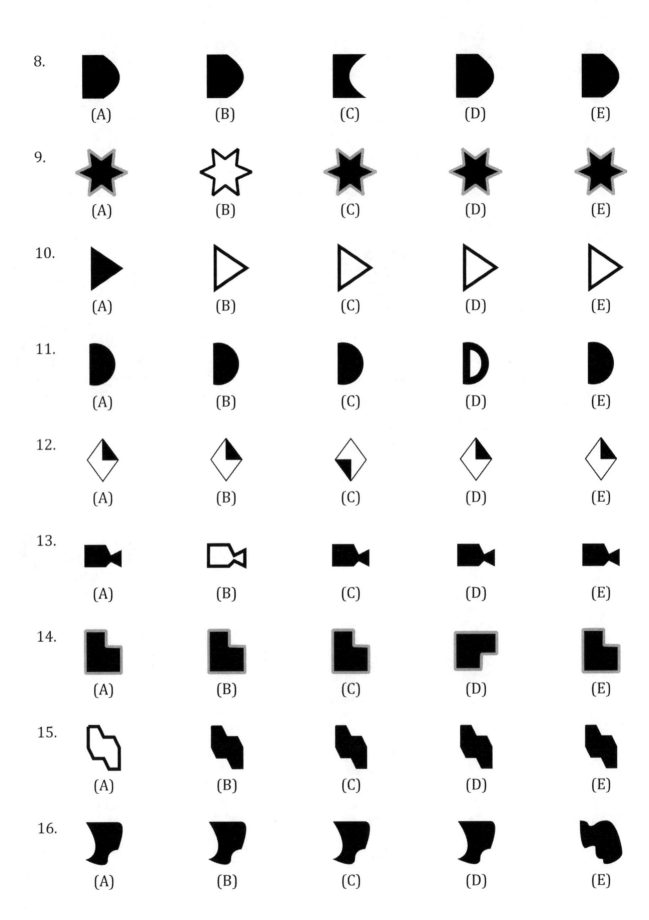

8. (A) (B) (C) (D) (E)

9. (A) (B) (C) (D) (E)

10. (A) (B) (C) (D) (E)

11. (A) (B) (C) (D) (E)

12. (A) (B) (C) (D) (E)

13. (A) (B) (C) (D) (E)

14. (A) (B) (C) (D) (E)

15. (A) (B) (C) (D) (E)

16. (A) (B) (C) (D) (E)

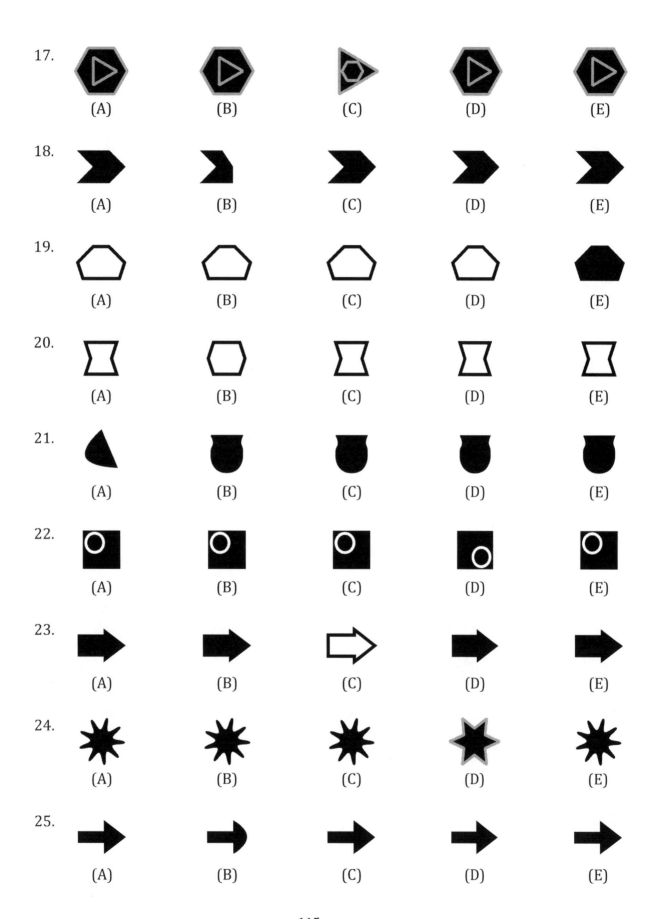

26.

(A)   (B)   (C)   (D)   (E)

27.

(A)   (B)   (C)   (D)   (E)

28.

(A)   (B)   (C)   (D)   (E)

29.

(A)   (B)   (C)   (D)   (E)

30.

(A)   (B)   (C)   (D)   (E)

31.

(A)   (B)   (C)   (D)   (E)

32.

(A)   (B)   (C)   (D)   (E)

33.

(A)   (B)   (C)   (D)   (E)

34.

(A)   (B)   (C)   (D)   (E)

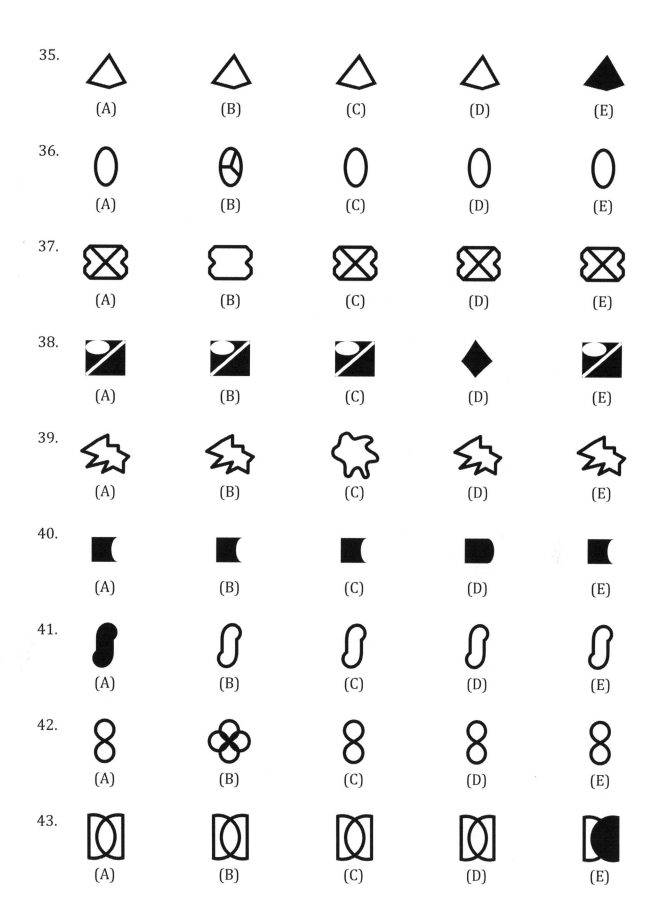

35.
(A)   (B)   (C)   (D)   (E)

36.
(A)   (B)   (C)   (D)   (E)

37.
(A)   (B)   (C)   (D)   (E)

38.
(A)   (B)   (C)   (D)   (E)

39.
(A)   (B)   (C)   (D)   (E)

40.
(A)   (B)   (C)   (D)   (E)

41.
(A)   (B)   (C)   (D)   (E)

42.
(A)   (B)   (C)   (D)   (E)

43.
(A)   (B)   (C)   (D)   (E)

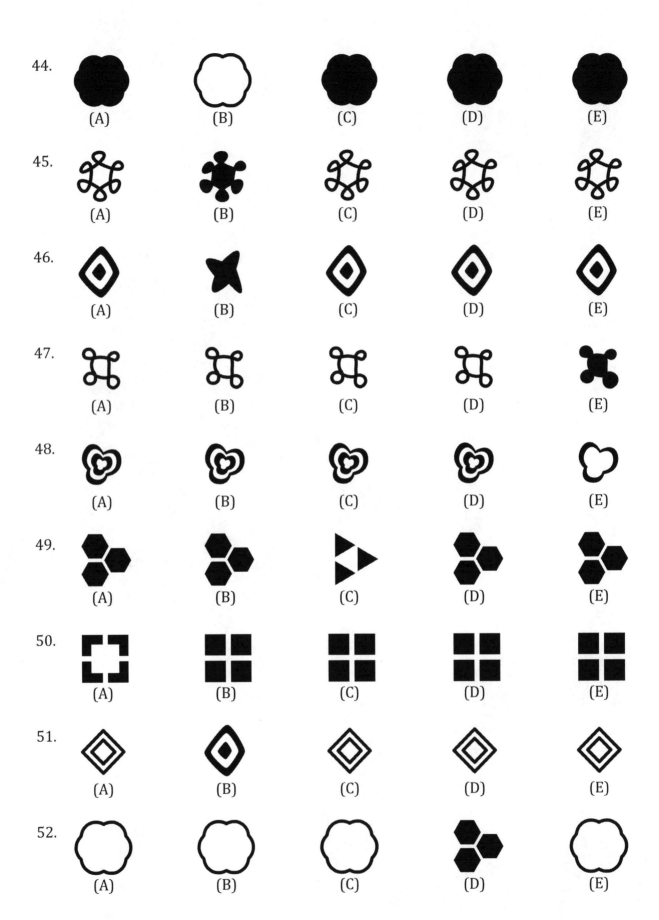

44. (A)   (B)   (C)   (D)   (E)

45. (A)   (B)   (C)   (D)   (E)

46. (A)   (B)   (C)   (D)   (E)

47. (A)   (B)   (C)   (D)   (E)

48. (A)   (B)   (C)   (D)   (E)

49. (A)   (B)   (C)   (D)   (E)

50. (A)   (B)   (C)   (D)   (E)

51. (A)   (B)   (C)   (D)   (E)

52. (A)   (B)   (C)   (D)   (E)

- 118 -

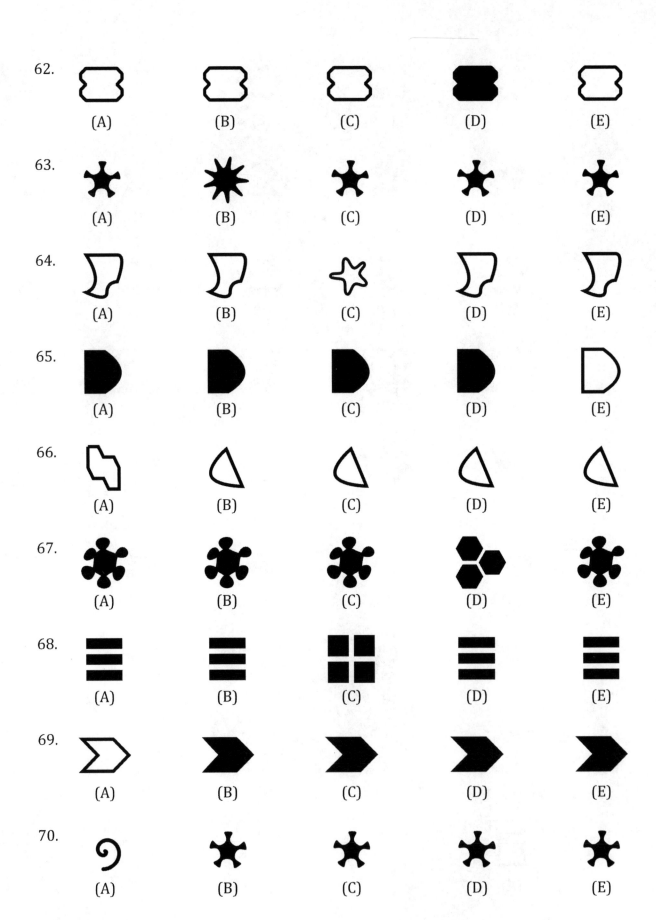

62.

(A)　　　(B)　　　(C)　　　(D)　　　(E)

63.

(A)　　　(B)　　　(C)　　　(D)　　　(E)

64.

(A)　　　(B)　　　(C)　　　(D)　　　(E)

65.

(A)　　　(B)　　　(C)　　　(D)　　　(E)

66.

(A)　　　(B)　　　(C)　　　(D)　　　(E)

67.

(A)　　　(B)　　　(C)　　　(D)　　　(E)

68.

(A)　　　(B)　　　(C)　　　(D)　　　(E)

69.

(A)　　　(B)　　　(C)　　　(D)　　　(E)

70.

(A)　　　(B)　　　(C)　　　(D)　　　(E)

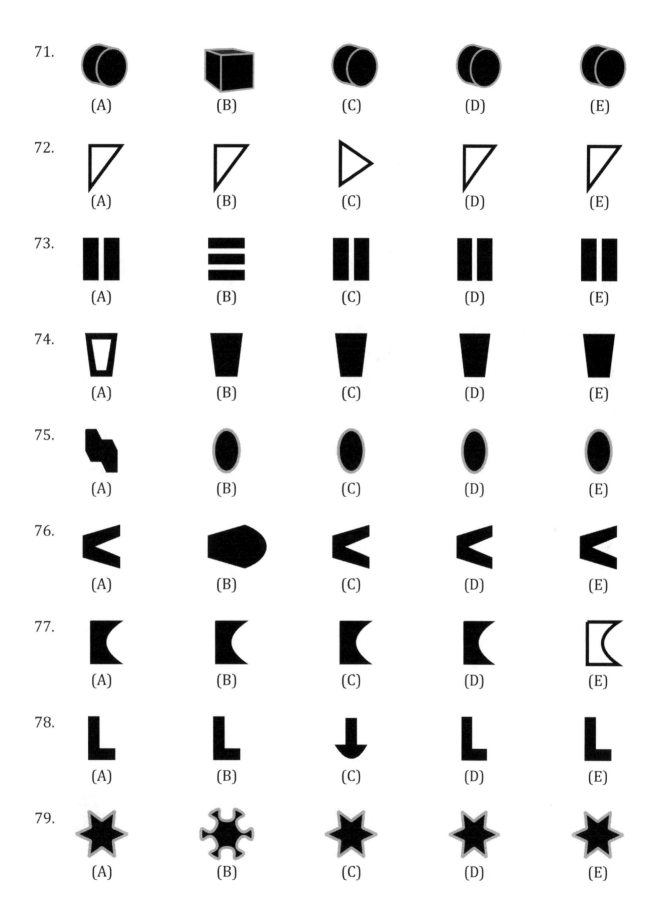

71.

(A) (B) (C) (D) (E)

72.

(A) (B) (C) (D) (E)

73.

(A) (B) (C) (D) (E)

74.

(A) (B) (C) (D) (E)

75.

(A) (B) (C) (D) (E)

76.

(A) (B) (C) (D) (E)

77.

(A) (B) (C) (D) (E)

78.

(A) (B) (C) (D) (E)

79.

(A) (B) (C) (D) (E)

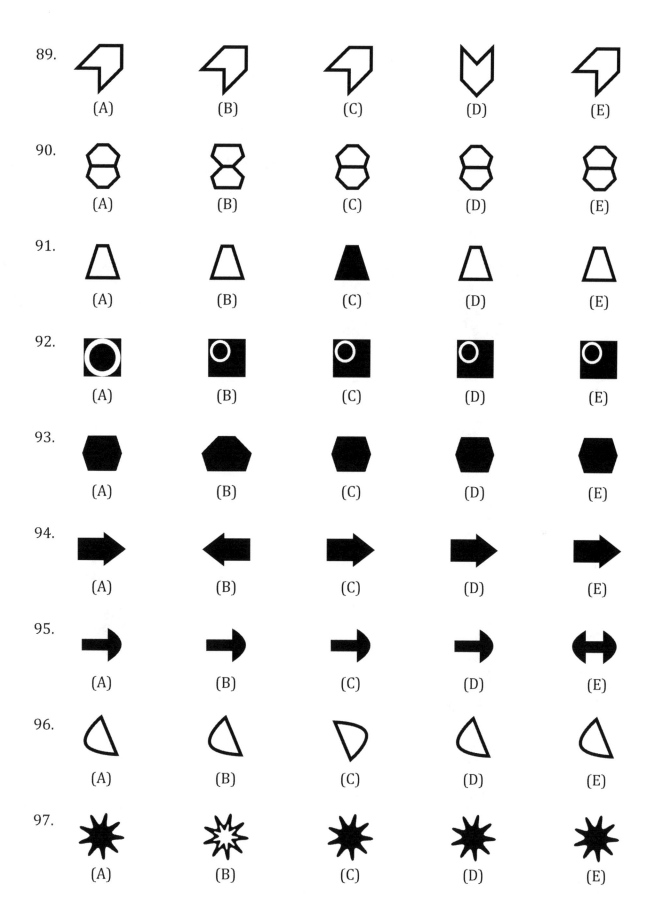

89.

(A)　(B)　(C)　(D)　(E)

90.

(A)　(B)　(C)　(D)　(E)

91.

(A)　(B)　(C)　(D)　(E)

92.

(A)　(B)　(C)　(D)　(E)

93.

(A)　(B)　(C)　(D)　(E)

94.

(A)　(B)　(C)　(D)　(E)

95.

(A)　(B)　(C)　(D)　(E)

96.

(A)　(B)　(C)　(D)　(E)

97.

(A)　(B)　(C)　(D)　(E)

98.

(A) (B) (C) (D) (E)

99.

(A) (B) (C) (D) (E)

100.

(A) (B) (C) (D) (E)

Hidden Figures Test

Instructions: For each question, select the answer letter of the figure at the top of the page that appears within the image shown. The figure that appears within the image will have the same size and orientation as the figure shown at the top of the page.

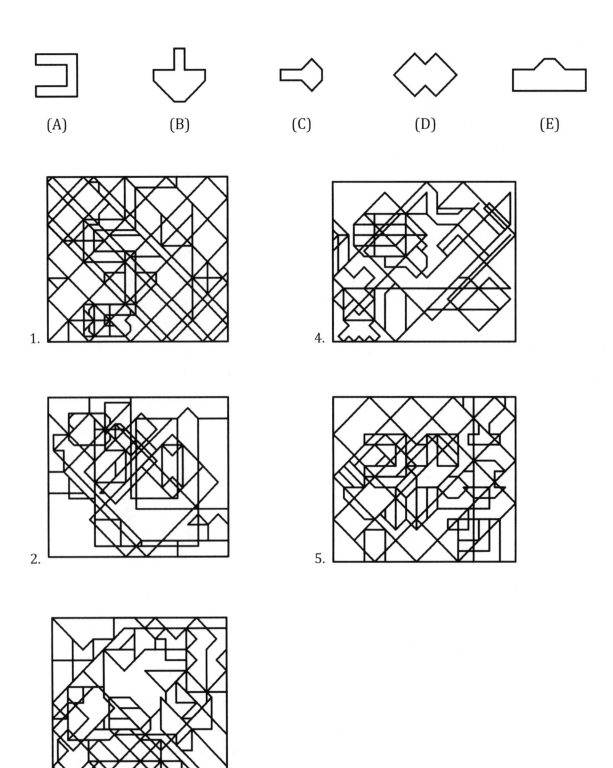

(A)　　　(B)　　　(C)　　　(D)　　　(E)

1.

2.

3.

4.

5.

6.

7.

8.

9.

10.

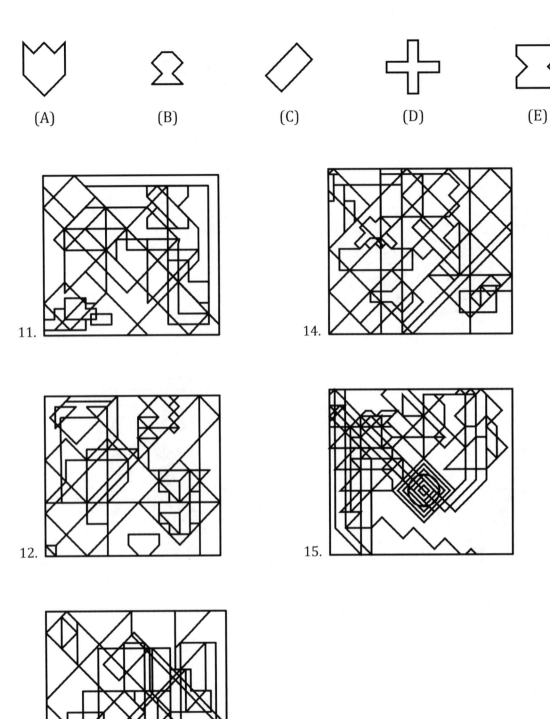

11.

14.

12.

15.

13.

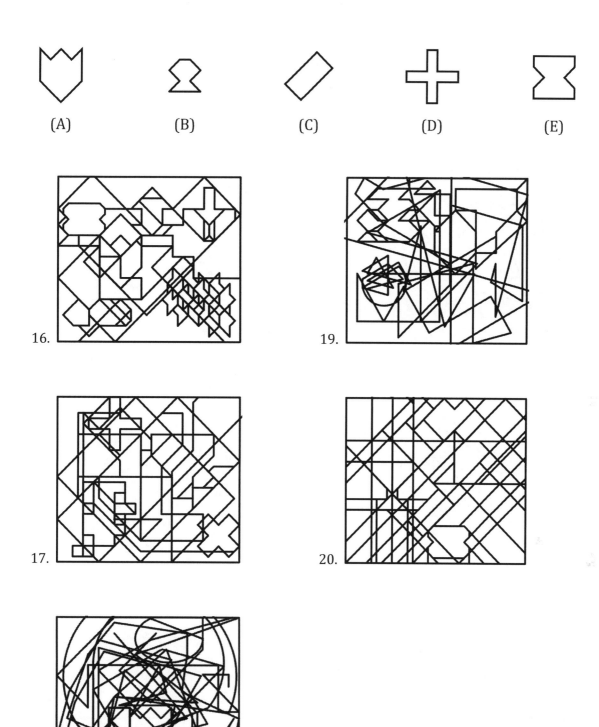

(A)   (B)   (C)   (D)   (E)

16.

17.

18.

19.

20.

- 129 -

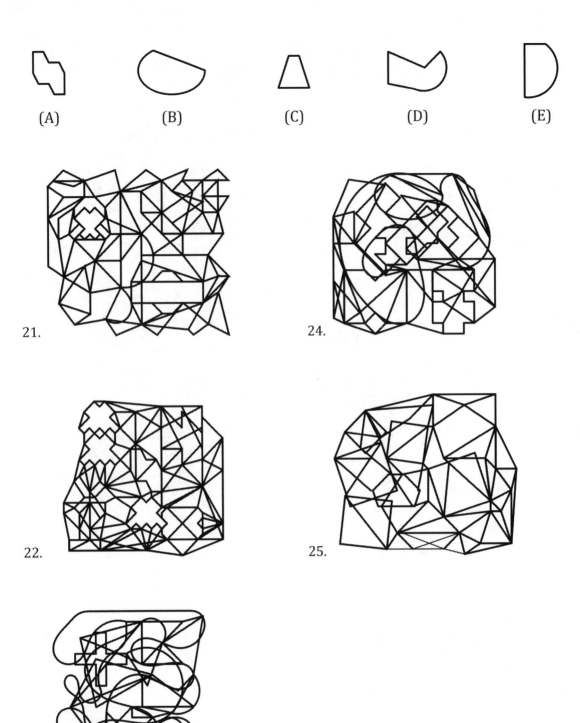

21.

22.

23.

24.

25.

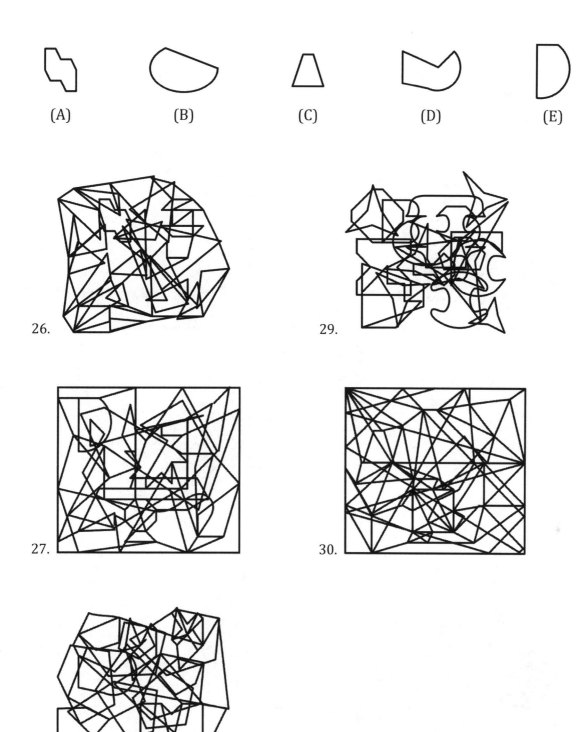

(A)　　　　(B)　　　　(C)　　　　(D)　　　　(E)

26.

29.

27.

30.

28.

- 131 -

(A)   (B)   (C)   (D)   (E)

31.

34.

32.

35.

33.

- 132 -

(A)   (B)   (C)   (D)   (E)

36.

39.

37.

40.

38.

- 133 -

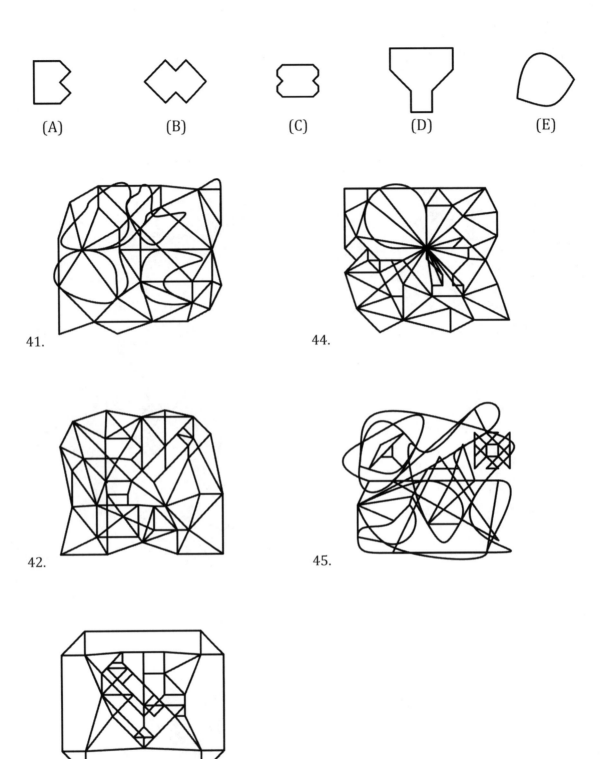

(A)　　　(B)　　　(C)　　　(D)　　　(E)

41.

44.

42.

45.

43.

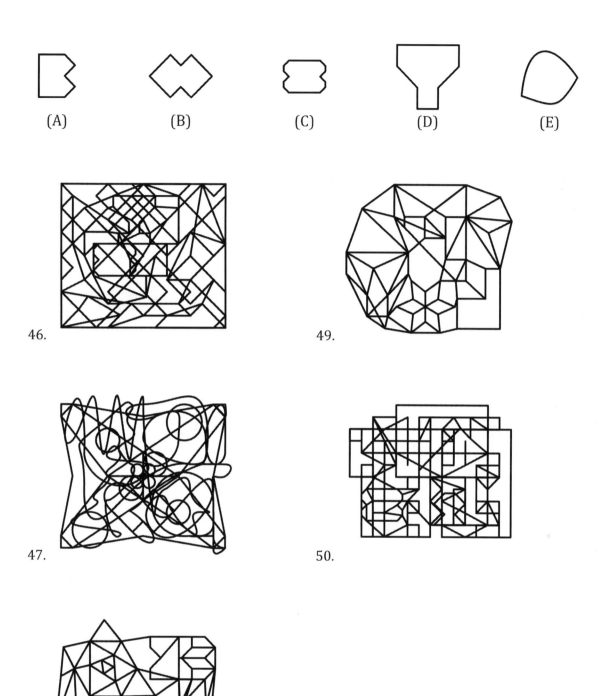

(A) (B) (C) (D) (E)

46.

49.

47.

50.

48.

1. Which of these is one of the three types of drag that constitute total drag?
a. Inversion
b. Paradox
c. Subduction
d. Accelerated
e. Parasite

2. Which of the following is common to all turbine helicopters, but is only on some piston powered helicopters?
a. Governor
b. Thrust control
c. Heading control
d. Antitorque rotor
e. Intermeshing rotor

3. Where is the horizontal reference datum located?
a. Three feet forward of the helicopter's nose
b. The tip of the helicopter's nose
c. The rotor mast
d. One foot forward of the rotor mast
e. It varies by helicopter

4. The _____ position relative to the horizon determines the helicopter's travel and attitude
a. Main rotor
b. Cyclic
c. Nose
d. Tail rotor
e. Collective

5. When training for a rapid deceleration, in most helicopters the entry speed should be approximately:
a. 30 knots
b. 35 knots
c. 40 knots
d. 45 knots
e. 50 knots

6. Which of the following has been the Army's primary training helicopter since 1993?
a. Eurocopter UH-72
b. Bell TH-67
c. Bell OH-58
d. Boeing AH-64
e. Sikorsky UH-60

7. Which of the following occurs when the tail rotor becomes more aerodynamically efficient during the transition from hover to forward flight?
a. Downwash
b. In Ground Effect
c. Out of Ground Effect
d. Translational thrust
e. Coning

8. The solidity ratio is the:
a. Ratio of thrust to drag
b. Ratio of lift to thrust
c. Ratio of the total rotor blade area to the total rotor disk area
d. Ratio of the total rotor disk area to the total rotor blade area squared
e. Ratio of the helicopter's total length to its total width

9. Which of the following is NOT one of the controls used by a helicopter pilot during flight?
a. Collective pitch
b. Torque pedals
c. Antitorque pedals
d. Cyclic pitch
e. Throttle

10. Each gallon of reciprocating engine oil weighs _____ lbs.
a. 6.5
b. 7.0
c. 7.5
d. 8.0
e. 8.5

11. To maintain airspeed in a 2G/60° turn, rotor thrust/engine power must increase by ___ percent.
a. 25
b. 50
c. 75
d. 100
e. 150

12. A high reconnaissance should be flown at an altitude of ___ to ___ feet above the surface.
a. 100 and 200
b. 150 and 250
c. 200 and 400
d. 300 and 500
e. 500 and 750

13. The twin-engine, tandem rotor helicopter that came to prominence in the Vietnam War and is still in current use is the:
a. UH-60 Black Hawk
b. OH-58 Kiowa
c. CH-47 Chinook
d. AH-64 Apache
e. UH-72 Lakota

14. _____ changes angle of incidence differentially around the rotor system.
a. Lift coefficient
b. Collective feathering
c. Cyclic feathering
d. Increased velocity
e. Decrease velocity

15. Which of the following describes the relationship between internal fluid pressure and fluid velocity?
a. Venturi Flow Theory
b. Newton's Third Law of Motion
c. Bernoulli's Principle
d. Kensington's Rule of Lift
e. Reynolds' Theory

16. What power setting should be used during terminations to a hover?
a. 25% of maximum
b. 50% of maximum
c. 75% of maximum
d. 100% of maximum
e. The correct power setting varies by make and model.

17. During the approach to a pinnacle, the apparent rate of closure:
a. Should not be a critical factor
b. Should be steadily increasing
c. Should be about the pace of a brisk walk
d. Should be about the pace of a fast run
e. Should vary by make and model of the aircraft

18. Which of these Army helicopters is the lightest (i.e., has the lowest empty weight)?
a. UH-60 Black Hawk
b. Bell TH-67
c. OH-58A Kiowa
d. AH-64 Apache
e. UH-72 Lakota

19. During hovering flight, a single main rotor helicopter tends to move in the direction of tail rotor thrust. This sideward movement is called _____ _____ .
a. Sideward tendency
b. Translating tendency
c. Lateral tendency
d. Translating bias
e. Lateral bias

20. Which of the following changes the helicopter's angle of attack?
a. Collective pitch
b. Torque pedals
c. Antitorque pedals
d. Cyclic pitch
e. Throttle

21. Which of these has the same meaning as *load factor*?
a. Weight
b. Effective weight
c. Basic empty weight
d. Cargo
e. Maximum gross weight

22. Which of the following is <u>false</u> regarding most helicopters?
a. During left turns, torque increases.
b. During right turns, torque decreases.
c. During application of aft cyclic, torque decreases and rotor speed increases.
d. During application of forward cyclic, torque increases and rotor speed decreases.
e. None of these are false.

23. When climbing to a ridgeline, the approach flightpath should be:
a. Parallel to the ridgeline and into the wind
b. Parallel to the ridgeline and with the wind
c. Diagonal to the ridgeline and with the wind
d. Perpendicular to the ridgeline and into the wind
e. Perpendicular to the ridgeline and with the wind

24. Which of these helicopters is the US Army's primary light utility helicopter?
a. UH-60 Black Hawk
b. OH-58 Kiowa
c. CH-47 Chinook
d. AH-64 Apache
e. UH-72 Lakota

25. The law of conservation of angular momentum is another name for the:
a. Coriolis Effect
b. Law of Hovering
c. Friedrich Momentum Principle
d. Principle of Autonomy
e. Angle of Attack Theorem

26. Which of the following is located on the left of the pilot's seat?
a. Collective pitch
b. Torque pedals
c. Antitorque pedals
d. Cyclic pitch
e. Throttle

27. A forward CG is not obvious when:
a. Hovering in a crosswind
b. Taking off in a crosswind
c. Hovering in a strong tailwind
d. Hovering in a strong headwind
e. A forward CG is always obvious.

28. Which of the following is a required action while entering a climb while maintaining air speed?
a. Increase right antitorque pedal pressure
b. Apply forward cyclic
c. Increase the collective
d. Lower the collective
e. Apply aft cyclic

29. An approach angle of approximately __ to __ degrees is considered a steep approach.
a. 3 and 5
b. 6 and 8
c. 10 and 12
d. 13 and 15
e. 16 and 18

30. Which of the following is an attack helicopter that features four hardpoints mounted on stub-wing pylons, and usually carries a combination of AGM-114 Hellfire missiles and Hydra 70 rocket pods?
a. UH-60 Black Hawk
b. OH-58 Kiowa
c. CH-47 Chinook
d. AH-64 Apache
e. UH-72 Lakota

31. Which of these conditions can make it hazardous to operate the helicopter at or near its maximum gross weight?
a. High altitude
b. Low temperature
c. Low humidity
d. B and C
e. A, B, and C

32. In a standard airplane traffic pattern, which of the five legs is known as the crosswind leg?
a. 1st
b. 2nd
c. 3rd
d. 4th
e. 5th

33. For slope landings, a slope of ___ degrees is considered maximum for normal operation of most helicopters.
a. 2
b. 5
c. 8
d. 10
e. 12

34. Which of these Army helicopters has the highest maximum speed?
a. UH-60 Black Hawk
b. OH-58 Kiowa
c. CH-47 Chinook
d. AH-64 Apache
e. AH-6 Little Bird

35. While transitioning to forward flight at about ___ to ___ knots, the helicopter goes through effective translational lift (ETL).
a. 5 and 10
b. 10 and 20
c. 16 and 24
d. 6 and 12
e. 5 and 15

36. Which of the following controls the direction in which the nose of the helicopter points?
a. Collective pitch
b. Torque pedals
c. Antitorque pedals
d. Cyclic pitch
e. Throttle

37. Each gallon of JP-4 jet fuel weighs _____ lbs.
a. 5.0
b. 5.5
c. 6.0
d. 6.5
e. 7.0

38. A hover taxi is used when operating below ___ feet above ground level (AGL).
a. 15
b. 20
c. 25
d. 30
e. 35

39. During a steep approach, the helicopter should be kept in trim just prior to loss of effective translational lift (approximately 25 knots). Below ____ feet AGL, the antitorque pedals should be adjusted to align the helicopter with the intended touchdown point.
a. 75
b. 100
c. 125
d. 150
e. 200

40. The primary use of OH-58 Kiowa helicopters is:
a. Armed reconnaissance in support of ground troops
b. Electronic warfare and special operations
c. Troop movement, battlefield resupply, and artillery placement
d. Tactical transport and special operations
e. Attack and multi-role combat

Spatial Apperception Test

Instructions: The view shown on each question is a view from the cockpit of an aircraft in flight. Select the answer letter that best represents the orientation of the aircraft as seen from the ground.

1.

| (A) | (B) | (C) | (D) | (E) |

2.

| (A) | (B) | (C) | (D) | (E) |

3.

| (A) | (B) | (C) | (D) | (E) |

4.

(A)   (B)   (C)   (D)   (E)

5.

(A)   (B)   (C)   (D)   (E)

6.

(A)   (B)   (C)   (D)   (E)

7.

(A)   (B)   (C)   (D)   (E)

8.

(A)   (B)   (C)   (D)   (E)

9.

(A)   (B)   (C)   (D)   (E)

- 145 -

10.

(A)   (B)   (C)   (D)   (E)

11.

(A)   (B)   (C)   (D)   (E)

12.

(A)   (B)   (C)   (D)   (E)

13.

(A) (B) (C) (D) (E)

14.

(A) (B) (C) (D) (E)

15.

(A) (B) (C) (D) (E)

- 147 -

16.

(A)

(B)

(C)

(D)

(E)

17.

(A)

(B)

(C)

(D)

(E)

18.

(A)

(B)

(C)

(D)

(E)

- 148 -

19.

(A)   (B)   (C)   (D)   (E)

20.

(A)   (B)   (C)   (D)   (E)

21.

(A)   (B)   (C)   (D)   (E)

- 149 -

22.

(A)   (B)   (C)   (D)   (E)

23.

(A)   (B)   (C)   (D)   (E)

24.

(A)   (B)   (C)   (D)   (E)

25.

(A)

(B)

(C)

(D)

(E)

Reading Comprehension Test

1. Although helicopters were developed and built during the first half-century of flight, some even reaching limited production; it was not until 1942 that a helicopter designed by Igor Sikorsky reached full-scale production, with 131 aircraft built. Even though most previous designs used more than one main rotor, it was the single main rotor with an antitorque tail rotor configuration design that would come to be recognized worldwide as the helicopter. In 1951, at the urging of his contacts at the Department of the Navy, Charles H. Kaman modified his K-225 helicopter with a new kind of engine, the turbo-shaft engine. This adaptation of the turbine engine provided a large amount of horsepower to the helicopter with a lower weight penalty than piston engines, heavy engine blocks, and auxiliary components. On December 11, 1951, the K-225 became the first turbine-powered helicopter in the world. Two years later, on March 26, 1954, a modified Navy HTK-1, another Kaman helicopter, became the first twin-turbine helicopter to fly. However, it was the Sud Aviation Alouette II that would become the first helicopter to be produced with a turbine engine. Reliable helicopters capable of stable hover flight were developed decades after fixed-wing aircraft. This is largely due to higher engine power density requirements than fixed-wing aircraft. Improvements in fuels and engines during the first half of the 20th century were a critical factor in helicopter development. The availability of lightweight turbo-shaft engines in the second half of the 20th century led to the development of larger, faster, and higher-performance helicopters. The turbine engine has the following advantages over a reciprocating engine: less vibration, increased aircraft performance, reliability, and ease of operation. While smaller and less expensive helicopters still use piston engines, turboshaft engines are the preferred powerplant for helicopters today.

Which of these is most responsible for a huge increase in the number of helicopters in use?
   a. The military demand for helicopters in World War I
   b. The military demand for helicopters in World War II
   c. The development of an antitorque tail rotor configuration design
   d. The development of turbine engine powered helicopters
   e. The development of piston engine helicopters

2. The helicopter rotor system is the rotating part of a helicopter that generates lift. A rotor system may be mounted horizontally, as main rotors are, providing lift vertically; it may be mounted vertically, such as a tail rotor, to provide lift horizontally as thrust to counteract torque effect. In the case of tilt rotors, the rotor is mounted on a nacelle that rotates at the edge of the wing to transition the rotor from a horizontal mounted position, providing lift horizontally as thrust, to a vertical mounted position providing lift exactly as a helicopter. Tandem rotor (sometimes referred to as dual rotor) helicopters have two large horizontal rotor assemblies; a twin rotor system, instead of one main assembly and a smaller tail rotor. Single rotor helicopters need a tail rotor to neutralize the twisting momentum produced by the single large rotor. Tandem rotor helicopters, however, use counter-rotating rotors, with each canceling out the other's torque. Counter-rotating rotor blades won't collide with and destroy each other if they flex into the other rotor's pathway. This configuration also has the advantage of being able to hold more weight with shorter blades, since there are two sets. Also, all of the power from the engines can be used for lift, whereas a single rotor helicopter uses power to counter the torque. Because of this, tandem helicopters are among some of the most powerful and fastest.

Which of these is not discussed in the passage?
    a. A horizontal rotor
    b. A vertical rotor
    c. Twin horizontal rotors
    d. Twin tilt rotors
    e. Tandem rotor helicopters

3. Displacing the cyclic forward causes the nose to pitch down initially, with a resultant increase in airspeed and loss of altitude. Aft cyclic causes the nose to pitch up initially, slowing the helicopter and causing it to climb; however, as the helicopter reaches a state of equilibrium, the horizontal stabilizer levels the helicopter airframe to minimize drag, unlike an airplane. Therefore, the helicopter has very little pitch deflection up or down when the helicopter is stable in a flight mode. The variation from absolutely level depends on the particular helicopter and the horizontal stabilizer function. Increasing collective (power) while maintaining a constant airspeed induces a climb while decreasing collective causes a descent. Coordinating these two inputs, down collective plus aft cyclic or up collective plus forward cyclic, results in airspeed changes while maintaining a constant altitude. The pedals serve the same function in both a helicopter and a fixed-wing aircraft, to maintain balanced flight. This is done by applying a pedal input in whichever direction is necessary to center the ball in the turn and bank indicator.
According to this article, what is one of the main factors when it comes to variation from absolute level?
    a. The horizontal stabilizer
    b. The direction of the wind
    c. The speed of the wind
    d. How much experience the pilot has
    e. Whether the weight of passengers and cargo is properly balanced

4. Making good choices sounds easy enough. However, there are a multitude of factors that come into play when these choices, and subsequent decisions, are made in the aeronautical world. Many tools are available for pilots to become more self-aware and assess the options available, along with the impact of their decision. Yet, with all the available resources, accident rates are not being reduced. Poor decisions continue to be made, frequently resulting in lives being lost and/or aircraft damaged or destroyed. The Risk Management Handbook discusses aeronautical decision-making (ADM) and single-pilot resource management (SRM) in detail and should be thoroughly read and understood. While progress is continually being made in the advancement of pilot training methods, aircraft equipment and systems, and services for pilots, accidents still occur. Historically, the term "pilot error" has been used to describe the causes of these accidents. Pilot error means an action or decision made by the pilot was the cause of, or a contributing factor that led to, the accident. This definition also includes the pilot's failure to make a decision or take action. From a broader perspective, the phrase "human factors related" more aptly describes these accidents since it is usually not a single decision that leads to an accident, but a chain of events triggered by a number of factors. The poor judgment chain, sometimes referred to as the "error chain," is a term used to describe this concept of contributing factors in a human factors related accident. Breaking one link in the chain is often the only event necessary to change the outcome of the sequence of events.

Which of the following statements would the author be most likely to agree with?
   a. The problem of aircraft accidents has never been worse.
   b. Realistically, the number of aircraft accidents is probably about as low as it's ever going to be.
   c. There is still much room for improvement when it comes to reducing aircraft accidents.
   d. The FAA is too lax, and often gives licenses to pilots who are not fully qualified.
   e. Great strides have been made in recent years in reducing the number of aircraft accidents.

5. The roots of aviation are firmly based on curiosity. Where would we be today had it not been for the dreams of Leonardo da Vinci, the Wright Brothers, and Igor Sikorsky? They all were infatuated with flight, a curiosity that led to the origins of aviation. The tale of aviation is full of firsts: first flight, first helicopter, first trans-Atlantic flight, and so on. But, along the way there were many setbacks, fatalities, and lessons learned. Today, we continue to learn and investigate the limits of aviation. We've been to the moon, and soon beyond. Our curiosity will continue to drive us to search for the next challenge. However, curiosity can also have catastrophic consequences. Despite over 100 years of aviation practice, we still see accidents that are caused by impaired judgment formed from curious behavior. Pilots commonly seek to determine the limits of their ability as well as the limits of the aircraft. Unfortunately, too often this leads to mishaps with deadly results. Inquisitive behavior must be harnessed and displayed within personal and material limits. Deadly curiosity may not seem as obvious to some as it is to others. Simple thoughts such as, "Is visibility really as bad as what the ATIS is reporting?" or "Does the 20 minute fuel light really indicate only 20 minutes worth of fuel?" can lead to poor decisions and disastrous outcomes. Some aviators blatantly violate rules and aircraft limitations without thinking through the consequences. "What indications and change in flight characteristics will I see if I fly this helicopter above its maximum gross weight?" or "I've heard this helicopter can do aerobatic flight. Why is it prohibited?" are examples of extremely harmful curiosity. Even more astounding is their ignoring the fact that the damage potentially done to the aircraft will probably manifest later in the aircraft's life, affecting other crews. Spontaneous excursions in aviation can be deadly. Curiosity is natural, and promotes learning. Airmen should abide by established procedures until proper and complete hazard assessment and risk management can be completed.

Which of these statements most closely matches the theme of this passage?
    a. Fortune favors the bold.
    b. A stitch in time saves nine.
    c. Curiosity killed the cat.
    d. Fools rush in where angels fear to tread.
    e. An ounce of prevention is worth a pound of cure.

6. As found in the Pilot's Handbook of Aeronautical Knowledge, the FAA has designed a personal minimums checklist. To help pilots with self-assessment, which in turn helps mitigate risk, the acronym PAVE divides the risks of flight into four categories. For each category, think of the applicability specific to helicopter operations:

- Pilot (pilot in command)
  - o Physical, emotional readiness.
  - o Flight experience, recency, currency, total time in type.
- Aircraft
  - o Is the helicopter capable of performing the task?
  - o Can it carry the necessary fuel?
  - o Does it provide adequate power margins for the task to be accomplished?
  - o Can it carry the weight and remain within CG?
  - o Will there be external loads?
- EnVironment
  - o Helicopters are susceptible to the impact of changing weather conditions.
  - o How will the change in moderating temperatures and DA affect performance?
  - o Will controllability be jeopardized by winds, terrain, and turbulence?
- External pressures
  - o Do not let the notion to accomplish "the mission" override good judgment and safety.
  - o Many jobs include time lines. How often do we hear "time is money" or "time is wasting"?
  - o Don't sacrifice safety for an implied or actual need to meet the deadline!
  - o Do not allow yourself to feel pressured by coworkers, family events, or friends.

Incorporated into preflight planning, the PAVE checklist provides the pilot with a simple way to remember each category to examine for risk prior to each flight. Once the pilot identifies the risks of a flight, he or she needs to decide whether the risk or combination of risks can be managed safely and successfully. Remember, the PIC is responsible for deciding about canceling the flight. If the pilot decides to continue with the flight, he or she should develop strategies to mitigate the risks. One way to control risk is by setting personal minimums for items in each risk category. Remember, these are limits unique to an individual pilot's current level of experience and proficiency. They should be reevaluated periodically based upon experience and proficiency.

Which category of PAVE does the pilot have the least control over?
- a. Pilot
- b. Aircraft
- c. EnVironment
- d. External Pressures
- e. The pilot has equal control over all four PAVE categories.

- 156 -

7. Many of the concepts utilized in crew resource management (CRM) have been successfully applied to single-pilot operations which led to the development of single-pilot resource management (SRM). Defined as the art and science of managing all the resources (both on board the aircraft and from outside resources) available to a single pilot (prior to and during flight), SRM ensures the successful outcome of the flight. This includes risk management, situational awareness, and controlled flight into terrain (CFIT) awareness. SRM training helps the pilot maintain situational awareness by managing automation, associated control, and navigation tasks. This enables the pilot to accurately assess hazards, manage resulting risk potential, and make good decisions. To make informed decisions during flight operations, a pilot must be aware of the resources found both inside and outside the cockpit. Since useful tools and sources of information may not always be readily apparent, learning to recognize these resources is an essential part of SRM training. Resources must not only be identified, but a pilot must also develop the skills to evaluate whether he or she has the time to use a particular resource and the impact its use has upon the safety of flight.

What is the author's purpose in writing this passage?
    a. To describe single-pilot resource management
    b. To compare single-pilot resource management to crew resource management
    c. To persuade readers to use single-pilot resource management
    d. To answer objections to single-pilot resource management
    e. To raise questions about single-pilot resource management

8. Checklists are essential cockpit resources used to verify the aircraft instruments and systems are checked, set, and operating properly. They also ensure proper procedures are performed if there is a system malfunction or inflight emergency. Pilots at all levels of experience refer to checklists. The more advanced the aircraft is, the more crucial checklists are.

Many accidents could and should be avoided by simply using the resources, internal and external, that are available. Internal resources are found in the cockpit during flight. Since some of the most valuable internal resources are ingenuity, knowledge, and skill, a pilot can expand cockpit resources immensely by improving these capabilities. This can be accomplished by frequently reviewing flight information publications, such as 14 CFR and the AIM, as well as by pursuing additional training. No other internal resource is more important than the pilot's ability to control the situation, thereby controlling the aircraft. Helicopter pilots quickly learn that it is not possible to hover, single pilot, and pick up the checklist, a chart, or publication without endangering themselves, the aircraft, or those nearby. Checklists are essential cockpit resources used to verify the aircraft instruments and systems are checked, set, and operating properly. They also ensure proper procedures are performed if there is a system malfunction or inflight emergency. Pilots at all levels of experience refer to checklists. The more advanced the aircraft is, the more crucial checklists are.

The author of this passage would most strongly agree with which of these statements?
- a. As technology brings us more and more advanced aircraft, checklists become less important.
- b. Checklists should be referred to frequently during operation of the aircraft.
- c. Autopilot technology has significantly reduced the importance of pilots' skill level.
- d. Checklists are used primarily by pilots who do not yet have enough experience to operate by instinct.
- e. Improving a pilot's knowledge and skills is an effective way to promoting safe operation.

9. When an operator requests a Minimum Equipment List (MEL), and a Letter of Authorization (LOA) is issued by the FAA, then the use of the MEL becomes mandatory for that helicopter. All maintenance deferrals must be accomplished in accordance with the terms and conditions of the MEL and the operator-generated procedures document. Exercise extreme caution when hovering near buildings or other aircraft. The use of an MEL for rotorcraft operated under part 91 also allows for the deferral of inoperative items or equipment. The primary guidance becomes the FAA-approved MEL issued to that specific operator and N-numbered helicopter. The FAA has developed master minimum equipment lists (MMELs) for rotorcraft in current use. Upon written request by a rotorcraft operator, the local FAA Flight Standards District Office (FSDO) may issue the appropriate make and model MMEL, along with an LOA, and the preamble. The operator then develops operations and maintenance (O&M) procedures from the MMEL. This MMEL with O&M procedures now becomes the operator's MEL. The MEL, LOA, preamble, and procedures document developed by the operator must be on board the helicopter when it is operated. The FAA considers an approved MEL to be a supplemental type certificate (STC) issued to an aircraft by serial number and registration number. It therefore becomes the authority to operate that aircraft in a condition other than originally type certificated. With an approved MEL, if the position lights were discovered inoperative prior to a daytime flight, the pilot would make an entry in the maintenance record or discrepancy record provided for that purpose. The item is then either repaired or deferred in accordance with the MEL. Upon confirming that daytime flight with inoperative position lights is acceptable in accordance with the provisions of the MEL, the pilot would leave the position lights switch OFF, open the circuit breaker (or whatever action is called for in the procedures document), and placard the position light switch as INOPERATIVE.

What resource would a pilot use to determine if an inoperative part or system rendered daytime flight unacceptable?
   a. LOA
   b. O&M
   c. FSDO
   d. MEL
   e. Any of the above

- 159 -

10. Since few helicopters carry cabin attendants, the pilot must conduct the pretakeoff and prelanding briefings, usually before takeoff due to noise and cockpit layout. The type of operation dictates what sort of briefing is necessary. All briefings should include the following:
1. The use and operation of seatbelts for takeoff, en route, and landing.
2. For over water flights, the location and use of flotation gear and other survival equipment that might be on board. Also include how and when to abandon the helicopter should ditching become necessary.
3. For flights over rough or isolated terrain, all occupants should be told where maps and survival gear are located.
4. Passengers should be informed as to what actions and precautions to take in the event of an emergency, such as the body position for best spinal protection against a high vertical impact landing (erect with back firmly against the seat back); and when and how to exit after landing. Ensure that passengers are aware of the location of the fire extinguisher, survival equipment and, if equipped, how to use and locate the Emergency Position Indicator Radio Beacon (EPIRB).
5. Smoking should not be permitted within 50 feet of an aircraft on the ground. Smoking could be permitted upwind from any possible fuel fumes, at the discretion of the pilot, except under the following conditions:
- During all ground operations.
- During takeoff or landing.
- When carrying flammable or hazardous materials.

When passengers are approaching or leaving a helicopter that is sitting on a slope with the rotors turning, they should approach and depart downhill. This affords the greatest distance between the rotor blades and the ground. If this involves walking around the helicopter, they should always go around the front—never the rear.

After listening to a briefing that follows these guidelines, which of the following issues might a passenger be unsure about?
- a. Which direction to head when exiting the aircraft
- b. Where to light a cigarette during a refueling stop
- c. Where to find terrain maps of the flight area
- d. How long to wait before exiting the aircraft
- e. Where to collect items stowed for the flight

11. Many helicopter operators have been lured into a "quick turnaround" ground operation to avoid delays at airport terminals and to minimize stop/start cycles of the engine. As part of this quick turn-around, the pilot might leave the cockpit with the engine and rotors turning. Such an operation can be extremely hazardous if a gust of wind disturbs the rotor disk, or the collective flight control moves causing lift to be generated by the rotor system. Either occurrence may cause the helicopter to roll or pitch, resulting in a rotor blade striking the tail boom or the ground. Good operating procedures dictate that, generally, pilots remain at the flight controls whenever the engine is running and the rotors are turning. If operations require the pilot to leave the cockpit to refuel, the throttle should be rolled back to flight idle and all controls firmly frictioned to prevent uncommanded control movements. The pilot should be well trained on setting controls and exiting the cockpit without disturbing the flight or power controls.

When the flight is terminated, park the helicopter where it does not interfere with other aircraft and is not a hazard to people during shutdown. For many helicopters, it is advantageous to land with the wind coming from the right over the tail boom (counterrotating blades). This tends to lift the blades over the tail boom, but lowers the blades in front of the helicopter. This action decreases the likelihood of a main rotor strike to the tail boom due to gusty winds. Rotor downwash can cause damage to other aircraft in close proximity, and spectators may not realize the danger or see the rotors turning. Passengers should remain in the helicopter with their seats belts secured until the rotors have stopped turning. During the shutdown and postflight inspection, follow the manufacturer's checklist. Any discrepancies should be noted and, if necessary, reported to maintenance personnel.

What is the main reason leaving the cockpit with the engines running and rotors going during turnarounds should be avoided?
    a. It violates FAA regulations.
    b. It adds wear and tear to the engine and rotors.
    c. It is unsafe.
    d. It wastes fuel.
    e. It looks unprofessional.

12. Today, helicopters are quite reliable. However, emergencies do occur, whether as a result of mechanical failure or pilot error, and should be anticipated. Regardless of the cause, the recovery needs to be quick and precise. By having a thorough knowledge of the helicopter and its systems, a pilot is able to handle the situation more readily. Helicopter emergencies and the proper recovery procedures should be discussed and, when possible, practiced in flight. In addition, by knowing the conditions that can lead to an emergency, many potential accidents can be avoided. Emergencies should always be anticipated. Knowledge of the helicopter, possible malfunctions and failures, and methods of recovery can help the pilot avoid accidents and be a safer pilot. Helicopter pilots should always expect the worst hazards and possible aerodynamic effects and plan for a safe exit path or procedure to compensate for the hazard.

Which of the following best sums up this passage?
  a. Helicopters are extremely reliable these days.
  b. Planning ahead is the best way to prepare for emergencies.
  c. Many helicopter emergencies are due to faulty equipment.
  d. In helicopter emergencies, there is little margin for error.
  e. Helicopter emergencies can arise at any time and for a variety of reasons.

13. Medium-frequency vibrations (1,000–2,000 cycles per minute) range between the low frequencies of the main rotor (100–500 cycles per minute) and the high frequencies (2,100 cycles per minute or higher) of the engine and tail rotor. Depending on the helicopter, medium-frequency vibration sources may be engine and transmission cooling fans, and accessories such as air conditioner compressors, or driveline components. Medium-frequency vibrations are felt through the entire airframe, and prolonged exposure to the vibrations will result in greater pilot fatigue. Most tail rotor vibrations fall into the high-frequency range (2,100 cycles per minute or higher) and can be felt through the tail rotor pedals as long as there are no hydraulic actuators to dampen out the vibration. This vibration is felt by the pilot through his or her feet, which are usually "put to sleep" by the vibration. The tail rotor operates at approximately a 6:1 ratio with the main rotor, meaning for every one rotation of the main rotor the tail rotor rotates 6 times. A main rotor operating rpm of 350 means the tail rotor rpm would be 2,100 rpm. Any imbalance in the tail rotor system is very harmful as it can cause cracks to develop and rivets to work loose. Piston engines usually produce a normal amount of high-frequency vibration, which is aggravated by engine malfunctions, such as spark plug fouling, incorrect magneto timing, carburetor icing and/or incorrect fuel/air mixture. Vibrations in turbine engines are often difficult to detect as these engines operate at a very high rpm. Turbine engine vibration can be at 30,000 rpm internally, but common gearbox speeds are in the 1,000 to 3,000 rpm range for the output shaft. The vibrations in turbine engines may be short lived as the engine disintegrates rapidly when damaged due to high rpm and the forces present.

Which frequencies can result in the pilot experiencing numbness in the pilot's leg?
  a. Low frequency vibrations
  b. Medium frequency vibrations
  c. High frequency vibrations
  d. Both low and medium frequency vibrations
  e. Both medium and high frequency vibrations

14. Under certain conditions of high weight, high temperature, or high density altitude, a pilot may get into a low rotor rpm situation. Although the pilot is using maximum throttle, the rotor rpm is low and the lifting power of the main rotor blades is greatly diminished. In this situation, the main rotor blades have an AOA that has created so much drag that engine power is not sufficient to maintain or attain normal operating rpm. When rotor rpm begins to decrease, it is essential to recover and maintain it. As soon as a low rotor rpm condition is detected, apply additional throttle if it is available. If there is no throttle available, lower the collective. The amount the collective can be lowered depends on altitude. Rotor rpm is life! If the engine rpm is too low, it cannot produce its rated power for the conditions because power generation is defined at a qualified rpm value. An rpm that is too low equals low power. Main rotor rpm must be maintained. When operating at altitude, the collective may need to be lowered only once to regain rotor speed. If power is available, throttle can be added and the collective raised. Once helicopter rotor blades cone excessively due to low rotor rpm, return the helicopter to the surface to allow the main rotor rpm to recover. Maintain precise landing gear alignment with the direction of travel in case a landing is necessary. Low inertia rotor systems can become unrecoverable in 2 seconds or less if the rpm is not regained immediately. Since the tail rotor is geared to the main rotor, low main rotor rpm may prevent the tail rotor from producing enough thrust to maintain directional control. If pedal control is lost and the altitude is low enough that a landing can be accomplished before the turning rate increases dangerously, slowly decrease collective pitch, maintain a level attitude with cyclic control, and land.

According to this passage, what is the primary determining factor when it comes to how much the collective can be lowered?
   a. Wind speed and direction
   b. The altitude of the helicopter
   c. The attitude of the helicopter
   d. The angle of attack of the main rotor blades
   e. The amount of throttle available

15. Control of the helicopter is the result of accurately interpreting the flight instruments and translating these readings into correct control responses. Helicopter control involves adjustment to pitch, bank, power, and trim in order to achieve a desired flightpath. Pitch attitude control is control of the movement of the helicopter about its lateral axis. After interpreting the helicopter's pitch attitude by reference to the pitch instruments (attitude indicator, altimeter, airspeed indicator, and VSI), cyclic control adjustments are made to affect the desired pitch attitude. A pilot transitioning from airplanes to helicopters must understand that the attitude indicator is mounted in the airframe beneath the main rotor system and does not directly indicate what the main rotor system is doing to the flightpath. Therefore, the helicopter can take off and climb with the nose below the horizon. The helicopter can slow down and land with the nose above the horizon. In contrast, the airplane must be pointed generally in the direction of travel (up or down) since the attitude indicator is firmly attached to the airframe that is firmly attached to the wings. The helicopter tends to fly through the air at some stabilized attitude, an effect developed by the horizontal stabilizer and designed to minimize drag in forward flight. As a helicopter begins to take off, acceleration begins. As the airflow increases over the horizontal stabilizer, it produces a downward force to bring the nose into a stabilized attitude to streamline the airframe into the relative wind. Therefore, the helicopter's attitude indicator is about level when at a stable airspeed and altitude. A nose-low attitude indicates acceleration, not necessarily a descent, and a nose-high attitude indicates a decelerating attitude, not necessarily a climb. These effects make the helicopter pilot interpretation of the instruments even more important because the pilot must integrate the results of the entire instrument scan to achieve complete situational awareness of the helicopter's to flightpath.

Which of the following is the best definition of *attitude*?
   a.   The relation of the helicopter to the horizon
   b.   The distance between the helicopter and the surface of the earth
   c.   The angle of the helicopter
   d.   The ratio of the helicopter's speed to its altitude
   e.   The angle of the main rotor blades

16. Common Errors of Attitude Instrument Flying

Fixation

Fixation, or staring at one instrument, is a common error observed in pilots first learning to utilize instruments. The pilot may initially fixate on an instrument and make adjustments with reference to that instrument alone.

Omission

Another common error associated with attitude instrument flying is omission of an instrument from the cross-check. Pilots tend to omit the stand-by instruments, as well as the magnetic compass from their scans. The position of the instrument is often the reason for the omission. One of the most commonly omitted instruments from the scan is the slip/skid indicator.

Emphasis

In initial training, placing emphasis on a single instrument is very common and can become a habit if not corrected. When the importance of a single instrument is elevated above another, the pilot begins to rely solely on that instrument for guidance. When rolling out of a 180° turn, the attitude indicator, heading indicator, slip/skid indicator, and altimeter need to be referenced. If a pilot omits the slip/skid indicator, coordination is sacrificed.

Inadvertent Entry into IMC

Prior to any flight, day or night, an inadvertent IMC plan should be carefully planned and, if possible, rehearsed. Many aircraft mishaps can be blamed on the pilot's inability to recover an aircraft after inadvertently entering IMC. The desire to stay outside visually is very strong and can only be overcome through training. IMC-trained helicopter pilots should climb to a safe altitude free of obstacles and obtain an instrument clearance from ATC. However, for the nonrated pilot and, more importantly, a non-IFR equipped helicopter, remaining VMC is critical. Pilots who are not trained in IMC have a tendency to try and chase favorable weather by flying just above the tree tops or following roads. The thought process is that as long as they can see what is below them, then they can fly to their intended destination. Experience shows us that continuing VFR flight in IMC is often fatal. Pilots get too fixated on what they see below them and fail to see what is ahead of them, such as power lines, towers, and taller trees. By the time the pilot sees the obstacle, it is too close to avoid collision. Helicopter pilots should always remain aware of flight visibility by comparing how much can be seen ahead. As soon as the pilot notices a marked decrease in visibility, that pilot must reevaluate the flight plan and landing options. A suitable landing area can always be used to sit out bad weather and let conditions improve.

Which of these errors is the most dangerous during attitude instrument flying?
- a. Fixation
- b. Omission
- c. Emphasis
- d. Inadvertent Entry into IMC
- e. All of these errors can be equally dangerous.

17. A semirigid rotor system is usually composed of two blades that are rigidly mounted to the main rotor hub. The main rotor hub is free to tilt with respect to the main rotor shaft on what is known as a teetering hinge. This allows the blades to flap together as a unit. As one blade flaps up, the other flaps down. Since there is no vertical drag hinge, lead/lag forces are absorbed and mitigated by blade ending. The semirigid rotor is also capable of feathering, which means that the pitch angle of the blade changes. This is made possible by the feathering hinge. [Figure 4-2] The underslung rotor system mitigates the lead/lag forces by mounting the blades slightly lower than the usual plane of rotation, so the lead and lag forces are minimized. As the blades cone upward, the center of pressures of the blades are almost in the same plane as the hub. Whatever stresses are remaining bend the blades for compliance. If the semirigid rotor system is an underslung rotor, the center of gravity (CG) is below where it is attached to the mast. This underslung mounting is designed to align the blade's center of mass with a common flapping hinge so that both blades' centers of mass vary equally in distance from the center of rotation during flapping. The rotational speed of the system tends to change, but this is restrained by the inertia of the engine and flexibility of the drive system. Only a moderate amount of stiffening at the blade root is necessary to handle this restriction. Simply put, underslinging effectively eliminates geometric imbalance. Helicopters with semirigid rotors are vulnerable to a condition known as mast bumping which can cause the rotor flap stops to shear the mast. The mechanical design of the semirigid rotor system dictates downward flapping of the blades must have some physical limit. Mast bumping is the result of excessive rotor flapping. Each rotor system design has a maximum flapping angle. If flapping exceeds the design value, the static stop will contact the mast. It is the violent contact between the static stop and the mast during flight that causes mast damage or separation. This contact must be avoided at all costs. Mast bumping is directly related to how much the blade system flaps. In straight and level flight, blade flapping is minimal, perhaps 2° under usual flight conditions. Flapping angles increase slightly with high forward speeds, at low rotor rpm, at high-density altitudes, at high gross weights, and when encountering turbulence. Maneuvering the aircraft in a sideslip or during low-speed flight at extreme CG positions can induce larger flapping angles.

Feathering means:
    a. Mounting the blades slightly lower than the usual plane of rotation
    b. Both blades flapping together as a unit
    c. The slight increase of flapping angles at high forward speeds
    d. Changing the pitch angle of the blade
    e. Excessive rotor flapping

- 166 -

18. Rigid rotor systems tend to behave like fully articulated systems through aerodynamics, but lack flapping or lead/ lag hinges. Instead, the blades accommodate these motions by bending. They cannot flap or lead/lag but they can be feathered. As advancements in helicopter aerodynamics and materials continue to improve, rigid rotor systems may become more common because the system is fundamentally easier to design and offers the best properties of both semirigid and fully articulated systems. The rigid rotor system is very responsive and is usually not susceptible to mast bumping like the semirigid or articulated systems because the rotor hubs are mounted solid to the main rotor mast. This allows the rotor and fuselage to move together as one entity and eliminates much of the oscillation usually present in the other rotor systems. Other advantages of the rigid rotor include a reduction in the weight and drag of the rotor hub and a larger flapping arm, which significantly reduces control inputs. Without the complex hinges, the rotor system becomes much more reliable and easier to maintain than the other rotor configurations. A disadvantage of this system is the quality of ride in turbulent or gusty air. Because there are no hinges to help absorb the larger loads, vibrations are felt in the cabin much more than with other rotor head designs. There are several variations of the basic three rotor head designs. The bearingless rotor system is closely related to the articulated rotor system, but has no bearings or hinges. This design relies on the structure of blades and hub to absorb stresses. The main difference between the rigid rotor system and the bearingless system is that the bearingless system has no feathering bearing—the material inside the cuff is twisted by the action of the pitch change arm. Nearly all bearingless rotor hubs are made of fiber-composite materials.

The author of this passage would probably agree most strongly with which statement about rigid rotor systems?
  a. They are less popular than they used to be.
  b. They result in fewer vibrations than semirigid and fully articulated systems.
  c. Overall, they're superior to semirigid and fully articulated systems.
  d. Overall, they're inferior to semirigid and fully articulated systems.
  e. They are not as safe as semirigid and fully articulated systems.

19. While RFMs may appear similar for the same make and model of aircraft, each flight manual is unique since it contains specific information about a particular aircraft, such as the equipment installed, and weight and balance information. Therefore, manufacturers are required to include the serial number and registration on the title page to identify the aircraft to which the flight manual belongs. If a flight manual does not indicate a specific aircraft registration and serial number, it is limited to general study purposes only.

The general information section provides the basic descriptive information on the rotorcraft and the powerplant. In some manuals there is a three-view drawing of the rotorcraft that provides the dimensions of various components, including the overall length and width, and the diameter of the rotor systems. This is a good place for pilots to quickly familiarize themselves with the aircraft. Pilots need to be aware of the dimensions of the helicopter since they often must decide the suitability of an operations area for themselves, as well as hanger space, landing pad, and ground handling needs. Pilots can find definitions, abbreviations, explanations of symbology, and some of the terminology used in the manual at the end of this section. At the option of the manufacturer, metric and other conversion tables may also be included.

The operating limitations section contains only those limitations required by regulation or that are necessary for the safe operation of the rotorcraft, powerplant, systems, and equipment. It includes operating limitations, instrument markings, color coding, and basic placards. Some of the areas included are: airspeed, altitude, rotor, and powerplant limitations, including fuel and oil requirements; weight and loading distribution; and flight limitations. Concise checklists describing the recommended procedures and airspeeds for coping with various types of emergencies or critical situations can be found in this section. Some of the emergencies covered include: engine failure in a hover and at altitude, tail rotor failures, fires, and systems failures. The procedures for restarting an engine and for ditching in the water might also be included. Manufacturers may first show the emergencies checklists in an abbreviated form with the order of items reflecting the sequence of action. This is followed by amplified checklists providing additional information to clarify the procedure. To be prepared for an abnormal or emergency situation, learn the first steps of each checklist, if not all the steps. If time permits, refer to the checklist to make sure all items have been covered. For more information on emergencies, refer to Chapter 11, Helicopter Emergencies. Manufacturers are encouraged to include an optional area titled Abnormal Procedures, which describes recommended procedures for handling malfunctions that are not considered to be emergencies. This information would most likely be found in RFMs for larger helicopters.

According to this passage, which of the following information is not usually found in most RFMs?
   a. How to deal with engine failure in a hover
   b. The dimensions of the rotor systems
   c. Operating limitations
   d. How to deal with non-emergency malfunctions
   e. How to deal with tail rotor failures

20. Prior to departing an unfamiliar location, make a detailed analysis of the area. There are several factors to consider during this evaluation. Besides determining the best departure path and identifying all hazards in the area, select a route that gets the helicopter from its present position to the takeoff point while avoiding all hazards, especially to the tail rotor and landing gear. Some things to consider while formulating a takeoff plan are the aircraft load, height of obstacles, the shape of the area, direction of the wind, and surface conditions. Surface conditions can consist of dust, sand and snow, as well as mud and rocks. Dust landings and snow landings can lead to a brownout or whiteout condition, which is the loss of the horizon reference. Disorientation may occur, leading to ground contact, often with fatal results. Taking off or landing on uneven terrain, mud, or rocks can cause the tail rotor to strike the surface or if the skids get caught can lead to dynamic rollover. If the helicopter is heavily loaded, determine if there is sufficient power to clear the obstacles. Sometimes it is better to pick a path over shorter obstacles than to take off directly into the wind. Also evaluate the shape of the area so that a path can be chosen that will provide you the most room to maneuver and abort the takeoff if necessary. Positioning the helicopter to the most downwind portion of the confined area gives the pilot the most distance to clear obstacles. Wind analysis also helps determine the route of takeoff. The prevailing wind can be altered by obstructions on the departure path and can significantly affect aircraft performance. There are several ways to check the wind direction before taking off. One technique is to watch the tops of the trees; another is to look for any smoke in the area. If there is a body of water in the area, look to see which way the water is rippling. If wind direction is still in question revert back to the last report that was received by either ATIS or airport tower.

The main theme of this passage is:
   a. How to come up with a takeoff plan in an unfamiliar location
   b. The biggest risks of taking off from an unfamiliar location
   c. The importance of relying on past experience when taking off from an unfamiliar location
   d. How critical wind analysis becomes when taking off from an unfamiliar location
   e. Listing the different problems that can occur when taking off from an unfamiliar location

Math Skills Test

1. If 16x +4 = 100, what is the value of x?
        a. 6
        b. 7
        c. 8
        d. 9

2. Simplify the following expression:
$(2x - 20) (5x + 10)$
        a. $10x^2 - 80x - 200$
        b. $70x - 200$
        c. $10x^2 - 80x + 200$
        d. $10x^2 - 120x - 200$

3. Which of the following are complementary angles?
        a. 71° and 19°
        b. 90° and 90°
        c. 90° and 45°
        d. 15° and 30°

4. Simply the following expression:
$(2x^4)^3 + 2(y^5)^5$
        a. $8x^{64} + 2y^{3125}$
        b. $6x^7 + 2y^{10}$
        c. $6x^{12} + 2y^{25}$
        d. $8x^{12} + 2y^{25}$

5. If the measures of the three angles in a triangle are 2 : 6 : 10, what is the measure of the smallest angle?
        a. 20 degrees
        b. 40 degrees
        c. 60 degrees
        d. 80 degrees

6. If a circle has a diameter of 12cm, what is its area?
        a. $38cm^2$
        b. $113cm^2$
        c. $276cm^2$
        d. $452cm^2$

7. The length of a square is 15cm. What is its area?
        a. $30cm^2$
        b. $60cm^2$
        c. $150cm^2$
        d. $225cm^2$

8. A rectangular solid measures 12cm by 3cm by 9cm. What is its volume?
     a. 36cm³
     b. 108cm³
     c. 324cm³
     d. 407cm³

9. If $2x^2 = -4x^2 + 216$, what is the value of x?
     a. 4
     b. 5
     c. 6
     d. 7

10. The perimeter of a square is 24 m. What is its area?
     a. 30m²
     b. 36m²
     c. 42m²
     d. 24m²

11. If a rectangle has a length of 5cm and a width of 7cm, what is its area?
     a. 24cm²
     b. 35cm²
     c. 42cm²
     d. 56cm²

12. On a six-sided die, each side has a number between 1 and 6. What is the probability of throwing a 3 or a 4?
     a. 1 in 6
     b. 1 in 3
     c. 1 in 2
     d. 1 in 4

13. Solve for y in the following inequality:
$-2y \geq 24 + 6$
     a. $y \leq 15$
     b. $y \geq 15$
     c. $y \leq -15$
     d. $y \geq -15$

14. If $2x = 5x - 30$, what is the value of x?
     a. 10
     b. -10
     c. 4.3
     d. -4.3

15. Given the functions, $f(x) = 3x + 6$ and $g(x) = 2x - 8$, what is the solution of the equation, $f(x) = g(x)$?
     a. $x = -12$
     b. $x = -8$
     c. $x = -14$
     d. $x = -10$

16. Suppose the area of the square in the diagram to the right is 64 in². (The square is not shown actual size.) What is the area of the circle?

       a. 16π in^2
       b. 64π in^2
       c. $\frac{64}{\pi}$ in^2
       d. $(64 + \pi)$ in^2

17. Solve for x in the following inequality:
4x + 23 > -3x – 6
       a. x > -4.14
       b. x < -4.14
       c. x > 4.14
       d. x < 4.14

18. If 2x + 5x = 3x + x + 30, what is the value of x?
       a. 2.72
       b. 4.29
       c. 6
       d. 10

19. 3x²y + y/2 – 6x
If x=4 and y=10, what is the value of the expression
       a. 221
       b. 461
       c. 872
       d. 1916

20. At a school carnival, three students spend an average of $10. Six other students spend an average of $4. What is the average amount of money spent by all nine students?
       a. $5
       b. $6
       c. $7
       d. $8

21. If w=7, calculate the value of the following expression:
8w² – 12w + (4w – 5) + 6
       a. 279
       b. 285
       c. 337
       d. 505

22. If x/3 + 7 = 35, what is the value of x?
       a. 9.33
       b. 14
       c. 84
       d. 126

23. In the following equation, solve for x by factoring:
$2x^2 - 7x = x^2 - 12$
       a. x = -3, -4
       b. x = 3, 4
       c. x = 3, -4
       d. x = -3, 4

24. If x is 25% of 250, what is the value of x?
       a. 62.5
       b. 100
       c. 1000
       d. 6250

25. Which of the following inequalities is correct?
       a. $\frac{1}{3} < \frac{2}{7} < \frac{5}{12}$
       b. $\frac{2}{7} < \frac{1}{3} < \frac{5}{12}$
       c. $\frac{5}{12} < \frac{2}{7} < \frac{1}{3}$
       d. $\frac{5}{12} < \frac{1}{3} < \frac{2}{7}$

26. If the volume of a cube is 8cm³, what is the length of the cube?
       a. 1cm
       b. 2cm
       c. 3cm
       d. 4cm

27. Simply the following expression:
$(2x^2 + 3)(2x - 1)$
       a. $4x^3 - 2x^2 + 6x - 3$
       b. $2x^2 + 6x - 3$
       c. $4x^3 - 2x^2 + 6x + 3$
       d. $4x^3 - 2x^2 - 6x - 3$

28. Simply the following expression
$(2x^4y^7m^2z) * (5x^2y^3m^8)$
       a. $10x^6y^9m^{10}z$
       b. $7x^6y^{10}m^{10}z$
       c. $10x^5y^{10}m^{10}z$
       d. $10x^6y^{10}m^{10}z$

29. A classroom contains 13 boys and 18 girls. If a student's name is chosen randomly, what is the probability it will be a girl's name?

    a. 36%
    b. 42%
    c. 58 %
    d. 72%

30. What is 10% of 40%?

    a. 4%
    b. 30%
    c. 50%
    d. 400%

Mechanical Comprehension Test

1. A cannon fires off a ship up towards a mountain range. Neglecting air resistance, where will the velocity of the projectile be greatest?

a. Exiting the muzzle
b. Halfway to the mountains
c. As it impacts the mountains

2. These pulleys are connected by belts. Which pulley travels the fastest?

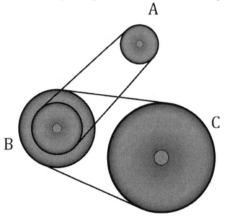

a. Pulley A
b. Pulley B
c. Pulley C

3. If Gear A is traveling at 10 rpm, how many times will Gear C rotate in 3 minutes?

a. 1.7 times
b. 3 times
c. 30 times

4. Where should the fulcrum be located to balance this beam?

a. closer to the large mass
b. closer to the small mass
c. exactly between the two masses

5. Which orientation will require more force to pull?

a. with the rope at an angle to the table
b. with the rope parallel to the table
c. both orientations are equal

6. The larger piston has four times as much horizontal area as the smaller piston. If the small piston is compressed 8 inches, how far will the larger piston move?

a. 8 inches
b. 2 inches
c. 32 inches

7. A wing in flight has a set of pressures causing the overall forces on the top and bottom of the wing. Where will the total force on the wing point?

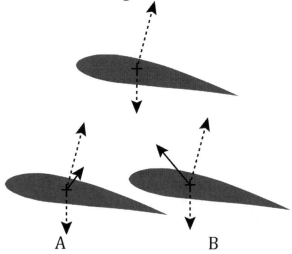

a. up and to the right
b. up and to the left
c. neither A or B

8. River water enters a section where the water spreads out into a wide, deep area. Is the water likely to speed up, slow down, or remain at a constant speed?

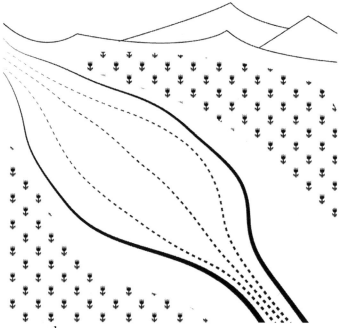

a. speed up
b. slow down
c. remain at a constant speed

9. A magnet is placed in the middle of two identical, anchored magnets. Which direction will the magnet go?

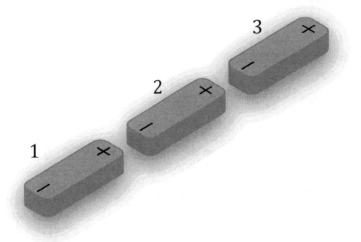

a. towards magnet 1
b. towards magnet 2
c. the magnet won't move

10. A solid substance melts at -21°C. If the object is known to change phase at 81°C, will the object be a solid, liquid, or gas at 90°C?

a. solid
b. liquid
c. gas

11. If the resistors in the circuits are identical, which circuit will have the greatest overall resistance?

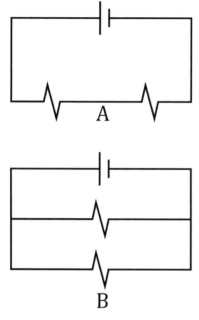

a. circuit A
b. circuit B
c. circuit A and B have the same overall resistance

12. A pendulum swings back and forth once per second. The pendulum is shortened by removing half of the string. The new frequency is 1.4 Hz (Hz=1/sec). How often will the pendulum swing back and forth in a minute?

a. 84
b. 92
c. 72

13. Two identical pistons are connected by a pipe. What is the mechanical advantage of the piston system?

a. 0.5
b. 1
c. 2

14. A ball is thrown horizontally off a cliff at the same time that an identical ball is dropped off a cliff. How long after the dropped ball hits the ground will the thrown ball hit?

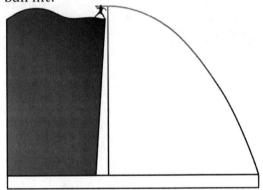

a. approximately 1 second after
b. approximately 2 seconds after
c. they will hit at the same time

15. The cam rotates at 5 rpm. How many times will the follower (needle) move up and down in a minute?

a. 20
b. 72
c. 140

16. Which of the following are not ways to increase the torque applied to a wrench?

a. increase the length from the center to the applied force
b. increase the force
c. angle the force toward the center

17. A ball is pushed down into a vertical spring. The ball is released and flies upward. Which best describes the states of energy the ball underwent?

a. convective energy to potential energy
b. potential energy to kinetic energy
c. kinetic energy to potential energy

18. A vacuum tank is held by weights at a depth of 50 feet underwater. If the tank is raised to a depth of 25 feet, will the pressure on the walls of the tank increase, decrease, or stay the same?

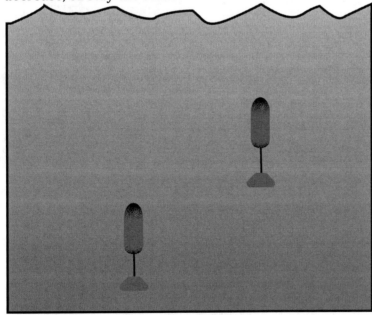

a. increase
b. decrease
c. stay the same

19. Adding salt to water raises its density. Will salt water have a lower, higher, or the same specific gravity than 1?

a. lower
b. higher
c. the same

20. Which of the following is an example of convective heat transfer?

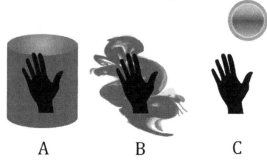

| A | B | C |

a. a man burns his hand on a hot pot
b. a man burns his hand in steam
c. a man gets a sun burn

21. Which of the following is the electrical component which holds a voltage across a gap between two conductive materials?
a. resistor
b. inductor
c. capacitor

22. Which of these wrenches is likely to provide the greatest torque with a set force?

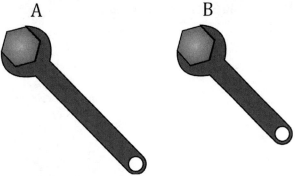

a. wrench A
b. wrench B
c. both wrenches will provide the same torque

23. Which of the following is true of this circuit?

a. the voltage is the same everywhere
b. the current is the same everywhere
c. there is no current

24. Which device does not measure current in an electrical system?
a. ammeter
b. multimeter
c. voltmeter

25. A ball is thrown straight into the air with an initial kinetic energy of 100 ft-lb. What is the potential energy of the ball at half of the height of the flight path?

a. 33 ft-lb
b. 50 ft-lb
c. 66 ft-lb

26. An increase in mechanical advantage with a set motion for the load and a set applied force necessitates an increase in _____ the applied force?
a. the distance traveled by
b. the angle of action of
c. the potential energy behind

27. A windlass drum has two sections with different circumferences. When winding the drum, one side of the rope winds around the large section and the other unwinds from the small section. If the large section of the drum has a circumference of 3.5 ft and the other section has a circumference of 1 ft, how far will the weight lift with two full turns of the drum?

a. 2.5 feet
b. 9 feet
c. 4.5 feet

28. Which type of situation will lead to condensation on the outside of pipes?
a. hot liquid in the pipe and cold air outside the pipe
b. cold liquid in the pipe and colder air outside the pipe
c. cold liquid in the pipe and hot air outside the pipe

29. Which color will absorb the most radiation?
a. black
b. green
c. dark yellow

30. Two gears (30 and 18 teeth) mesh. If the smaller gear rotates 3 times, how many times will the larger gear rotate?

a. 1.6 times
b. 1.8 times
c. 3 times

Answer Key and Explanations

Simple Drawings Test

1. C	35. E	69. A
2. B	36. B	70. A
3. E	37. B	71. B
4. A	38. D	72. C
5. B	39. C	73. B
6. A	40. D	74. A
7. D	41. A	75. A
8. C	42. B	76. B
9. B	43. E	77. E
10. A	44. B	78. C
11. D	45. B	79. B
12. C	46. B	80. A
13. B	47. E	81. B
14. D	48. E	82. D
15. A	49. C	83. E
16. E	50. A	84. A
17. C	51. B	85. C
18. B	52. D	86. D
19. E	53. E	87. E
20. B	54. C	88. C
21. A	55. B	89. D
22. D	56. A	90. B
23. C	57. A	91. C
24. D	58. C	92. A
25. B	59. D	93. B
26. C	60. B	94. B
27. A	61. A	95. E
28. E	62. D	96. C
29. C	63. B	97. B
30. D	64. C	98. E
31. D	65. E	99. B
32. A	66. A	100. C
33. C	67. D	
34. A	68. C	

Hidden Figures Test

(A)   (B)   (C)   (D)   (E)

1. **(B)**

4. **(C)**

2. **(D)**

5. **(A)**

3. **(E)**

- 188 -

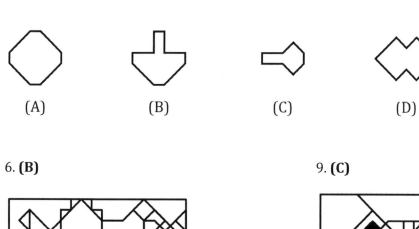

(A)   (B)   (C)   (D)   (E)

6. **(B)**

9. **(C)**

7. **(E)**

10. **(A)**

8. **(D)**

- 189 -

(A)　　 (B)　　 (C)　　 (D)　　 (E)

11. **(E)**

14. **(C)**

12. **(B)**

15. **(E)**

13. **(C)**

(A)   (B)   (C)   (D)   (E)

16. **(A)**

19. **(B)**

17. **(D)**

20. **(C)**

18. **(A)**

- 191 -

(A)　　　　　(B)　　　　　(C)　　　　　(D)　　　　　(E)

21. **(E)**

24. **(B)**

22. **(A)**

25. **(C)**

23. **(D)**

- 192 -

(A)   (B)   (C)   (D)   (E)

26. **(A)**

27. **(E)**

28. **(D)**

29. **(B)**

30. **(C)**

- 193 -

(A)   (B)   (C)   (D)   (E)

31. **(A)**

34. **(B)**

32. **(D)**

35. **(D)**

33. **(C)**

(A) (B) (C) (D) (E)

36. **(C)**

39. **(D)**

37. **(A)**

40. **(A)**

38. **(E)**

(A)   (B)   (C)   (D)   (E)

41. **(D)**

44. **(A)**

42. **(A)**

45. **(E)**

43. **(B)**

- 196 -

(A) (B) (C) (D) (E)

46. **(C)**

49. **(D)**

47. **(B)**

50. **(C)**

48. **(A)**

Army Aviation Information Test

1. E: Parasite. The force that resists the movement of a helicopter through the air and is produced when lift is developed is called drag. Drag must be overcome by the engine to turn the rotor. Drag always acts parallel to the relative wind. Total drag is composed of three types of drag: profile, induced, and parasite.

2. A: Governors are common on all turbine helicopters (as it is a function of the fuel control system of the turbine engine), and used on some piston powered helicopters.

3. E: The horizontal reference datum is an imaginary vertical plane or point, arbitrarily fixed somewhere along the longitudinal axis of the helicopter, from which all horizontal distances are measured for weight and balance purposes. There is no fixed rule for its location. It is established by the helicopter manufacturer.

4. B: The cyclic position relative to the horizon determines the helicopter's travel and attitude.

5. D: 45 knots. Training maneuvers for rapid deceleration should always be done into the wind. After leveling off at an altitude between 25 and 40 feet, depending upon the manufacturer's recommendations, accelerate to the desired entry speed, which is approximately 45 knots for most training helicopters.

6. B: The Bell TH-67 has been the Army's primary training helicopter since 1993.

7. D: Translational thrust occurs when the tail rotor becomes more aerodynamically efficient during the transition from hover to forward flight. As the tail rotor works in progressively less turbulent air, this improved efficiency produces more antitorque thrust, causing the nose of the aircraft to yaw left (with a main rotor turning counterclockwise) and forces the pilot to apply right pedal (decreasing the AOA in the tail rotor blades) in response.

8. C: The solidity ratio is the ratio of the total rotor blade area, which is the combined area of all the main rotor blades, to the total rotor disk area. This ratio provides a means to measure the potential for a rotor system to provide thrust and lift.

9. B: Torque pedals. There are three major controls in a helicopter that the pilot must use during flight. They are the collective pitch control, the cyclic pitch control, and the antitorque pedals or tail rotor control. In addition to these major controls, the pilot must also use the throttle control, which is usually mounted directly to the collective pitch control in order to fly the helicopter.

10. C: Each gallon of reciprocating engine oil weighs 7.5 pounds.

11. D: 100. In steep turns, the nose drops. In most cases, energy (airspeed) must be traded to maintain altitude as the required excess engine power may not be available (to maintain airspeed in a 2G/60° turn, rotor thrust/engine power must increase by 100 percent).

12. D: 300 and 500. It is important to strike a balance between a reconnaissance conducted too high and one too low. It should not be flown so low that a pilot must divide attention between studying the area and avoiding obstructions to flight. A high reconnaissance should be flown at an altitude of 300 to 500 feet above the surface.

13. C: The CH-47 Chinook came to prominence in the Vietnam War and is still in current use.

14. C: Cyclic feathering changes angle of incidence differentially around the rotor system. Cyclic feathering creates a differential lift in the rotor system by changing the AOA differentially across the rotor system. Aviators use cyclic feathering to control attitude of the rotor system.

15. C: Bernoulli's principle describes the relationship between internal fluid pressure and fluid velocity. It is a statement of the law of conservation of energy and helps explain why an airfoil develops an aerodynamic force.

16. D: 100% of maximum. Normal helicopter landings usually require high power settings, with terminations to a hover requiring the highest power setting.

17. C: Should be about the pace of a brisk walk. During an approach to a pinnacle or ridgeline, groundspeed is more difficult to judge because visual references are farther away than during approaches over trees or flat terrain. Pilots must continually perceive the apparent rate of closure by observing the apparent change in size of the landing zone features. Avoid the appearance of an increasing rate of closure to the landing site. The apparent rate of closure should be that of a brisk walk.

18. C: The OH-58A Kiowa has an empty weight of 1,583 pounds.

19. B: Translating tendency. During hovering flight, a single main rotor helicopter tends to move in the direction of tail rotor thrust. This lateral (or sideward) movement is called translating tendency.

20. D: Cyclic pitch. An increase in pitch angle increases angle of attack; a decrease in pitch angle decreases angle of attack.

21. B: Effective weight. When a helicopter is maneuvering, centrifugal force adds extra weight to the fuselage. This extra weight, when added to the weight of the helicopter, crew, passengers, and cargo, becomes the effective weight of the helicopter, or load factor.

22. E: None - the first four answers are all true in most helicopters.

23. A: Parallel to the ridgeline and into the wind. If there is a need to climb to a pinnacle or ridgeline, it should be done on the upwind side, when practicable, to take advantage of any updrafts. The approach flightpath should be parallel to the ridgeline and into the wind as much as possible.

24. E: The UH-72 Lakota is the US Army's primary light utility helicopter.

25. A: The Coriolis Effect is also referred to as the law of conservation of angular momentum. It states that the value of angular momentum of a rotating body does not change unless an external force is applied. In other words, a rotating body continues to rotate with the same rotational velocity until some external force is applied to change the speed of rotation.

26. A: The collective pitch control (or simply "collective" or "thrust lever") is located on the left side of the pilot's seat and is operated with the left hand.

27. D: Hovering in a strong headwind. A forward CG is easily recognized when coming to a hover following a vertical takeoff, but not as obvious when hovering into a strong wind, since less rearward cyclic displacement is required than when hovering with no wind.

28. C: Increase the collective. To enter a climb in a helicopter while maintaining airspeed, the first actions are increasing the collective and throttle, and adjusting the pedals as necessary to maintain a centered ball in the slip/skid indicator.

29. D: 13 and 15. An approach angle of approximately 13° to 15° is considered a steep approach.

30. D: The AH-64 Apache features four hardpoints mounted on stub-wing pylons, and usually carries a combination of AGM-114 Hellfire missiles and Hydra 70 rocket pods.

31. A: Factors that can make it unsafe to take off operating at maximum gross weight include high altitude, high temperature, and high humidity conditions, which result in a high density altitude.

32. B: In a standard airplane traffic pattern, the second of the five legs is known as the crosswind leg.

33. B: 5. The slope must be shallow enough to hold the helicopter against it with the cyclic during the entire landing. A slope of 5° is considered maximum for normal operation of most helicopters. Pilots should always consult the RFM or POH for the specific limitations of the helicopter being flown.

34. C: The CH-47 Chinook has a maximum speed of 170 knots.

35. C: 16 and 24. While transitioning to forward flight at about 16 to 24 knots, the helicopter goes through effective translational lift (ETL).

36. C: The antitorque pedals control in which direction the nose of the helicopter is pointing.

37. D: Each gallon of JP-4 jet fuel weighs 6.5 pounds.

38. C: 25. A hover taxi is used when operating below 25 feet above ground level (AGL).

39. B: 100. The helicopter should be kept in trim just prior to loss of effective translational lift (approximately 25 knots). Below 100' AGL, the antitorque pedals should be adjusted to align the helicopter with the intended touchdown point.

40. A: The primary use of OH-58 Kiowa helicopters is armed reconnaissance in support of ground troops.

Spatial Apperception Test

Problem	Answer	Description
1	B	out to sea, diving, and banking right
2	D	coastline right, diving, and wings level
3	E	coastline right, level flight, and banking left
4	B	coastline right, diving, and banking right
5	E	coastline left, climbing, and wings level
6	D	out to sea, level flight, and banking left
7	A	out to sea, diving, and banking left
8	A	out to sea, climbing, and wings level
9	B	coastline left, diving, and banking right
10	B	coastline left, level flight, and banking right
11	B	coastline right, climbing, and wings level
12	D	out to sea, climbing, and banking left
13	C	coastline left, diving, and banking left
14	B	coastline left, climbing, and banking right
15	D	out to sea, climbing, and banking right
16	C	coastline right, level flight, and banking right
17	C	coastline right, level flight, and wings level
18	B	coastline left, level flight, and banking left
19	C	coastline left, level flight, and wings level
20	D	coastline left, climbing, and banking left
21	D	coastline left, diving, and wings level
22	C	coastline right, climbing, and banking right
23	A	out to sea, level flight, and wings level
24	D	out to sea, diving, and wings level
25	B	out to sea, level flight, and banking right

Reading Comprehension Test

1. C: Taking the entire passage as a whole, it shows that the development of turbine engine powered helicopters is the factor that was most responsible for a huge increase in the number of helicopters in use.

2. D: Twin tilt rotors are not mentioned in the passage, while all the other answer choices are.

3. A: The passages states: "The variation from absolutely level depends on the particular helicopter and the horizontal stabilizer function."

4. C: This statement is the only one backed up by the contents of the passage.

5. D: Fools rush in where angels fear to tread expresses the idea that people who are new or inexperienced at something will often take dangerous chances that wiser or more experienced people would steer clear of, which most closely matches the author's theme that unbridled curiosity in a pilot can lead to disaster. He is not saying curiosity is bad in and of itself; only that it needs to have limits. That's why Curiosity killed the cat is incorrect.

6. C: EnVironment. While the pilot has less control over external pressures than over himself/herself and the aircraft, a pilot still has some control over these pressures. A pilot can refuse to yield to pressure to take risky chances in order to meet a schedule or accomplish a mission. However, when it comes to weather and other environmental factors, the pilot has no control whatsoever, and must deal with them as they are.

7. A: The passage is a broad overview of single-pilot resource management (SRM).

8. E: Improving a pilot's knowledge and skills is an effective way to promoting safe operation is a good summary of the message the author is trying to get across.

9. D: The Minimum Equipment List (MEL) is the correct answer, based on this part of the passage: The FAA considers an approved MEL to be a supplemental type certificate (STC) issued to an aircraft by serial number and registration number. It therefore becomes the authority to operate that aircraft in a condition other than originally type certificated.

10. E: The briefing covers the information in the first four answer choices, but does not instruct passengers on where to collect items stowed for the flight.

11. C: The main reason pilots should avoid leaving the cockpit with the engines running and rotors going during turnarounds is that it's unsafe.

12. B: The author's main point in this passage is that pilots can best prepare for emergencies by planning ahead – taking the time to master the helicopter and its systems, and anticipating emergencies and how to respond to them before they happen.

13. C: The passage states that high frequency vibrations can cause numbness in the pilot's leg.

14. B: According to the passage, the amount the collective can be lowered depends on altitude.

15. A: While many factors go into an exact technical definition of attitude, the relation of the helicopter to the horizon is a good thumbnail description.

16. E: While some of the errors listed are more common during attitude instrument flying, that doesn't imply that the less common ones are any less dangerous. Any of the mistakes listed can be extremely dangerous, and can lead to an accident.

17. D: From the passage: The semirigid rotor is also capable of feathering, which means that the pitch angle of the blade changes.

18. C: The author says that rigid rotor systems offer the best properties of semirigid and fully articulated systems, and are easier to design, too.

19. D: The passage states that information on how to deal with non-emergency malfunctions are usually found in RFMs for larger helicopters, which implies that this information doesn't appear in most RFMs.

20. A: This passage is mainly about how to create a takeoff plan in an unfamiliar location.

Math Skills Test

1. A: First, subtract 4 from both sides to isolate x:
$16x + 4 - 4 = 100 - 4$
$16x = 96$
Then, divide both sides by 16 to solve for x:
$16x/16 = 96/16$
$x = 6$

2. A: Use the FOIL method (first, outside, inside, and last) to get rid of the brackets:
$10x^2 + 20x - 100x - 200$
Then, combine like terms to simplify the expression:
$10x^2 - 80x - 200$

3. A: Complementary angles are two angles that equal 90° when added together.

4. D: To simplify this expression, the law of exponents that states that $(x^m)^n = x^{m*n}$ must be observed:
$2^3 x^{4*3} + 2 (y^{5*5})$
$8x^{12} + 2y^{25}$

5. A: The sum of the measures of the three angles of any triangle is 180. The equation of the angles of this triangle can be written as $2x + 6x + 10x = 180$, or $18x = 180$. Therefore, x = 10. Therefore, the measure of the smallest angle is 20.

6. B: The formula for the area of a circle is πr^2. The diameter of a circle is equal to twice its radius. Therefore, to find the radius of this circle, it is necessary to divide the diameter by 2: 12 / 2 = 6cm
Then, use the formula to find the area of the circle: $\pi 6^2$
$\pi *36 = 113cm^2$

7. D: The general equation to find the area of a quadrilateral is length * width.
Since the length and width of a square are equal, we can calculate the area of the square described in the question:
$A = l * w$
$A = 15cm * 15cm$
$A = 225cm^2$

8. C: To find the volume of a rectangular solid, the formula is length * width * height.
Therefore, this solid's volume = 12cm * 3cm * 9cm = 324cm³

9. C: First, add $4x^2$ to both sides to isolate x:
$2x^2 + 4x^2 = -4x^2 + 4x^2 + 216$
$6x^2 = 216$
Then, divide both sides by 6:
$6x^2/6 = 216/6$
$x^2 = 36$
Finally, take the square root of both sides to solve for x:
$\sqrt{x^2} = \sqrt{36}$
$x = 6$

10. B: The general equation to find the area of a quadrilateral is length * width. Since the length and width of a square are equal, we can calculate the area of the square described in the question. We can divide the perimeter by 4 since all sides are equal length. Once we know each side is 6 m we can multiply 6*6 to get an area of 36 m^2.

11. B: The formula for the area of a rectangle is length * width. Using the measurements given in the question, the area of the rectangle can be calculated:
A = length * width
A = 5cm * 7cm
A = 35cm²

12. B: On a six-sided die, the probability of throwing any number is 1 in 6. The probability of throwing a 3 or a 4 is double that, or 2 in 6. This can be simplified by dividing both 2 and 6 by 2. Therefore, the probability of throwing either a 3 or 4 is 1 in 3.

13. C: First, add the 24 and the 6:
-2y ≥ 30
Then, divide both sides by -2 to solve for y:
-2y/-2 ≥ 30/-2
y ≥ -15
Finally, when both sides are divided by a negative number, the direction of the sign must be reversed:
y ≤ -15

14. A: First, bring the 5x to the left side of the equation to make it easier to solve:
2x – 5x = -30
-3x = -30
Then, divide both sides by -3 to solve for x:
-3x/-3 = -30/-3
x = 10

15. C: The solution of $f(x) = g(x)$ can be determined by setting the two functions equal to one another. Thus, the following may be written $3x + 6 = 2x - 8$. Solving for x gives $x = -14$.

16. A: The area of a square is equal to the square of the length of one side. If the area is 64 in², the side length must therefore be $\sqrt{64\text{in}^2} = 8$ in. The circle is inscribed in the square, so the side length of the square is the same as the circle's diameter. If the circle's diameter is 8 in, then the circle's radius must be half of that, or 4 in. The area of a circle is equal to $A = \pi r^2 = \pi(4 \text{ in})^2 = 16\pi \text{ in}^2$.

17. A: First, bring the -3x to the left side of the equation and the 23 to the right side of the equation to make it easier to solve:
4x + 3x > -6 – 23
7x > -29
Then, divide both side by 7 to solve for x:
7x/7> -29/7
x > -4.14

18. D: First, bring all of the terms containing x to the left side of the equation to make it easier to solve: 2x + 5x – 3x – x = 30
7x – 4x = 30

3x = 30
Then, divide both sides by 3 to solve for x:
3x/3 = 30/3
x=10

19. B: First, substitute the given values for x and y into the expression:
$3(4)^2 10 + 10/2 - 6(4)$
Then, calculate the value of the expression:
According to the order of operations, any multiplying and dividing must be done first:
3*16*10 + 5 – 24
480 + 5 – 24
Then, any addition or subtraction should be completed:
485 – 24
461

20. B: The average is the total amount spent divided by the number of students. The first three students spend an average of $10, so the total amount they spend is $3 \times \$10 = \$30$. The other six students spend an average of $4, so the total amount they spend is $6 \times \$4 = \$24$. The total amount spent by all nine students is $\$30 + \$24 = \$54$, and the average amount they spend is $\$54 \div 9 = \$6$.

21. C: First, substitute the given value of w (7) into the expression each time it appears.
$8*7^2 - 12(7) + (4*7 - 5) + 6$
According to the order of operations, any calculations inside of the brackets must be done first:
$8*7^2 - 12(7) + (23) + 6$
Finally, calculate the value of the expression:
8*49 – 84 + 23 + 6
392 – 84 + 23 + 6
337

22. C: First, subtract 7 from both sides to isolate x:
x/3 + 7 – 7 = 35 – 7
x/3 = 28
Then, multiply both sides by three to solve for x:
x/3 * 3 = 28 * 3
x = 84

23. B: First, bring all terms to the left side of the equation to make it easier to solve:
$2x^2 -7x - x^2 +12 = 0$
Combine like terms:
$x^2 -7x + 12 = 0$
Then, factor the equation:
(x – 4) (x – 3) =0
Finally, solve for x in both instances:
x – 4 = 0
x = 4
x – 3 = 0
x = 3
x = 3, 4

24. A: Another way of expressing the fact that x is 25% of 250 is:

x = (0.25)250

Then, it is simply a matter of multiplying out the right side of the equation to calculate the value of x: x = 62.5

25. B: The volume of a cube is calculated by cubing the length, width, or height of the cube (the value for all three of these is the same.

Therefore, the volume of a cube equals = length^3

In this case 8cm^3= x * x * x, where x can represent the length of the cube.

To find the length, we must figure out which number cubed equals 8.

The answer is 2cm: 2cm * 2cm * 2cm = 8cm^3

26. B: One way to compare fractions is to convert them to equivalent fractions which have common denominators. In this case the lowest common denominator of the three fractions is $7 \times 12 = 84$. Converting each of the fractions to this denominator, $\frac{1}{3} = \frac{1 \times 28}{3 \times 28} = \frac{28}{84}$, $\frac{2}{7} = \frac{2 \times 12}{7 \times 12} = \frac{24}{84}$, and $\frac{5}{12} = \frac{5 \times 7}{12 \times 7} = \frac{35}{84}$. Since $24 < 28 < 35$, it must be the case that $\frac{2}{7} < \frac{1}{3} < \frac{5}{12}$.

27. A: Use the FOIL (first, outside, inside, last) to expand the expression:
4x^3 -2x^2 +6x – 3
There are no like terms, so the expression cannot be simplified any further.

28. D: To simplify this expression, the law of exponents that states that x^m * x^n = x^{m+n} must be observed.
10x^{4+2}y^{7+3}m^{2+8}z
Therefore, 10x^{6}y^{10}m^{10}z is the simplified expression.

29. C: First, find the total number of students in the classroom: 13 + 18 = 31
There is an 18 in 31 chance that a name chosen randomly will be a girl's name.
To express this as a percentage, divide 18 by 31, then multiply that number by 100:
18/31 * 100% = 58%

30. A: x percent is the same thing as $\frac{x}{100}$, and finding x percent of a number is the same as multiplying that number by x percent. This is true even when the number is itself a percent. So, 10% of 40% is $40\% \times 10\% = 40\% \times \frac{10}{100} = 40\% \times \frac{1}{10} = 4\%$.

Mechanical Comprehension Test

1. A, The velocity is made up of two components, the x and y components. The x component is not changing during flight, but the weight of the projectile decreases the positive y component of the velocity. Thus, the total velocity will be greatest before the y component has decreased.

2. A, Because the linear speed of two connected pulleys is the same, the pulley with the smaller radius spins faster. The largest pulley will spin slower than the middle pulley. The smallest pulley will spin faster than the middle pulley, making it the fastest pulley.

3. C, Gear A and gear C have the same number of teeth. Thus, gears A and C will have the same speed. Since gear C is rotating at 10 rpm, the total number of rotations is calculated by multiplying the rpm by the number of minutes.

4. A, Because the large mass will produce a greater torque at the same distance from the fulcrum as the small mass, the distance from the large mass to the fulcrum should be shortened. Then, the torque produced by the large mass will decrease and the torque produced by the small mass will increase.

5. A, When the rope is not parallel to the intended path of motion, the force is divided into useful force (x direction) and not useful force (y direction). If only some of the force is useful, then the man will need to apply more force to achieve the same pulling force as if the rope were parallel to the table.

6. B, Because the volume of the liquid doesn't change, when the small piston is compressed, the volume decrease in one piston is the volume increase in the other piston. As the volume is the area times the height, the height of the larger piston only needs to raise one fourth the height that the small piston moved.

7. A, The downward force decreases part of the y component of the top force, but does not affect the x component of the force. Thus, the resultant force is up and to the right.

8. B, because the same volume of water has to flow through all parts of the river, the water will slow down to fill the wide section.

9. C, The negative side of magnet 2 will be attracted to the positive side of magnet 1. The positive side of magnet 2 will be attracted to the negative side of magnet 3 with the same force. Because the magnitudes of the forces are equal and the directions are opposite, the sum of the forces will be zero.

10. C, The first phase change is from solid to liquid at -21°C. The next phase change is from liquid to gas at 81°C. 90°C is only slightly higher than 81°C, making it safe to say that the substance is still a gas.

11. A, Substitute token values for the resistors to solve. Using 1 Ω resistors, the resistance of circuit A, having resistors in series, is the simple sum of the two resistors: 2 Ω. Because the resistors in circuit B are in parallel, the resistance of circuit B is the reciprocal of the sum of the reciprocals of the resistances, or $\frac{1}{\frac{1}{1}+\frac{1}{1}}$. the result is 1/2 Ω.

12. A, To find the number of swings in a time period from the frequency, multiply the frequency times the time period, after converting the time period into seconds to match the frequency. The final calculation is $\frac{1.4\ swings}{second} * 1\ minute * \frac{60\ seconds}{1\ minute} = 84\ swings$

13. B, The mechanical advantage is calculated by the output force divided by the input force. Because both pistons are the same size, the output force will equal the input force, resulting in a mechanical advantage of one.

14. C, Because the horizontal component of the thrown ball's velocity will not affect the vertical component, the vertical component of the thrown ball's velocity will be identical to the dropped ball's velocity. The balls will hit at the same time.

15. A, The cam has four bumps on it. The needle will move up and down for each bump. The cam will rotate five times in the time period of one minute. The total times the needle will move up and down will be five times four.

16. C, Torque is the product of a force perpendicular to the arm and the length of the arm. Options A and B each increase one part of the torque calculation. However, angling the force towards the center would decrease the part of the force that is acting perpendicular to the arm, as some of the force will be acting inward.

17. B, When the ball is compressed into the spring, the ball has potential stored in the spring. When the ball is flying upwards, the ball has kinetic energy associated with the motion.

18. B, Pressure increases with depth in water. When the tank was lower it experienced more pressure. Thus, when the tank is higher it experiences less pressure.

19. B, Specific gravity can be calculated as the ratio of the density of the liquid in question to the density of water. Because salt water has a higher density than water, the ratio will be greater than one.

20. B, Convective heat transfer deals with the transfer of heat by fluids (including gas). Steam is a fluid which transfers heat to objects, like a hand, with lower temperatures than it.

21. C, A capacitor stores voltage across a gap between two conductive materials.

22. A, Torque is the product of a force perpendicular to the arm and the length of the arm. Wrench A, with the longer arm, will be able to achieve greater amounts of torque with a set force.

23. B, Because the circuit only has one path and the two resistors are in series, the current is the same everywhere in the circuit. The voltage will drop over both resistors. Also, because the circuit is complete, there is current in the circuit.

24. C, Ammeters measure current (think amps). Multimeters measure current and voltage. Voltmeters only measure voltage.

25. B, When the ball is flying upwards, the kinetic energy is being converted into potential energy. Potential energy increases linearly with height, meaning that an object at 2 feet over the ground has twice the potential energy of the object at 1 foot over the ground. Thus, if all of the energy of the ball

will be converted from kinetic energy, and half of the energy will be converted at half the height, the potential energy of the ball will be 50 ft-lb.

26. A, Because mechanical advantage is the ratio of output force to input force, an increase in mechanical advantage means, in this case, that the output force will be increasing. However, energy in simple machines is conserved. This means that the work, or force times distance, done to the input will need to increase, while keeping the force the same. Increasing the distance of the applied force will increase the work, allowing for an increased force for the output.

27. A, As the drum spins one full turn, the hanging rope increases length by 1 foot and decreases length by 3.5 feet. Thus, every spin decreases the rope length by 2.5 feet. In two turns, the rope will decrease length by 5 feet. The pulley makes the weight lift half the distance that the rope decreased. Thus, the weight raises 2.5 feet.

28. C, Condensation from the air occurs when the water vapor in the air cools down enough to change phase from vapor to liquid water. If a pipe is cold and the air is warm, the water vapor will condense on the pipe.

29. A, The color, black, will absorb the most heat from radiation.

30. B, The gear ratio between the small and large gears is 18/30 or 3/5. Multiply the number of rotations of the small gear times the gear ratio to get (3 rotations)*(3/5) = 1.8 rotations.

- 210 -

Secret Key #1 - Time is Your Greatest Enemy

Pace Yourself

Wear a watch. At the beginning of the test, check the time (or start a chronometer on your watch to count the minutes), and check the time after every few questions to make sure you are "on schedule."

If you are forced to speed up, do it efficiently. Usually one or more answer choices can be eliminated without too much difficulty. Above all, don't panic. Don't speed up and just begin guessing at random choices. By pacing yourself, and continually monitoring your progress against your watch, you will always know exactly how far ahead or behind you are with your available time. If you find that you are one minute behind on the test, don't skip one question without spending any time on it, just to catch back up. Take 15 fewer seconds on the next four questions, and after four questions you'll have caught back up. Once you catch back up, you can continue working each problem at your normal pace.

Furthermore, don't dwell on the problems that you were rushed on. If a problem was taking up too much time and you made a hurried guess, it must be difficult. The difficult questions are the ones you are most likely to miss anyway, so it isn't a big loss. It is better to end with more time than you need than to run out of time.

Lastly, sometimes it is beneficial to slow down if you are constantly getting ahead of time. You are always more likely to catch a careless mistake by working more slowly than quickly, and among very high-scoring test takers (those who are likely to have lots of time left over), careless errors affect the score more than mastery of material.

Secret Key #2 - Guessing is not Guesswork

You probably know that guessing is a good idea. Unlike other standardized tests, there is no penalty for getting a wrong answer. Even if you have no idea about a question, you still have a 20-25% chance of getting it right.

Most test takers do not understand the impact that proper guessing can have on their score. Unless you score extremely high, guessing will significantly contribute to your final score.

Monkeys Take the Test

What most test takers don't realize is that to insure that 20-25% chance, you have to guess randomly. If you put 20 monkeys in a room to take this test, assuming they answered once per question and behaved themselves, on average they would get 20-25% of the questions correct. Put 20 test takers in the room, and the average will be much lower among guessed questions. Why?

1. The test writers intentionally write deceptive answer choices that "look" right. A test taker has no idea about a question, so he picks the "best looking" answer, which is often wrong. The monkey has no idea what looks good and what doesn't, so it will consistently be right about 20-25% of the time.
2. Test takers will eliminate answer choices from the guessing pool based on a hunch or intuition. Simple but correct answers often get excluded, leaving a 0% chance of being correct. The monkey has no clue, and often gets lucky with the best choice.

This is why the process of elimination endorsed by most test courses is flawed and detrimental to your performance. Test takers don't guess; they make an ignorant stab in the dark that is usually worse than random.

$5 Challenge

Let me introduce one of the most valuable ideas of this course—the $5 challenge:

- *You only mark your "best guess" if you are willing to bet $5 on it.*
- *You only eliminate choices from guessing if you are willing to bet $5 on it.*

Why $5? Five dollars is an amount of money that is small yet not insignificant, and can really add up fast (20 questions could cost you $100). Likewise, each answer choice on one question of the test will have a small impact on your overall score, but it can really add up to a lot of points in the end.

The process of elimination IS valuable. The following shows your chance of guessing it right:

If you eliminate wrong answer choices until only this many remain:	Chance of getting it correct:
1	100%
2	50%
3	33%

However, if you accidentally eliminate the right answer or go on a hunch for an incorrect answer, your chances drop dramatically—to 0%. By guessing among all the answer choices, you are GUARANTEED to have a shot at the right answer.

That's why the $5 test is so valuable. If you give up the advantage and safety of a pure guess, it had better be worth the risk.

What we still haven't covered is how to be sure that whatever guess you make is truly random. Here's the easiest way:

- *Always pick the first answer choice among those remaining.*

Such a technique means that you have decided, **before you see a single test question**, exactly how you are going to guess, and since the order of choices tells you nothing about which one is correct, this guessing technique is perfectly random.

This section is not meant to scare you away from making educated guesses or eliminating choices; you just need to define when a choice is worth eliminating. The $5 test, along with a pre-defined random guessing strategy, is the best way to make sure you reap all of the benefits of guessing.

Secret Key #3 - Practice Smarter, Not Harder

Many test takers delay the test preparation process because they dread the awful amounts of practice time they think necessary to succeed on the test. We have refined an effective method that will take you only a fraction of the time.

There are a number of "obstacles" in the path to success. Among these are answering questions, finishing in time, and mastering test-taking strategies. All must be executed on the day of the test at peak performance, or your score will suffer. The test is a mental marathon that has a large impact on your future.

Just like a marathon runner, it is important to work your way up to the full challenge. So first you just worry about questions, and then time, and finally strategy:

Success Strategy

1. Find a good source for practice tests.
2. If you are willing to make a larger time investment, consider using more than one study guide. Often the different approaches of multiple authors will help you "get" difficult concepts.
3. Take a practice test with no time constraints, with all study helps, "open book." Take your time with questions and focus on applying strategies.
4. Take a practice test with time constraints, with all guides, "open book."
5. Take a final practice test without open material and with time limits.

If you have time to take more practice tests, just repeat step 5. By gradually exposing yourself to the full rigors of the test environment, you will condition your mind to the stress of test day and maximize your success.

Secret Key #4 - Prepare, Don't Procrastinate

Let me state an obvious fact: if you take the test three times, you will probably get three different scores. This is due to the way you feel on test day, the level of preparedness you have, and the version of the test you see. Despite the test writers' claims to the contrary, some versions of the test WILL be easier for you than others.

Since your future depends so much on your score, you should maximize your chances of success. In order to maximize the likelihood of success, you've got to prepare in advance. This means taking practice tests and spending time learning the information and test taking strategies you will need to succeed.

Never go take the actual test as a "practice" test, expecting that you can just take it again if you need to. Take all the practice tests you can on your own, but when you go to take the official test, be prepared, be focused, and do your best the first time!

Secret Key #5 - Test Yourself

Everyone knows that time is money. There is no need to spend too much of your time or too little of your time preparing for the test. You should only spend as much of your precious time preparing as is necessary for you to get the score you need.

Once you have taken a practice test under real conditions of time constraints, then you will know if you are ready for the test or not.

If you have scored extremely high the first time that you take the practice test, then there is not much point in spending countless hours studying. You are already there.

Benchmark your abilities by retaking practice tests and seeing how much you have improved. Once you consistently score high enough to guarantee success, then you are ready.

If you have scored well below where you need, then knuckle down and begin studying in earnest. Check your improvement regularly through the use of practice tests under real conditions. Above all, don't worry, panic, or give up. The key is perseverance!

Then, when you go to take the test, remain confident and remember how well you did on the practice tests. If you can score high enough on a practice test, then you can do the same on the real thing.

General Strategies

The most important thing you can do is to ignore your fears and jump into the test immediately- do not be overwhelmed by any strange-sounding terms. You have to jump into the test like jumping into a pool- all at once is the easiest way.

Make Predictions

As you read and understand the question, try to guess what the answer will be. Remember that several of the answer choices are wrong, and once you begin reading them, your mind will immediately become cluttered with answer choices designed to throw you off. Your mind is typically the most focused immediately after you have read the question and digested its contents. If you can, try to predict what the correct answer will be. You may be surprised at what you can predict.

Quickly scan the choices and see if your prediction is in the listed answer choices. If it is, then you can be quite confident that you have the right answer. It still won't hurt to check the other answer choices, but most of the time, you've got it!

Answer the Question

It may seem obvious to only pick answer choices that answer the question, but the test writers can create some excellent answer choices that are wrong. Don't pick an answer just because it sounds right, or you believe it to be true. It MUST answer the question. Once you've made your selection, always go back and check it against the question and make sure that you didn't misread the question, and the answer choice does answer the question posed.

Benchmark

After you read the first answer choice, decide if you think it sounds correct or not. If it doesn't, move on to the next answer choice. If it does, mentally mark that answer choice. This doesn't mean that you've definitely selected it as your answer choice, it just means that it's the best you've seen thus far. Go ahead and read the next choice. If the next choice is worse than the one you've already selected, keep going to the next answer choice. If the next choice is better than the choice you've already selected, mentally mark the new answer choice as your best guess.

The first answer choice that you select becomes your standard. Every other answer choice must be benchmarked against that standard. That choice is correct until proven otherwise by another answer choice beating it out. Once you've decided that no other answer choice seems as good, do one final check to ensure that your answer choice answers the question posed.

Valid Information

Don't discount any of the information provided in the question. Every piece of information may be necessary to determine the correct answer. None of the information in the question is there to throw you off (while the answer choices will certainly have information to throw you off). If two seemingly unrelated topics are discussed, don't ignore either. You can be confident there is a relationship, or it wouldn't be included in the question, and you are probably going to have to determine what is that relationship to find the answer.

Avoid "Fact Traps"

Don't get distracted by a choice that is factually true. Your search is for the answer that answers the question. Stay focused and don't fall for an answer that is true but incorrect. Always go back to the question and make sure you're choosing an answer that actually answers the question and is not just a true statement. An answer can be factually correct, but it MUST answer the question asked. Additionally, two answers can both be seemingly correct, so be sure to read all of the answer choices, and make sure that you get the one that BEST answers the question.

Milk the Question

Some of the questions may throw you completely off. They might deal with a subject you have not been exposed to, or one that you haven't reviewed in years. While your lack of knowledge about the subject will be a hindrance, the question itself can give you many clues that will help you find the correct answer. Read the question carefully and look for clues. Watch particularly for adjectives and nouns describing difficult terms or words that you don't recognize. Regardless of if you completely understand a word or not, replacing it with a synonym either provided or one you more familiar with may help you to understand what the questions are asking. Rather than wracking your mind about specific detailed information concerning a difficult term or word, try to use mental substitutes that are easier to understand.

The Trap of Familiarity

Don't just choose a word because you recognize it. On difficult questions, you may not recognize a number of words in the answer choices. The test writers don't put "make-believe" words on the test; so don't think that just because you only recognize all the words in one answer choice means that answer choice must be correct. If you only recognize words in one answer choice, then focus on that one. Is it correct? Try your best to determine if it is correct. If it is, that is great, but if it doesn't, eliminate it. Each word and answer choice you eliminate increases your chances of getting the question correct, even if you then have to guess among the unfamiliar choices.

Eliminate Answers

Eliminate choices as soon as you realize they are wrong. But be careful! Make sure you consider all of the possible answer choices. Just because one appears right, doesn't mean that the next one won't be even better! The test writers will usually put more than one good answer choice for every question, so read all of them. Don't worry if you are stuck between two that seem right. By getting down to just two remaining possible choices, your odds are now 50/50. Rather than wasting too much time, play the odds. You are guessing, but guessing wisely, because you've been able to knock out some of the answer choices that you know are wrong. If you are eliminating choices and realize that the last answer choice you are left with is also obviously wrong, don't panic. Start over and consider each choice again. There may easily be something that you missed the first time and will realize on the second pass.

Tough Questions

If you are stumped on a problem or it appears too hard or too difficult, don't waste time. Move on! Remember though, if you can quickly check for obviously incorrect answer choices, your chances of guessing correctly are greatly improved. Before you completely give up, at least try to knock out a couple of possible answers. Eliminate what you can and then guess at the remaining answer choices before moving on.

Brainstorm

If you get stuck on a difficult question, spend a few seconds quickly brainstorming. Run through the complete list of possible answer choices. Look at each choice and ask yourself, "Could this answer the question satisfactorily?" Go through each answer choice and consider it independently of the other. By systematically going through all possibilities, you may find something that you would otherwise overlook. Remember that when you get stuck, it's important to try to keep moving.

Read Carefully

Understand the problem. Read the question and answer choices carefully. Don't miss the question because you misread the terms. You have plenty of time to read each question thoroughly and make sure you understand what is being asked. Yet a happy medium must be attained, so don't waste too much time. You must read carefully, but efficiently.

Face Value

When in doubt, use common sense. Always accept the situation in the problem at face value. Don't read too much into it. These problems will not require you to make huge leaps of logic. The test writers aren't trying to throw you off with a cheap trick. If you have to go beyond creativity and make a leap of logic in order to have an answer choice answer the question, then you should look at the other answer choices. Don't overcomplicate the problem by creating theoretical relationships or explanations that will warp time or space. These are normal problems rooted in reality. It's just that the applicable relationship or explanation may not be readily apparent and you have to figure things out. Use your common sense to interpret anything that isn't clear.

Prefixes

If you're having trouble with a word in the question or answer choices, try dissecting it. Take advantage of every clue that the word might include. Prefixes and suffixes can be a huge help. Usually they allow you to determine a basic meaning. Pre- means before, post- means after, pro - is positive, de- is negative. From these prefixes and suffixes, you can get an idea of the general meaning of the word and try to put it into context. Beware though of any traps. Just because con is the opposite of pro, doesn't necessarily mean congress is the opposite of progress!

Hedge Phrases

Watch out for critical "hedge" phrases, such as likely, may, can, will often, sometimes, often, almost, mostly, usually, generally, rarely, sometimes. Question writers insert these hedge phrases to cover every possibility. Often an answer choice will be wrong simply because it leaves no room for exception. Avoid answer choices that have definitive words like "exactly," and "always".

Switchback Words

Stay alert for "switchbacks". These are the words and phrases frequently used to alert you to shifts in thought. The most common switchback word is "but". Others include although, however, nevertheless, on the other hand, even though, while, in spite of, despite, regardless of.

New Information

Correct answer choices will rarely have completely new information included. Answer choices typically are straightforward reflections of the material asked about and will directly relate to the question. If a new piece of information is included in an answer choice that doesn't even seem to relate to the topic being asked about, then that answer choice is likely incorrect. All of the information needed to answer the question is usually provided for you, and so you should not have to make guesses that are unsupported or choose answer choices that require unknown information that cannot be reasoned on its own.

Time Management

On technical questions, don't get lost on the technical terms. Don't spend too much time on any one question. If you don't know what a term means, then since you don't have a dictionary, odds are you aren't going to get much further. You should immediately recognize terms as whether or not you know them. If you don't, work with the other clues that you have, the other answer choices and terms provided, but don't waste too much time trying to figure out a difficult term.

Contextual Clues

Look for contextual clues. An answer can be right but not correct. The contextual clues will help you find the answer that is most right and is correct. Understand the context in which a phrase or statement is made. This will help you make important distinctions.

Don't Panic

Panicking will not answer any questions for you. Therefore, it isn't helpful. When you first see the question, if your mind goes blank, take a deep breath. Force yourself to mechanically go through the steps of solving the problem and using the strategies you've learned.

Pace Yourself

Don't get clock fever. It's easy to be overwhelmed when you're looking at a page full of questions, your mind is full of random thoughts and feeling confused, and the clock is ticking down faster than you would like. Calm down and maintain the pace that you have set for yourself. As long as you are on track by monitoring your pace, you are guaranteed to have enough time for yourself. When you get to the last few minutes of the test, it may seem like you won't have enough time left, but if you only have as many questions as you should have left at that point, then you're right on track!

Answer Selection

The best way to pick an answer choice is to eliminate all of those that are wrong, until only one is left and confirm that is the correct answer. Sometimes though, an answer choice may immediately look right. Be careful! Take a second to make sure that the other choices are not equally obvious. Don't make a hasty mistake. There are only two times that you should stop before checking other answers. First is when you are positive that the answer choice you have selected is correct. Second is when time is almost out and you have to make a quick guess!

Check Your Work

Since you will probably not know every term listed and the answer to every question, it is important that you get credit for the ones that you do know. Don't miss any questions through careless mistakes. If at all possible, try to take a second to look back over your answer selection and make sure you've selected the correct answer choice and haven't made a costly careless mistake (such as marking an answer choice that you didn't mean to mark). This quick double check should more than pay for itself in caught mistakes for the time it costs.

Beware of Directly Quoted Answers

Sometimes an answer choice will repeat word for word a portion of the question or reference section. However, beware of such exact duplication – it may be a trap! More than likely, the correct choice will paraphrase or summarize a point, rather than being exactly the same wording.

Slang

Scientific sounding answers are better than slang ones. An answer choice that begins "To compare the outcomes..." is much more likely to be correct than one that begins "Because some people insisted..."

Extreme Statements

Avoid wild answers that throw out highly controversial ideas that are proclaimed as established fact. An answer choice that states the "process should be used in certain situations, if..." is much more likely to be correct than one that states the "process should be discontinued completely." The first is a calm rational statement and doesn't even make a definitive, uncompromising stance, using a hedge word "if" to provide wiggle room, whereas the second choice is a radical idea and far more extreme.

Answer Choice Families

When you have two or more answer choices that are direct opposites or parallels, one of them is usually the correct answer. For instance, if one answer choice states "x increases" and another answer choice states "x decreases" or "y increases," then those two or three answer choices are very similar in construction and fall into the same family of answer choices. A family of answer choices is when two or three answer choices are very similar in construction, and yet often have a directly opposite meaning. Usually the correct answer choice will be in that family of answer choices. The "odd man out" or answer choice that doesn't seem to fit the parallel construction of the other answer choices is more likely to be incorrect.

How to Overcome Test Anxiety

The very nature of tests caters to some level of anxiety, nervousness or tension, just as we feel for any important event that occurs in our lives. A little bit of anxiety or nervousness can be a good thing. It helps us with motivation, and makes achievement just that much sweeter. However, too much anxiety can be a problem; especially if it hinders our ability to function and perform.

"Test anxiety," is the term that refers to the emotional reactions that some test-takers experience when faced with a test or exam. Having a fear of testing and exams is based upon a rational fear, since the test-taker's performance can shape the course of an academic career. Nevertheless, experiencing excessive fear of examinations will only interfere with the test-takers ability to perform, and his/her chances to be successful.

There are a large variety of causes that can contribute to the development and sensation of test anxiety. These include, but are not limited to lack of performance and worrying about issues surrounding the test.

Lack of Preparation

Lack of preparation can be identified by the following behaviors or situations:

Not scheduling enough time to study, and therefore cramming the night before the test or exam
Managing time poorly, to create the sensation that there is not enough time to do everything
Failing to organize the text information in advance, so that the study material consists of the entire text and not simply the pertinent information
Poor overall studying habits

Worrying, on the other hand, can be related to both the test taker, or many other factors around him/her that will be affected by the results of the test. These include worrying about:

Previous performances on similar exams, or exams in general
How friends and other students are achieving
The negative consequences that will result from a poor grade or failure

There are three primary elements to test anxiety. Physical components, which involve the same typical bodily reactions as those to acute anxiety (to be discussed below). Emotional factors have to do with fear or panic. Mental or cognitive issues concerning attention spans and memory abilities.

Physical Signals

There are many different symptoms of test anxiety, and these are not limited to mental and emotional strain. Frequently there are a range of physical signals that will let a test taker know that he/she is suffering from test anxiety. These bodily changes can include the following:

Perspiring
Sweaty palms
Wet, trembling hands
Nausea
Dry mouth
A knot in the stomach
Headache
Faintness
Muscle tension
Aching shoulders, back and neck
Rapid heart beat
Feeling too hot/cold

To recognize the sensation of test anxiety, a test-taker should monitor him/herself for the following sensations:

The physical distress symptoms as listed above
Emotional sensitivity, expressing emotional feelings such as the need to cry or laugh too much, or a sensation of anger or helplessness
A decreased ability to think, causing the test-taker to blank out or have racing thoughts that are hard to organize or control.

Though most students will feel some level of anxiety when faced with a test or exam, the majority can cope with that anxiety and maintain it at a manageable level. However, those who cannot are faced with a very real and very serious condition, which can and should be controlled for the immeasurable benefit of this sufferer.

Naturally, these sensations lead to negative results for the testing experience. The most common effects of test anxiety have to do with nervousness and mental blocking.

Nervousness

Nervousness can appear in several different levels:

The test-taker's difficulty, or even inability to read and understand the questions on the test
The difficulty or inability to organize thoughts to a coherent form
The difficulty or inability to recall key words and concepts relating to the testing questions (especially essays)
The receipt of poor grades on a test, though the test material was well known by the test taker
Conversely, a person may also experience mental blocking, which involves:

Blanking out on test questions
Only remembering the correct answers to the questions when the test has already finished.

Fortunately for test anxiety sufferers, beating these feelings, to a large degree, has to do with proper preparation. When a test taker has a feeling of preparedness, then anxiety will be dramatically lessened.

The first step to resolving anxiety issues is to distinguish which of the two types of anxiety are being suffered. If the anxiety is a direct result of a lack of preparation, this should be considered a normal reaction, and the anxiety level (as opposed to the test results) shouldn't be anything to worry about. However, if, when adequately prepared, the test-taker still panics, blanks out, or seems to overreact, this is not a fully rational reaction. While this can be considered normal too, there are many ways to combat and overcome these effects.

Remember that anxiety cannot be entirely eliminated, however, there are ways to minimize it, to make the anxiety easier to manage. Preparation is one of the best ways to minimize test anxiety. Therefore the following techniques are wise in order to best fight off any anxiety that may want to build.

To begin with, try to avoid cramming before a test, whenever it is possible. By trying to memorize an entire term's worth of information in one day, you'll be shocking your system, and not giving yourself a very good chance to absorb the information. This is an easy path to anxiety, so for those who suffer from test anxiety, cramming should not even be considered an option.

Instead of cramming, work throughout the semester to combine all of the material which is presented throughout the semester, and work on it gradually as the course goes by, making sure to master the main concepts first, leaving minor details for a week or so before the test.

To study for the upcoming exam, be sure to pose questions that may be on the examination, to gauge the ability to answer them by integrating the ideas from your texts, notes and lectures, as well as any supplementary readings.

If it is truly impossible to cover all of the information that was covered in that particular term, concentrate on the most important portions, that can be covered very well. Learn these concepts as best as possible, so that when the test comes, a goal can be made to use these concepts as presentations of your knowledge.

In addition to study habits, changes in attitude are critical to beating a struggle with test anxiety. In fact, an improvement of the perspective over the entire test-taking experience can actually help a test taker to enjoy studying and therefore improve the overall experience. Be certain not to overemphasize the significance of the grade - know that the result of the test is neither a reflection of self worth, nor is it a measure of intelligence; one grade will not predict a person's future success.

To improve an overall testing outlook, the following steps should be tried:

Keeping in mind that the most reasonable expectation for taking a test is to expect to try to demonstrate as much of what you know as you possibly can.
Reminding ourselves that a test is only one test; this is not the only one, and there will be others.
The thought of thinking of oneself in an irrational, all-or-nothing term should be avoided at all costs.
A reward should be designated for after the test, so there's something to look forward to. Whether it be going to a movie, going out to eat, or simply visiting friends, schedule it in advance, and do it no matter what result is expected on the exam.

Test-takers should also keep in mind that the basics are some of the most important things, even beyond anti-anxiety techniques and studying. Never neglect the basic social, emotional and biological needs, in order to try to absorb information. In order to best achieve, these three factors must be held as just as important as the studying itself.

Study Steps

Remember the following important steps for studying:

Maintain healthy nutrition and exercise habits. Continue both your recreational activities and social pass times. These both contribute to your physical and emotional well being.
Be certain to get a good amount of sleep, especially the night before the test, because when you're overtired you are not able to perform to the best of your best ability.
Keep the studying pace to a moderate level by taking breaks when they are needed, and varying the work whenever possible, to keep the mind fresh instead of getting bored.
When enough studying has been done that all the material that can be learned has been learned, and the test taker is prepared for the test, stop studying and do something relaxing such as listening to music, watching a movie, or taking a warm bubble bath.

There are also many other techniques to minimize the uneasiness or apprehension that is experienced along with test anxiety before, during, or even after the examination. In fact, there are a great deal of things that can be done to stop anxiety from interfering with lifestyle and performance. Again, remember that anxiety will not be eliminated entirely, and it shouldn't be. Otherwise that "up" feeling for exams would not exist, and most of us depend on that sensation to perform better than usual. However, this anxiety has to be at a level that is manageable.

Of course, as we have just discussed, being prepared for the exam is half the battle right away. Attending all classes, finding out what knowledge will be expected on the exam, and knowing the exam schedules are easy steps to lowering anxiety. Keeping up with work will remove the need to cram, and efficient study habits will eliminate wasted time. Studying should be done in an ideal location for concentration, so that it is simple to become interested in the material and give it complete attention. A method such as SQ3R (Survey, Question, Read, Recite, Review) is a wonderful key to follow to make sure that the study habits are as effective as possible, especially in the case of learning from a textbook. Flashcards are great techniques for memorization. Learning to take good notes will mean that notes will be full of useful information, so that less sifting will need to be done to seek out what is pertinent for studying. Reviewing notes after class and then again on occasion will keep the information fresh in the mind. From notes that have been taken summary sheets and outlines can be made for simpler reviewing.

A study group can also be a very motivational and helpful place to study, as there will be a sharing of ideas, all of the minds can work together, to make sure that everyone understands, and the studying will be made more interesting because it will be a social occasion.

Basically, though, as long as the test-taker remains organized and self confident, with efficient study habits, less time will need to be spent studying, and higher grades will be achieved.

To become self confident, there are many useful steps. The first of these is "self talk." It has been shown through extensive research, that self-talk for students who suffer from test anxiety, should be well monitored, in order to make sure that it contributes to self confidence as opposed to sinking the student. Frequently the self talk of test-anxious students is negative or self-defeating, thinking that everyone else is smarter and faster, that they always mess up, and that if they don't do well, they'll fail the entire course. It is important to decreasing anxiety that awareness is made of self talk. Try writing any negative self thoughts and then disputing them with a positive statement instead. Begin self-encouragement as though it was a friend speaking. Repeat positive statements to help reprogram the mind to believing in successes instead of failures.

Helpful Techniques

Other extremely helpful techniques include:

Self-visualization of doing well and reaching goals
While aiming for an "A" level of understanding, don't try to "overprotect" by setting your expectations lower. This will only convince the mind to stop studying in order to meet the lower expectations.
Don't make comparisons with the results or habits of other students. These are individual factors, and different things work for different people, causing different results.
Strive to become an expert in learning what works well, and what can be done in order to improve. Consider collecting this data in a journal.
Create rewards for after studying instead of doing things before studying that will only turn into avoidance behaviors.
Make a practice of relaxing - by using methods such as progressive relaxation, self-hypnosis, guided imagery, etc - in order to make relaxation an automatic sensation.
Work on creating a state of relaxed concentration so that concentrating will take on the focus of the mind, so that none will be wasted on worrying.
Take good care of the physical self by eating well and getting enough sleep.
Plan in time for exercise and stick to this plan.

Beyond these techniques, there are other methods to be used before, during and after the test that will help the test-taker perform well in addition to overcoming anxiety.
Before the exam comes the academic preparation. This involves establishing a study schedule and beginning at least one week before the actual date of the test. By doing this, the anxiety of not having enough time to study for the test will be automatically eliminated. Moreover, this will make the studying a much more effective experience, ensuring that the learning will be an easier process. This relieves much undue pressure on the test-taker.

Summary sheets, note cards, and flash cards with the main concepts and examples of these main concepts should be prepared in advance of the actual studying time. A topic should never be eliminated from this process. By omitting a topic because it isn't expected to be on the test is only setting up the test-taker for anxiety should it actually appear on the exam. Utilize the course syllabus for laying out the topics that should be studied. Carefully go over the notes that were made in class, paying special attention to any of the issues that the professor took special care to emphasize while lecturing in class. In the textbooks, use the chapter review, or if possible, the chapter tests, to begin your review.

It may even be possible to ask the instructor what information will be covered on the exam, or what the format of the exam will be (for example, multiple choice, essay, free form, true-false).

Additionally, see if it is possible to find out how many questions will be on the test. If a review sheet or sample test has been offered by the professor, make good use of it, above anything else, for the preparation for the test. Another great resource for getting to know the examination is reviewing tests from previous semesters. Use these tests to review, and aim to achieve a 100% score on each of the possible topics. With a few exceptions, the goal that you set for yourself is the highest one that you will reach.

Take all of the questions that were assigned as homework, and rework them to any other possible course material. The more problems reworked, the more skill and confidence will form as a result. When forming the solution to a problem, write out each of the steps. Don't simply do head work. By doing as many steps on paper as possible, much clarification and therefore confidence will be formed. Do this with as many homework problems as possible, before checking the answers. By checking the answer after each problem, a reinforcement will exist, that will not be on the exam. Study situations should be as exam-like as possible, to prime the test-taker's system for the experience. By waiting to check the answers at the end, a psychological advantage will be formed, to decrease the stress factor.

Another fantastic reason for not cramming is the avoidance of confusion in concepts, especially when it comes to mathematics. 8-10 hours of study will become one hundred percent more effective if it is spread out over a week or at least several days, instead of doing it all in one sitting. Recognize that the human brain requires time in order to assimilate new material, so frequent breaks and a span of study time over several days will be much more beneficial.

Additionally, don't study right up until the point of the exam. Studying should stop a minimum of one hour before the exam begins. This allows the brain to rest and put things in their proper order. This will also provide the time to become as relaxed as possible when going into the examination room. The test-taker will also have time to eat well and eat sensibly. Know that the brain needs food as much as the rest of the body. With enough food and enough sleep, as well as a relaxed attitude, the body and the mind are primed for success.

Avoid any anxious classmates who are talking about the exam. These students only spread anxiety, and are not worth sharing the anxious sentimentalities.

Before the test also involves creating a positive attitude, so mental preparation should also be a point of concentration. There are many keys to creating a positive attitude. Should fears become rushing in, make a visualization of taking the exam, doing well, and seeing an A written on the paper. Write out a list of affirmations that will bring a feeling of confidence, such as "I am doing well in my English class," "I studied well and know my material," "I enjoy this class." Even if the affirmations aren't believed at first, it sends a positive message to the subconscious which will result in an alteration of the overall belief system, which is the system that creates reality.

If a sensation of panic begins, work with the fear and imagine the very worst! Work through the entire scenario of not passing the test, failing the entire course, and dropping out of school, followed by not getting a job, and pushing a shopping cart through the dark alley where you'll live. This will place things into perspective! Then, practice deep breathing and create a visualization of the opposite situation - achieving an "A" on the exam, passing the entire course, receiving the degree at a graduation ceremony.

On the day of the test, there are many things to be done to ensure the best results, as well as the most calm outlook. The following stages are suggested in order to maximize test-taking potential:

Begin the examination day with a moderate breakfast, and avoid any coffee or beverages with caffeine if the test taker is prone to jitters. Even people who are used to managing caffeine can feel jittery or light-headed when it is taken on a test day.
Attempt to do something that is relaxing before the examination begins. As last minute cramming clouds the mastering of overall concepts, it is better to use this time to create a calming outlook.
Be certain to arrive at the test location well in advance, in order to provide time to select a location that is away from doors, windows and other distractions, as well as giving enough time to relax before the test begins.
Keep away from anxiety generating classmates who will upset the sensation of stability and relaxation that is being attempted before the exam.
Should the waiting period before the exam begins cause anxiety, create a self-distraction by reading a light magazine or something else that is relaxing and simple.

During the exam itself, read the entire exam from beginning to end, and find out how much time should be allotted to each individual problem. Once writing the exam, should more time be taken for a problem, it should be abandoned, in order to begin another problem. If there is time at the end, the unfinished problem can always be returned to and completed.

Read the instructions very carefully - twice - so that unpleasant surprises won't follow during or after the exam has ended.

When writing the exam, pretend that the situation is actually simply the completion of homework within a library, or at home. This will assist in forming a relaxed atmosphere, and will allow the brain extra focus for the complex thinking function.

Begin the exam with all of the questions with which the most confidence is felt. This will build the confidence level regarding the entire exam and will begin a quality momentum. This will also create encouragement for trying the problems where uncertainty resides.

Going with the "gut instinct" is always the way to go when solving a problem. Second guessing should be avoided at all costs. Have confidence in the ability to do well.

For essay questions, create an outline in advance that will keep the mind organized and make certain that all of the points are remembered. For multiple choice, read every answer, even if the correct one has been spotted - a better one may exist.

Continue at a pace that is reasonable and not rushed, in order to be able to work carefully. Provide enough time to go over the answers at the end, to check for small errors that can be corrected.

Should a feeling of panic begin, breathe deeply, and think of the feeling of the body releasing sand through its pores. Visualize a calm, peaceful place, and include all of the sights, sounds and sensations of this image. Continue the deep breathing, and take a few minutes to continue this with closed eyes. When all is well again, return to the test.

If a "blanking" occurs for a certain question, skip it and move on to the next question. There will be time to return to the other question later. Get everything done that can be done, first, to guarantee all the grades that can be compiled, and to build all of the confidence possible. Then return to the weaker questions to build the marks from there.

Remember, one's own reality can be created, so as long as the belief is there, success will follow. And remember: anxiety can happen later, right now, there's an exam to be written!

After the examination is complete, whether there is a feeling for a good grade or a bad grade, don't dwell on the exam, and be certain to follow through on the reward that was promised...and enjoy it! Don't dwell on any mistakes that have been made, as there is nothing that can be done at this point anyway.

Additionally, don't begin to study for the next test right away. Do something relaxing for a while, and let the mind relax and prepare itself to begin absorbing information again.

From the results of the exam - both the grade and the entire experience, be certain to learn from what has gone on. Perfect studying habits and work some more on confidence in order to make the next examination experience even better than the last one.

Learn to avoid places where openings occurred for laziness, procrastination and day dreaming. Use the time between this exam and the next one to better learn to relax, even learning to relax on cue, so that any anxiety can be controlled during the next exam. Learn how to relax the body. Slouch in your chair if that helps. Tighten and then relax all of the different muscle groups, one group at a time, beginning with the feet and then working all the way up to the neck and face. This will ultimately relax the muscles more than they were to begin with. Learn how to breathe deeply and comfortably, and focus on this breathing going in and out as a relaxing thought. With every exhale, repeat the word "relax."

As common as test anxiety is, it is very possible to overcome it. Make yourself one of the test-takers who overcome this frustrating hindrance.

How to Overcome Your Fear of Math

If this article started by saying "Math," many of us would feel a shiver crawl up our spines, just by reading that simple word. Images of torturous years in those crippling desks of the math classes can become so vivid to our consciousness that we can almost smell those musty textbooks, and see the smudges of the #2 pencils on our fingers.

If you are still a student, feeling the impact of these sometimes overwhelming classroom sensations, you are not alone if you get anxious at just the thought of taking that compulsory math course. Does your heart beat just that much faster when you have to split the bill for lunch among your friends with a group of your friends? Do you truly believe that you simply don't have the brain for math? Certainly you're good at other things, but math just simply isn't one of them? Have you ever avoided activities, or other school courses because they appear to involve mathematics, with which you're simply not comfortable?

If any one or more of these "symptoms" can be applied to you, you could very well be suffering from a very real condition called "Math Anxiety."

It's not at all uncommon for people to think that they have some sort of math disability or allergy, when in actuality, their block is a direct result of the way in which they were taught math!

In the late 1950's with the dawning of the space age, New Math - a new "fuzzy math" reform that focuses on higher-order thinking, conceptual understanding and solving problems - took the country by storm. It's now becoming ever more clear that teachers were not supplied with the correct, practical and effective way in which they should be teaching new math so that students will understand the methods comfortably. So is it any wonder that so many students struggled so deeply, when their teachers were required to change their entire math systems without the foundation of proper training? Even if you have not been personally, directly affected by that precise event, its impact is still as rampant as ever.

Basically, the math teachers of today are either the teachers who began teaching the new math in the first place (without proper training) or they are the students of the math teachers who taught new math without proper training. Therefore, unless they had a unique, exceptional teacher, their primary, consistent examples of teaching math have been teachers using methods that are not conducive to the general understanding of the entire class. This explains why your discomfort (or fear) of math is not at all rare.

It is very clear why being called up to the chalk board to solve a math problem is such a common example of a terrifying situation for students - and it has very little to do with a fear of being in front of the class. Most of us have had a minimum of one humiliating experience while standing with chalk dusted fingers, with the eyes of every math student piercing through us. These are the images that haunt us all the way through adulthood. But it does not mean that we cannot learn math. It just means that we could be developing a solid case of math anxiety.

But what exactly is math anxiety? It's an very strong emotional sensation of anxiety, panic, or fear that people feel when they think about or must apply their ability to understand mathematics. Sufferers of math anxiety frequently believe that they are incapable of doing activities or taking classes that involve math skills. In fact, some people with math anxiety have developed such a fear that it has become a phobia; aptly named math phobia.

The incidence of math anxiety, especially among college students, but also among high school students, has risen considerably over the last 10 years, and currently this increase shows no signs of slowing down. Frequently students will even chose their college majors and programs based specifically on how little math will be compulsory for the completion of the degree.

The prevalence of math anxiety has become so dramatic on college campuses that many of these schools have special counseling programs that are designed to assist math anxious students to deal with their discomfort and their math problems.

Math anxiety itself is not an intellectual problem, as many people have been lead to believe; it is, in fact, an emotional problem that stems from improper math teaching techniques that have slowly built and reinforced these feelings. However, math anxiety can result in an intellectual problem when its symptoms interfere with a person's ability to learn and understand math.

The fear of math can cause a sort of "glitch" in the brain that can cause an otherwise clever person to stumble over even the simplest of math problems. A study by Dr. Mark H. Ashcraft of Cleveland State University in Ohio showed that college students who usually perform well, but who suffer from math anxiety, will suffer from fleeting lapses in their working memory when they are asked to perform even the most basic mental arithmetic. These same issues regarding memory were not present in the same students when they were required to answer questions that did not involve numbers. This very clearly demonstrated that the memory phenomenon is quite specific to only math.

So what exactly is it that causes this inhibiting math anxiety? Unfortunately it is not as simple as one answer, since math anxiety doesn't have one specific cause. Frequently math anxiety can result of a student's either negative experience or embarrassment with math or a math teacher in previous years.

These circumstances can prompt the student to believe that he or she is somehow deficient in his or her math abilities. This belief will consistently lead to a poor performance in math tests and courses in general, leading only to confirm the beliefs of the student's inability. This particular phenomenon is referred to as the "self-fulfilling prophecy" by the psychological community. Math anxiety will result in poor performance, rather than it being the other way around.

Dr. Ashcraft stated that math anxiety is a "It's a learned, almost phobic, reaction to math," and that it is not only people prone to anxiety, fear, or panic who can develop math anxiety. The image alone of doing math problems can send the blood pressure and heart rate to race, even in the calmest person.

The study by Dr. Ashcraft and his colleague Elizabeth P. Kirk, discovered that students who suffered from math anxiety were frequently stumped by issues of even the most basic math rules, such as "carrying over" a number, when performing a sum, or "borrowing" from a number when doing a subtraction. Lapses such as this occurred only on working memory questions involving numbers.

To explain the problem with memory, Ashcraft states that when math anxiety begins to take its effect, the sufferer experiences a rush of thoughts, leaving little room for the focus required to perform even the simplest of math problems. He stated that "you're draining away the energy you need for solving the problem by worrying about it."

The outcome is a "vicious cycle," for students who are sufferers of math anxiety. As math anxiety is developed, the fear it promotes stands in the way of learning, leading to a decrease in self-confidence in the ability to perform even simple arithmetic.

A large portion of the problem lies in the ways in which math is taught to students today. In the US, students are frequently taught the rules of math, but rarely will they learn why a specific approach to a math problems work. Should students be provided with a foundation of "deeper understanding" of math, it may prevent the development of phobias.

Another study that was published in the Journal of Experimental Psychology by Dr. Jamie Campbell and Dr. Qilin Xue of the University of Saskatchewan in Saskatoon, Canada, reflected the same concepts. The researchers in this study looked at university students who were educated in Canada and China, discovering that the Chinese students could generally outperform the Canadian-educated students when it came to solving complex math problems involving procedural knowledge - the ability to know how to solve a math problem, instead of simply having ideas memorized.

A portion of this result seemed to be due to the use of calculators within both elementary and secondary schools; while Canadians frequently used them, the Chinese students did not.

However, calculators were not the only issue. Since Chinese-educated students also outperformed Canadian-educated students in complex math, it is suggested that cultural factors may also have an impact. However, the short-cut of using the calculator may hinder the development of the problem solving skills that are key to performing well in math.

Though it is critical that students develop such fine math skills, it is easier said than done. It would involve an overhaul of the training among all elementary and secondary educators, changing the education major in every college.

Math Myths

One problem that contributes to the progression of math anxiety, is the belief of many math myths. These erroneous math beliefs include the following:
- Men are better in math than women - however, research has failed to demonstrate that there is any difference in math ability between the sexes.
- There is a single best way to solve a math problem - however, the majority of math problems can be solved in a number of different ways. By saying that there is only one way to solve a math problem, the thinking and creative skills of the student are held back.
- Some people have a math mind, and others do not - in truth, the majority of people have much more potential for their math capabilities than they believe of themselves.
- It is a bad thing to count by using your fingers - counting by using fingers has actually shown that an understanding of arithmetic has been established.

- People who are skilled in math can do problems quickly in their heads - in actuality, even math professors will review their example problems before they teach them in their classes.

The anxieties formed by these myths can frequently be perpetuated by a range of mind games that students seem to play with themselves. These math mind games include the following beliefs:

- I don't perform math fast enough - actually everyone has a different rate at which he or she can learn. The speed of the solving of math problems is not important as long as the student can solve it.
- I don't have the mind for math - this belief can inhibit a student's belief in him or herself, and will therefore interfere with the student's real ability to learn math.
- I got the correct answer, but it was done the wrong way - there is no single best way to complete a math problem. By believing this, a student's creativity and overall understanding of math is hindered.
- If I can get the correct answer, then it is too simple - students who suffer from math anxiety frequently belittle their own abilities when it comes to their math capabilities.
- Math is unrelated to my "real" life - math anxiety sufferers are only limiting their choices and freedoms for the rest of their life.

Fortunately, there are many ways to help those who suffer from math anxiety. Since math anxiety is a learned, psychological response to doing or thinking about math, that interferes with the sufferer's ability to understand and perform math, it is not at all a reflection of the sufferer's true math skills and abilities.

Helpful Strategies

Many strategies and therapies have been developed to help students to overcome their math anxious responses. Some of these helpful strategies include the following:

- Reviewing and learning basic arithmetic principles, techniques and methods. Frequently math anxiety is a result of the experience of many students with early negative situations, and these students have never truly developed a strong base in basic arithmetic, especially in the case of multiplication and fractions. Since math is a discipline that is built on an accumulative foundation, where the concepts are built upon gradually from simpler concepts, a student who has not achieved a solid basis in arithmetic will experience difficulty in learning higher order math. Taking a remedial math course, or a short math course that focuses on arithmetic can often make a considerable difference in reducing the anxious response that math anxiety sufferers have with math.
- Becoming aware of any thoughts, actions and feelings that are related to math and responses to math. Math anxiety has a different effect on different students. Therefore it is very important to become familiar with any reactions that the math anxiety sufferer may have about him/herself and the situation when math has been encountered. If the sufferer becomes aware of any irrational or unrealistic thoughts, it's possible to better concentrate on replacing these thoughts with more positive and realistic ones.
- Find help! Math anxiety, as we've mentioned, is a learned response, that is reinforced repeatedly over a period of time, and is therefore not something that can be eliminated

instantaneously. Students can more effectively reduce their anxious responses with the help of many different services that are readily available. Seeking the assistance of a psychologist or counselor, especially one with a specialty in math anxiety, can assist the sufferer in performing an analysis of his/her psychological response to math, as well as learning anxiety management skills, and developing effective coping strategies. Other great tools are tutors, classes that teach better abilities to take better notes in math class, and other math learning aids.

- Learning the mathematic vocabulary will instantly provide a better chance for understanding new concepts. One major issue among students is the lack of understanding of the terms and vocabulary that are common jargon within math classes. Typically math classes will utilize words in a completely different way from the way in which they are utilized in all other subjects. Students easily mistake their lack of understanding the math terms with their mathematical abilities.

- Learning anxiety reducing techniques and methods for anxiety management. Anxiety greatly interferes with a student's ability to concentrate, think clearly, pay attention, and remember new concepts. When these same students can learn to relax, using anxiety management techniques, the student can regain his or her ability to control his or her emotional and physical symptoms of anxiety that interfere with the capabilities of mental processing.

- Working on creating a positive overall attitude about mathematics. Looking at math with a positive attitude will reduce anxiety through the building of a positive attitude.

- Learning to self-talk in a positive way. Pep talking oneself through a positive self talk can greatly assist in overcoming beliefs in math myths or the mind games that may be played. Positive self-talking is an effective way to replace the negative thoughts - the ones that create the anxiety. Even if the sufferer doesn't believe the statements at first, it plants a positive seed in the subconscious, and allows a positive outlook to grow.

Beyond this, students should learn effective math class, note taking and studying techniques. Typically, the math anxious students will avoid asking questions to save themselves from embarrassment. They will sit in the back of classrooms, and refrain from seeking assistance from the professor. Moreover, they will put off studying for math until the very last moment, since it causes them such substantial discomfort. Alone, or a combination of these negative behaviors work only to reduce the anxiety of the students, but in reality, they are actually building a substantially more intense anxiety.

There are many different positive behaviors that can be adopted by math anxious students, so that they can learn to better perform within their math classes:

- Sit near the front of the class. This way, there will be fewer distractions, and there will be more of a sensation of being a part of the topic of discussion.

- If any questions arise, ASK! If one student has a question, then there are certain to be others who have the same question but are too nervous to ask - perhaps because they have not yet learned how to deal with their own math anxiety.

- Seek extra help from the professor after class or during office hours.

- Prepare, prepare, prepare - read textbook material before the class, do the homework and work out any problems available within the textbook. Math skills are developed through practice and repetition, so the more practice and repetition, the better the math skills.

- 234 -

Copyright © Mometrix Media. You have been licensed one copy of this document for personal use only. Any other reproduction or redistribution is strictly prohibited. All rights reserved.

- Review the material once again after class, to repeat it another time, and to reinforce the new concepts that were learned.

Beyond these tactics that can be taken by the students themselves, teachers and parents need to know that they can also have a large impact on the reduction of math anxiety within students.

As parents and teachers, there is a natural desire to help students to learn and understand how they will one day utilize different math techniques within their everyday lives. But when the student or teacher displays the symptoms of a person who has had nightmarish memories regarding math, where hesitations then develop in the instruction of students, these fears are automatically picked up by the students and commonly adopted as their own.

However, it is possible for teachers and parents to move beyond their own fears to better educate students by overcoming their own hesitations and learning to enjoy math.

Begin by adopting the outlook that math is a beautiful, imaginative or living thing. Of course, we normally think of mathematics as numbers that can be added or subtracted, multiplied or divided, but that is simply the beginning of it.

By thinking of math as something fun and imaginative, parents and teachers can teach children different ways to manipulate numbers, for example in balancing a checkbook. Parents rarely tell their children that math is everywhere around us; in nature, art, and even architecture. Usually, this is because they were never shown these relatively simple connections. But that pattern can break very simply through the participation of parents and teachers.

The beauty and hidden wonders of mathematics can easily be emphasized through a focus that can open the eyes of students to the incredible mathematical patterns that arise everywhere within the natural world. Observations and discussions can be made into things as fascinating as spider webs, leaf patterns, sunflowers and even coastlines. This makes math not only beautiful, but also inspiring and (dare we say) fun!

Pappas Method

For parents and teachers to assist their students in discovering the true wonders of mathematics, the techniques of Theoni Pappas can easily be applied, as per her popular and celebrated book "Fractals, Googols and Other Mathematical Tales." Pappas used to be a math phobia sufferer and created a fascinating step-by-step program for parents and teachers to use in order to teach students the joy of math.

Her simple, constructive step-by-step program goes as follows:

Don't let your fear of math come across to your kids - Parents must be careful not to perpetuate the mathematical myth - that math is only for specially talented "math types." Strive not to make comments like; "they don't like math" or "I have never been good at math." When children overhear comments like these from their primary role models they begin to dread math before even considering a chance of experiencing its wonders. It is important to encourage your children to read and explore the rich world of mathematics, and to practice mathematics without imparting negative biases.

Don't immediately associate math with computation (counting) - It is very important to realize that math is not just numbers and computations, but a realm of exciting ideas that touch every part of our lives -from making a telephone call to how the hair grows on someone's head. Take your children outside and point out real objects that display math concepts. For example, show them the symmetry of a leaf or angles on a building. Take a close look at the spirals in a spider web or intricate patterns of a snowflake.

Help your child understand why math is important - Math improves problem solving, increases competency and should be applied in different ways. It's the same as reading. You can learn the basics of reading without ever enjoying a novel. But, where's the excitement in that? With math, you could stop with the basics. But why when there is so much more to be gained by a fuller understanding? Life is so much more enriching when we go beyond the basics. Stretch your children's minds to become involved in mathematics in ways that will not only be practical but also enhance their lives.

Make math as "hands on" as possible - Mathematicians participate in mathematics. To really experience math encourage your child to dig in and tackle problems in creative ways. Help them learn how to manipulate numbers using concrete references they understand as well as things they can see or touch. Look for patterns everywhere, explore shapes and symmetries. How many octagons do you see each day on the way to the grocery store? Play math puzzles and games and then encourage your child to try to invent their own. And, whenever possible, help your child realize a mathematical conclusion with real and tangible results. For example, measure out a full glass of juice with a measuring cup and then ask your child to drink half. Measure what is left. Does it measure half of a cup?

Read books that make math exciting:
Fractals, Googols and Other Mathematical Tales introduces an animated cat who explains fractals, tangrams and other mathematical concepts you've probably never heard of to children in terms they can understand. This book can double as a great text book by using one story per lesson.
A Wrinkle in Time is a well-loved classic, combining fantasy and science.
The Joy of Mathematics helps adults explore the beauty of mathematics that is all around.
The Math Curse is an amusing book for 4-8 year olds.
The Gnarly Gnews is a free, humorous bi-monthly newsletter on mathematics.
The Phantom Tollbooth is an Alice in Wonderland-style adventure into the worlds of words and numbers.
Use the internet to help your child explore the fascinating world of mathematics.
Web Math provides a powerful set of math-solvers that gives you instant answers to the stickiest problems.
Math League has challenging math materials and contests for fourth grade and above.
Silver Burdett Ginn Mathematics offers Internet-based math activities for grades K-6.
The Gallery of Interactive Geometry is full of fascinating, interactive geometry activities.

Math is very much like a language of its own. And like any second language, it will get rusty if it is not practiced enough. For that reason, students should always be looking into new ways to keep understanding and brushing up on their math skills, to be certain that foundations do not crumble, inhibiting the learning of new levels of math.

There are many different books, services and websites that have been developed to take the fear out of math, and to help even the most uncertain student develop self confidence in his or her math capabilities.

There is no reason for math or math classes to be a frightening experience, nor should it drive a student crazy, making them believe that they simply don't have the "math brain" that is needed to solve certain problems.

There are friendly ways to tackle such problems and it's all a matter of dispelling myths and creating a solid math foundation.

Concentrate on re-learning the basics and feeling better about yourself in math, and you'll find that the math brain you've always wanted was there all along.

Additional Bonus Material

Due to our efforts to try to keep this book to a manageable length, we've created a link that will give you access to all of your additional bonus material.

Please visit http://www.mometrix.com/bonus948/sift to access the information.